POSTCARD HISTORY SERIES

Robeson County

IN VINTAGE POSTCARDS

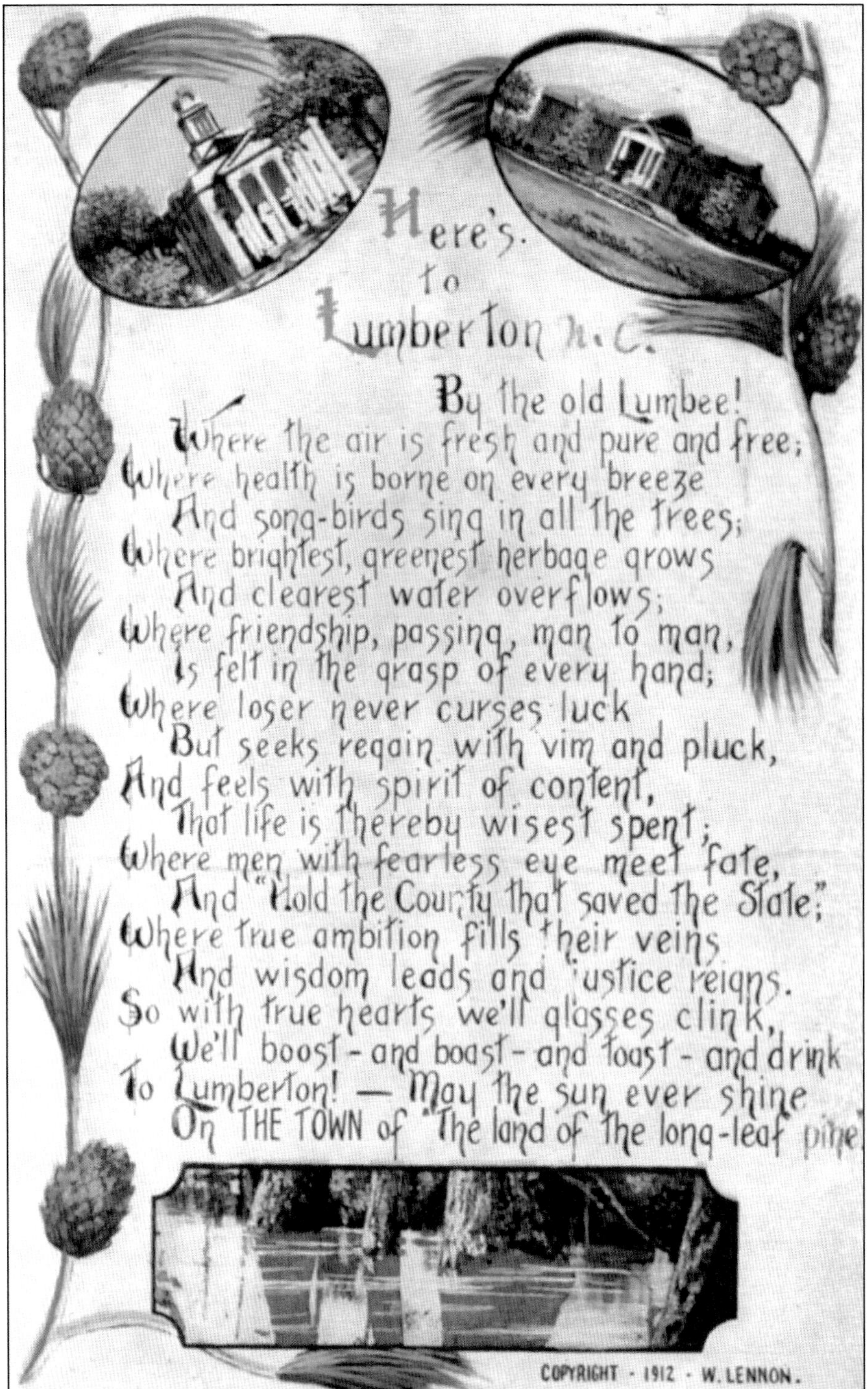

HERE'S TO LUMBERTON. This wonderful poem, which tells all of the positive aspects of Lumberton, was written by Woodberry Lennon in 1912.

POSTCARD HISTORY SERIES

Robeson County

IN VINTAGE POSTCARDS

K. Blake Tyner

ARCADIA
PUBLISHING

ISBN 978-0-7385-4162-4

Published by Arcadia Publishing
Charleston, South Carolina

Printed in the United States of America

Library of Congress Catalog Card Number: 2005927688

For all general information contact Arcadia Publishing at:
Telephone 843-853-2070
Fax 843-853-0044
E-mail sales@arcadiapublishing.com
For customer service and orders:
Toll-Free 1-888-313-2665

Visit us on the Internet at www.arcadiapublishing.com

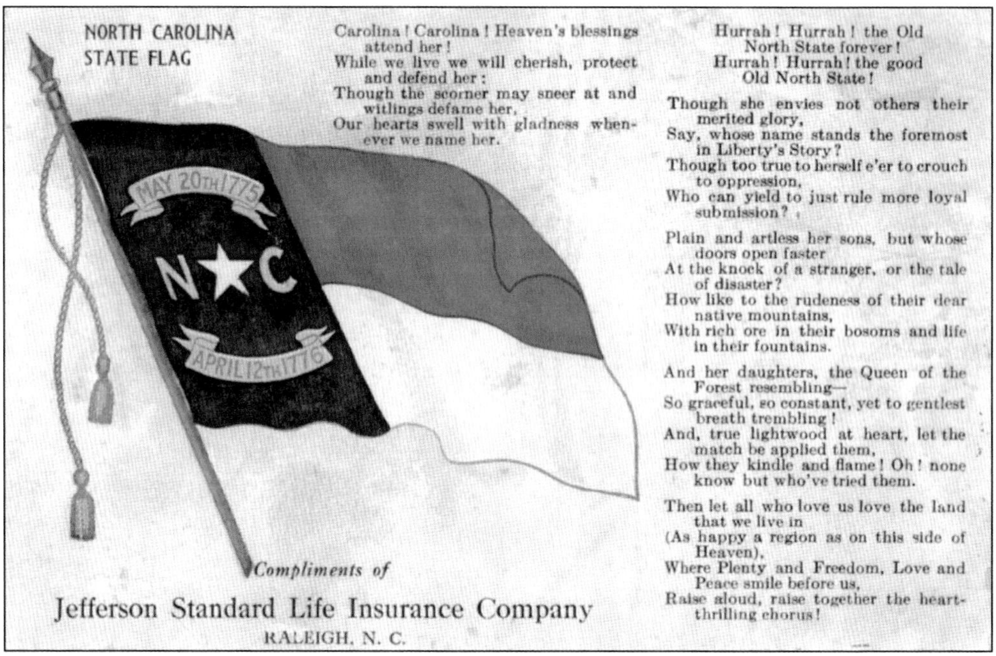

State Emblems. The North Carolina General Assembly adopted "The Old North State" as the state's official song in 1927. The words were written by William Gaston in 1840, and the music was arranged by Ora Randolph, wife of Dr. Edgar Eugene Randolph. North Carolina's official flag was adopted in 1885 and is made up of red, white, and blue fields. The letters N and C surround a white star. Above the letters is "May 20th, 1775," which is the date of the Mecklenburg Declaration of Independence. Below is "April 12th, 1776," which is the date of the Halifax Resolves.

Contents

ACKNOWLEDGMENTS

Robeson County in Vintage Postcards has been a labor of love and the fulfillment of a desire that I had after completing my first book on Robeson County: to be able to provide another resource on such a diverse and culturally rich county. I completed both of these books as an independent study for the University Honors College at the University of North Carolina at Pembroke. When my wife, Bess, and I returned to our roots in Robeson County in 1998, I began seeking any and all items that I could find dealing with the county's history. I managed to collect a number of vintage postcards that were the beginning of the Hubbard-Tyner Collection, but in the past two years, the collection has increased to over 200 scenes of Robeson County.

Not all of our collection appears in this volume, and noting certain gaps in our collection, I sought outside help in order to present a broad overview of the county. I want to thank all of individuals who opened their private collections and shared their cherished postcards with me. They include Rev. James Burt MacLeod and his daughter, Suzie MacLeod Dedrick (who loaned images from the postcard collection of Alexander Hamilton MacLeod); John and Betty Edens; Mutt McCoy; Paul Valenti; and Carla Baxley.

Special thanks are also due to Steve Massengill, supervisor of the Non-Textual Materials Unit of the North Carolina State Archives, and the staff of the Carolina Collection at UNC Chapel Hill for their efforts to gather and preserve a wonderful collection of North Carolina postcards. I found a wonderful general history of postcards at www.emotionscards.com, which served to answer many questions about how the postcard became an important part of correspondence.

The entire staff of Arcadia Publishing has been wonderful to work with, especially my editor, Adam Latham, who had to listen to sob stories about why deadlines were impossible to meet. At the University of North Carolina at Pembroke, I must thank my boss, art department chairman Janette Hopper, and Dr. Carolyn Thompson, dean of the University Honors College, who approved this project.

This book would not have been a possibility without one person, my wife. Bess has spent untold hours working with me on this publication. She first of all supported my sometimes-rapid desire to get just one more postcard that our collection really needed. She has read and reread every word of text. Bess, my darling, this book is dedicated to you for all of your love and support, on not only this project, but on all of my historical research projects. Thank you.

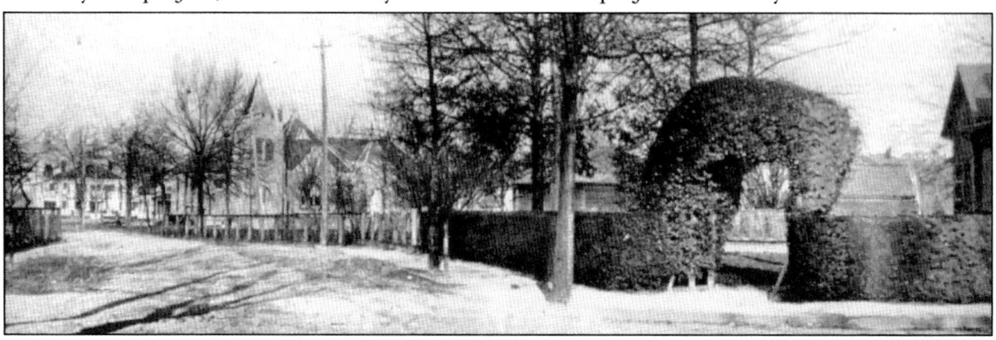

GRAHAM STREET. This view of Graham Street shows in the background the First Presbyterian Church, as well as the neoclassical residence that Maj. A. J. McKinnon built in 1904. Graham Street was originally known as Hughes Street. Robert Hughes had purchased 291 acres from his maternal uncle, Alexander McKay. Huges left no will but one sister and five half-siblings. He and his full sister has been born out of wedlock, and a fight revolved around the right of legitimate and illegitimate children. The case over the property lasted 11 years and ended up in the North Carolina Supreme Court twice. The final decision of the court was that legitimate children can inherit from their illegitimate siblings.

Introduction

The history of the area now known as Robeson County goes further back than when the county was carved out of fertile farmland along the border of the Carolinas in 1787. Robeson County is North Carolina's largest county, spanning 948 square miles. The county is called The State of Robeson not only because of its size, but because of its fierce independence and self-reliance. Robeson County is named for Col. Thomas Robeson, hero of the Revolutionary War Battle of Elizabethtown and proponent of creation of the county. Originally part of Bladen County, the residents of the area that was to become Robeson felt that their center of government needed to be closer and that the huge county of Bladen was simply too unwieldy. Situated in the verdant southeastern section of North Carolina, Robeson is bisected by Interstate 95 and is located near Fayetteville and Fort Bragg (the country's largest military installation).

Unique in its equally-balanced triracial population, the county combines in a rich heritage the Native American Lumbee tribe (largest Native American tribe east of the Mississippi), the African American community, and many descendants of the numerous Scottish and European settlers who arrived before and during the Revolution. Over the centuries, these people have worked together to create a culturally-diverse community.

This volume brings together a collection of vintage postcards that seek to take the reader on a trip through Robeson County's proud heritage. I have strived to include not only street scenes and business scenes from long ago but historical homes, churches, and, most importantly, community life. I gratefully acknowledge the overwhelming support of those interested in the preservation of Robeson County history and their generous assistance in sharing their images and stories. It has been a true joy to journey back and reconstruct the county's past. All postcards not listed as belonging to another individual or part of a collection are from the Hubbard-Tyner Collection. This collection was started by my wife and me in effort to purchase as many items relating to the history of the Carolinas as possible.

It is interesting to see what parts of Robeson County were chosen to grace postcards in the past. As you progress through this book, you will notice many landmarks that local residents pass each day without considering the importance that those landmarks have played in the county's history.

After gathering these Robeson County postcards, I was interested in the general history of postcards, so I set out to do some research. On May 19, 1898, Congress passed the Private Mailing Card Act to allow private firms to produce postcards. Until that time, only the United States could issue cards. The government-issued cards were prestamped postal cards that were first produced in 1873. Writing was not allowed on the back of the postcard until March 1, 1907, when a new law was issued. Before this time, any message was written across the front over the photographs or artwork on the card.

Around 1900, the first real photo postcards were seen. These were postcards that had actual photographs and were usually printed on film stock paper. Although most real photo postcards were advertising and trade cards, many were of entertainers and portraits of family members.

It is said that the publishing of printed postcards during this time period doubled every six months. By 1907, European card publishers began opening offices in the United States and produced over 75 percent of all postcards sold in the United States. At the end of this period, the hobby of collecting picture postcards became the greatest collection hobby that the world had ever known. The official figures from the U.S. Post Office for their fiscal year ending June 30, 1908, cite 677,777,798 postcards mailed. At that time, the total population of the United States was only 88,700,000.

The main purpose of this book, aside from the preservation and dissemination of these postcards, is to continue to build an interest in the study of Robeson County's history and to encourage others to seek out documents, photos, maps, and other ephemera relative to the county history while it still exists. Every 20 years represents a new generation and the potential loss of large amounts of our history and artifacts. If new generations of Robesonians are interested in their history and the study of their proud heritage, then the purpose of this book is fulfilled. Our future is truly rooted in our past, and preservation of this foundation is a sacred trust that we must uphold.

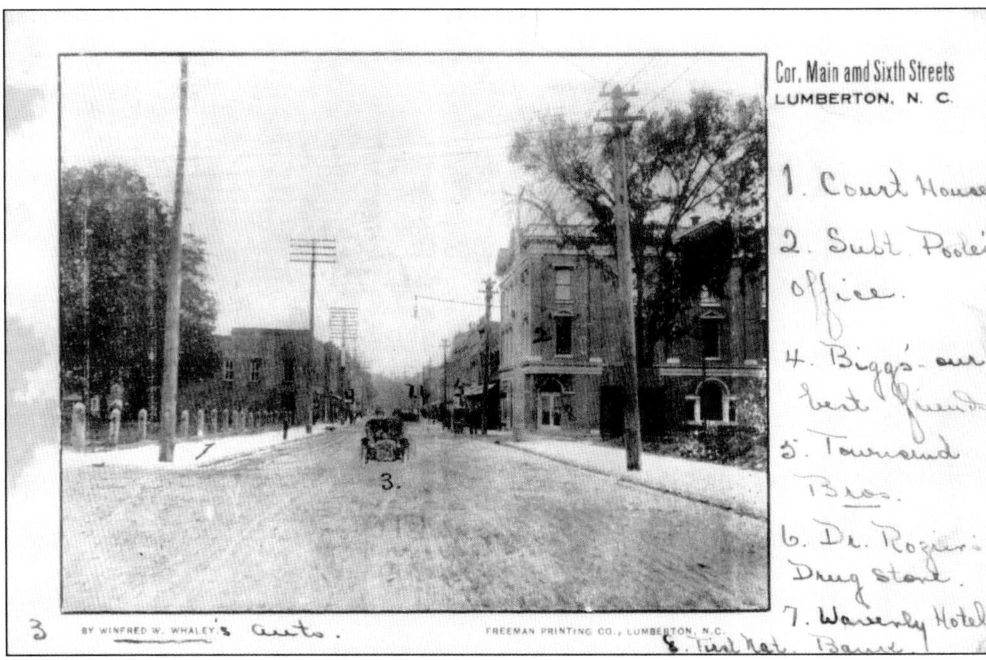

DOWNTOWN LUMBERTON. The sender of this postcard pointed out several places of interest for the recipient. Noted are the courthouse, Robeson County Superintendent Poole's office, the stores of K. M. Biggs and the Townsend Brothers, as well as Dr. Rozier's Drug Store and the Waverly Hotel. (Courtesy Carolina Collection, UNC-Chapel Hill.)

One

Street Scenes

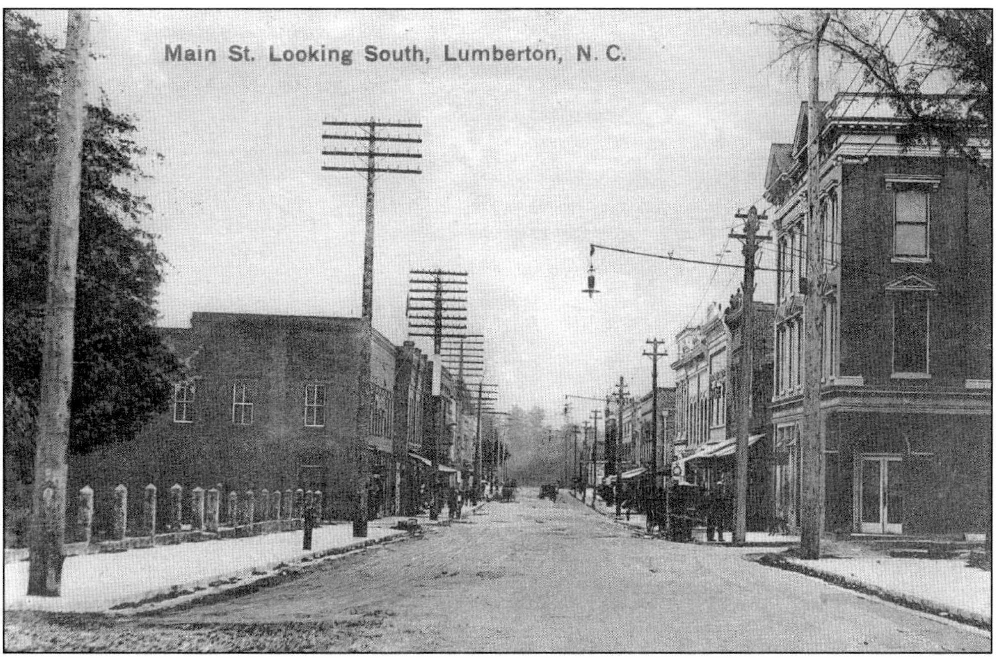

Main Street Looking South. This view of Main Street, now called Elm Street (in downtown Lumberton), was taken from in front of the courthouse. In the right foreground is the First National Bank of Lumberton building. The bank was established on September 14, 1904, and by April 1910 had paid had paid over $15,000 in dividends. In 1910, the officers were George B. McLeod (president), A. R. McEachern (vice president), H. M. McAllister (cashier), and R. McA. Nixon (assistant cashier).

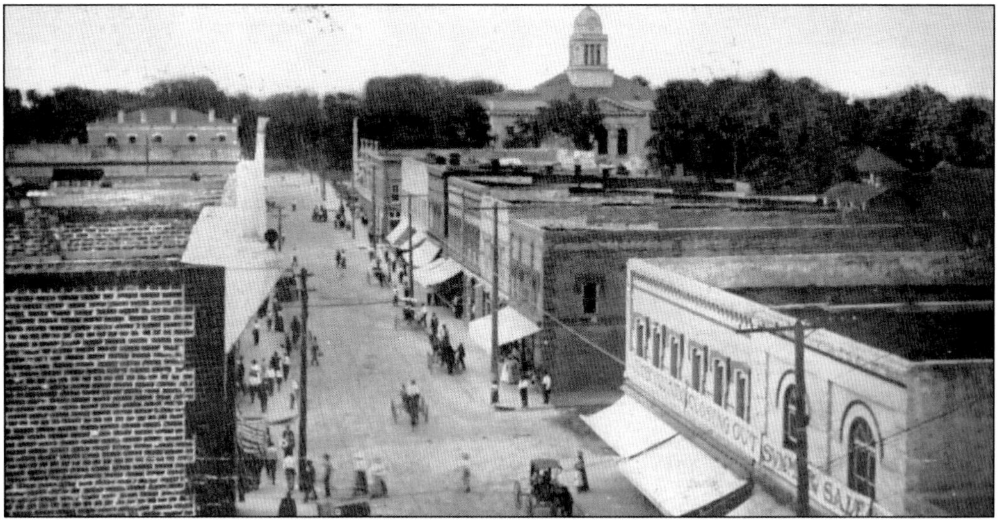

MAIN STREET. The wonderful aerial view of Lumberton's Main (now Elm) Street shows the 1908 courthouse in the background and a great view of the busy and wide dirt street with wagons and buggies. The building in the right-hand foreground housed the Caldwell and Carlyle Company. The business was started by R. D. Caldwell and W. W. Carlyle in January 1884 with $3,000 in stock, and by 1905, they boasted inventory between $80,000 and $100,000. They advertised that they carried everything needed by man from the cradle to the grave.

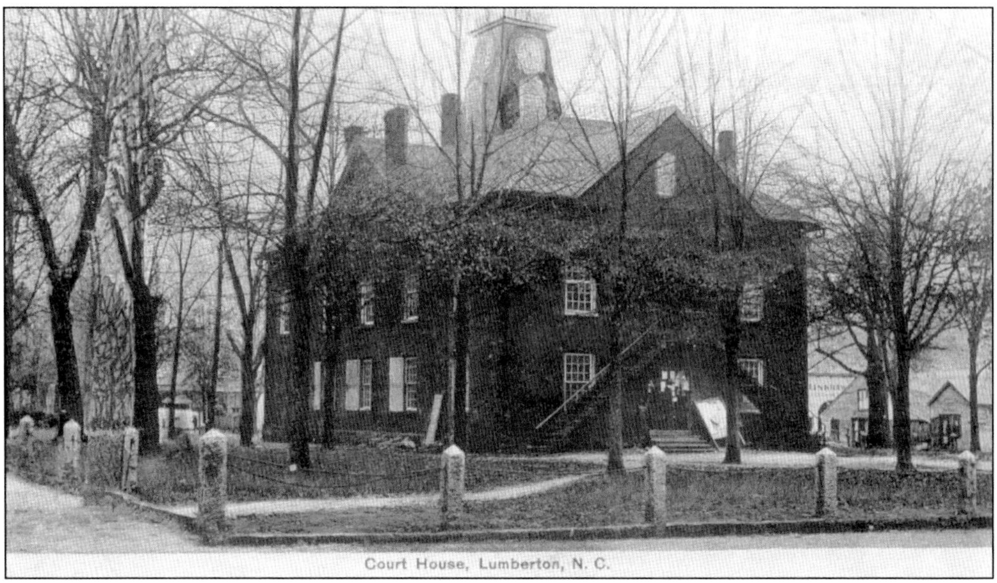

SECOND COURTHOUSE. In the 1872 book The Swamp Outlaws or The North Carolina Bandits is a description of this courthouse. "The Court House is built of brick, with a frame pediment above the eaves in the gable end, and the court room in the second story is covered with saw dust to keep the peace while Judge Clarke, one of the District Judges, goes through the comedy of justice. The court room is very crude, large and bare, and the Judge looks amazingly high up behind the long gallery where they expose him. Down before the Court House, where the people of the county are congregated, there is an old pole well in the public square, where white and negro fill their gourds at the dipping bucket." (Courtesy Rev. James Burt MacLeod and Suzie MacLeod Dedrick.)

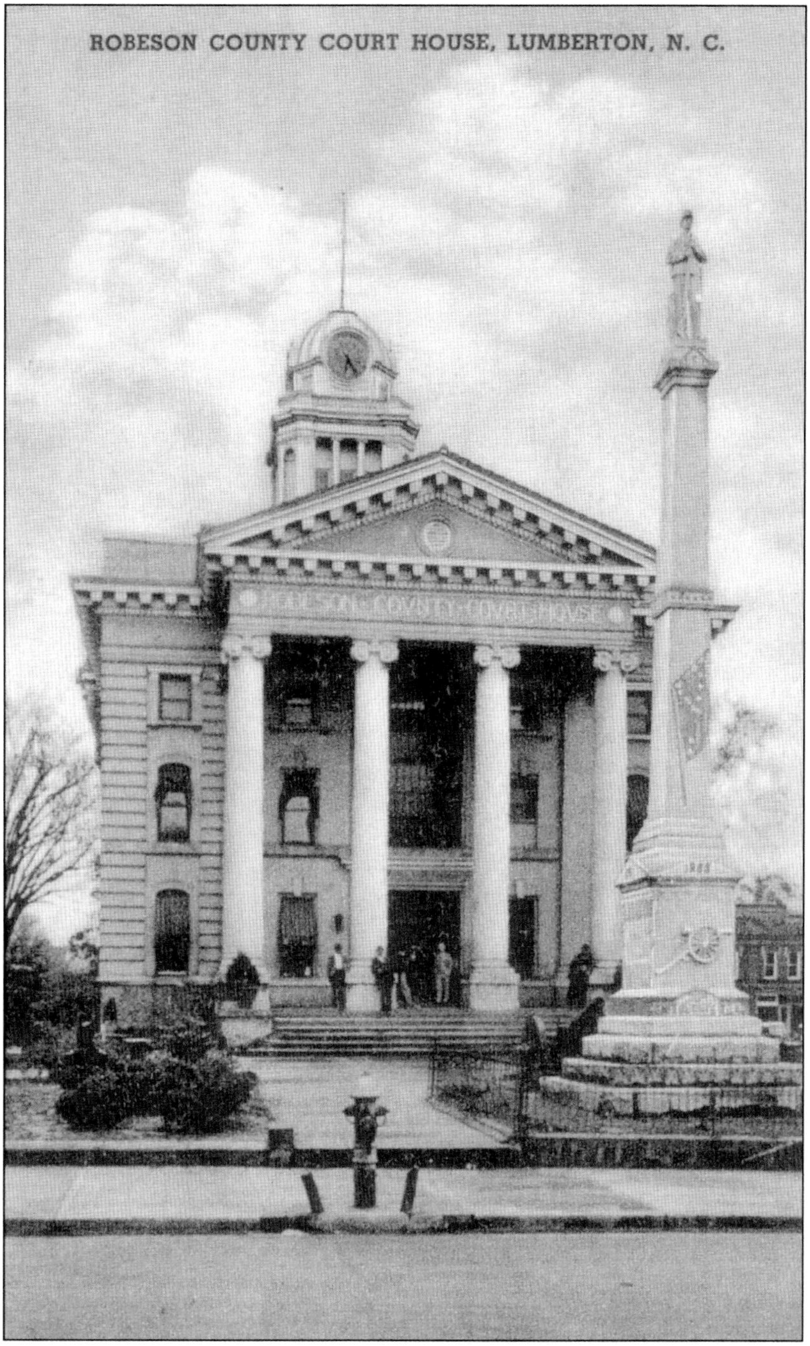

THIRD COURTHOUSE. Robeson County saw the need for a new courthouse, and in 1907, the North Carolina General Assembly voted to allow the county to issue $50,000 in bonds for construction. During the construction, court was held in Dr. Rudolph Vampill's Opera House at the corner of Elm and Sixth Streets. Construction costs were high, and the county issued $25,000 more in bonds to cover the costs. In 1950, additions were added to the back and both sides of the building at a cost of $162,000. The building was razed in 1976 to make room for the forth and current courthouse. (Courtesy Paul Valenti and Carla Baxley.)

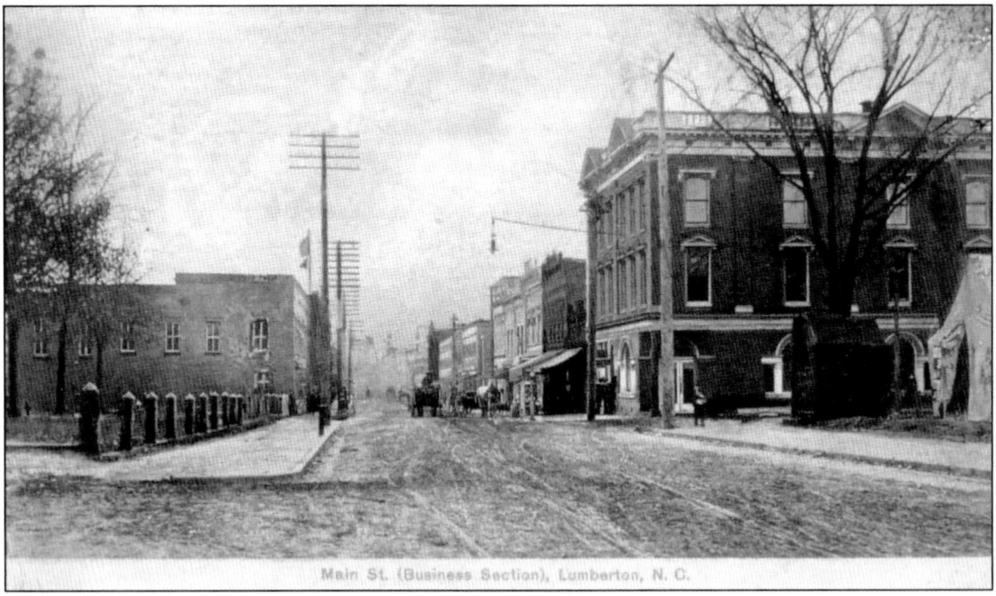

ELM STREET LOOKING SOUTH. This postcard shows the area in front and south of the courthouse. The first large building on the left was built in 1895 to house the mercantile business, White and Gough, which was owned by A. E. White and Frank Gough. In 1908, the facade was remolded to a neoclassical Revival. It was later the site of Rayless Department Store. Directly in front of the courthouse is a tent store, an unusual site considering all the permanent buildings that line Elm Street.

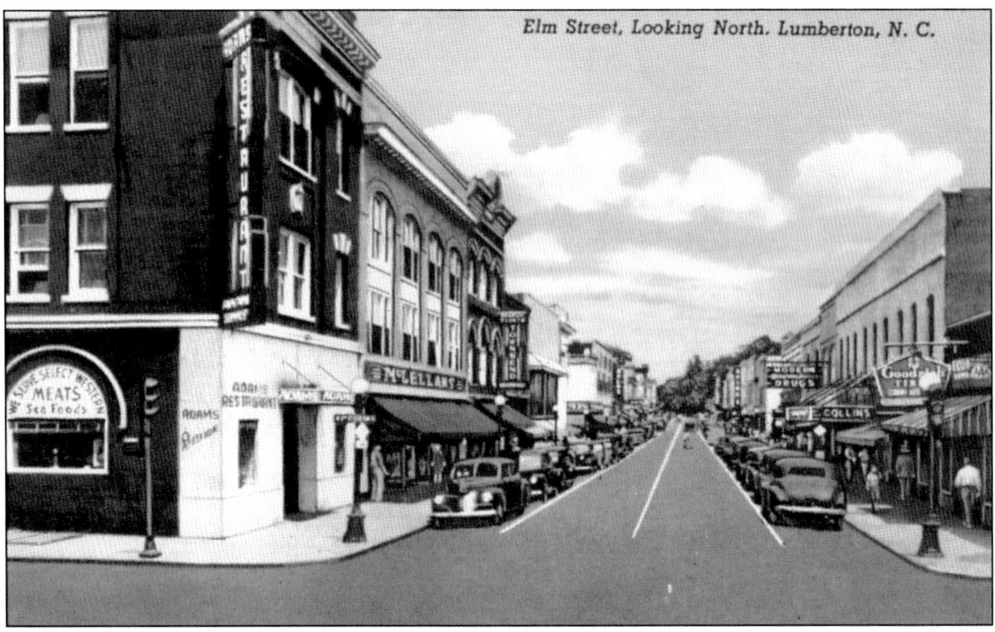

ELM STREET LOOKING NORTH. This section of Elm Street is shown from Second Street; the entire block on the right that housed Economy Auto, Modern Drug Store and Collins was torn down and is the site of the downtown plaza. The building on the left foreground that houses Adams Restaurant was built in 1908 to house the offices of the Lumberton and Dresden Cotton Mills. During World War I, that building was the site of Lyric Theatre.

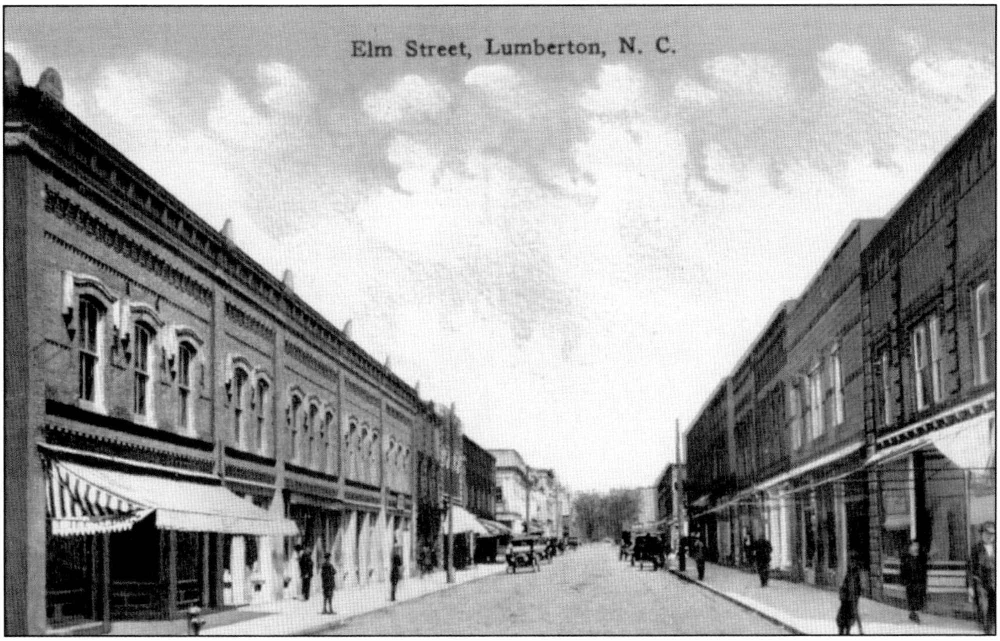

ELM STREET. Elm Street, which parallels the Lumber River one block east, has served Lumberton as a main street. The building in the left foreground is the L. H. Caldwell General Merchandise Store.

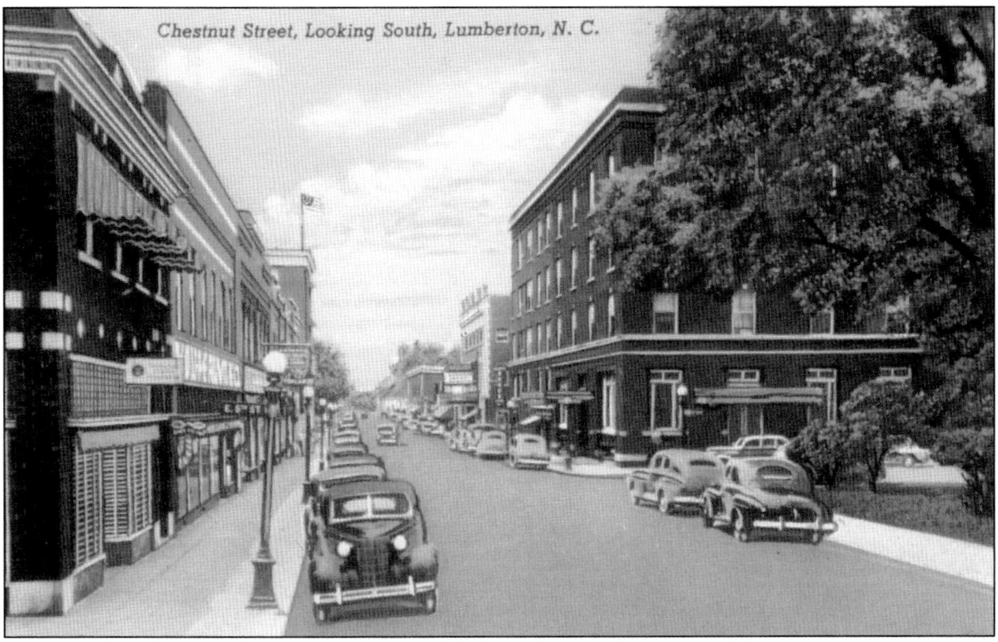

CHESTNUT STREET. Chestnut Street has always been an important retail center in Lumberton. Longtime businesses on this street were the Lorraine Hotel, McDuffie Furniture, and the Carolina Theatre. The building topped with the flag in the background was built in 1925 to house Planters Bank and was later the site of the Scottish Bank and First Union Bank. At the south end of Chestnut Street is the beginning of the tobacco market, which in its prime, sold millions of dollars worth of flue-cured tobacco every year.

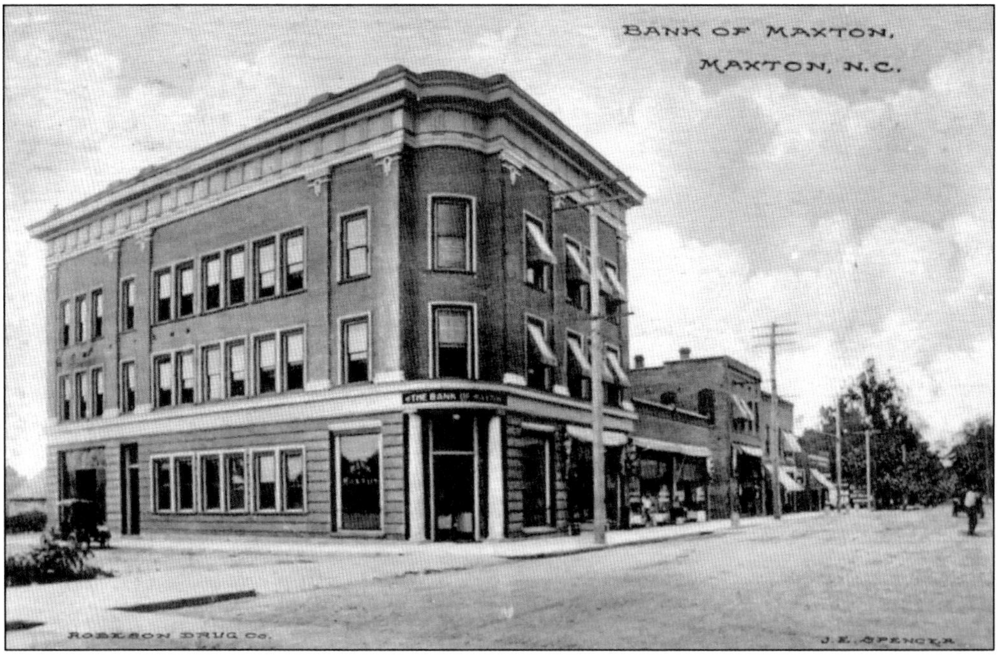

BANK OF MAXTON. Built to house the Bank of Maxton, this building became home to the Bank of Robeson in 1931. In 1932, the Bank of Robeson became a branch of the State Bank of Laurinburg.

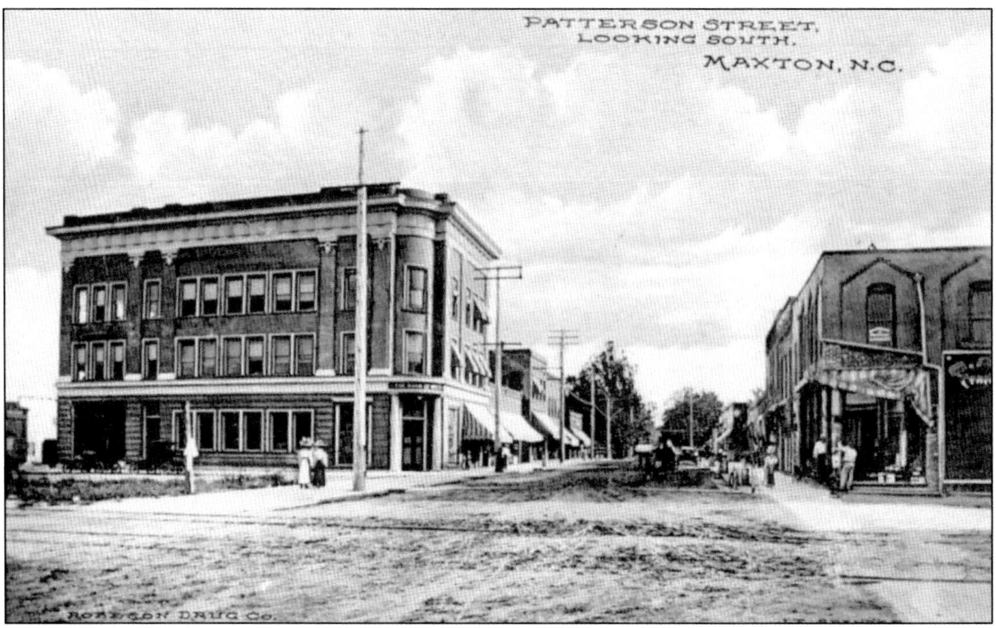

PATTERSON STREET LOOKING SOUTH. The foreground of this postcard shows the tracks of the Wilmington and Charlotte Railroad, which was the first railroad to cross Robeson County. On the left side of the street is the Bank of Maxton Building, which also housed a drug store; located next to it are the barber shop and a general merchandise store. On the right side of the street, the first building is a general merchandise store owned by Robert McDuffie Morton. Additional general merchandise stores filled the rest of the block.

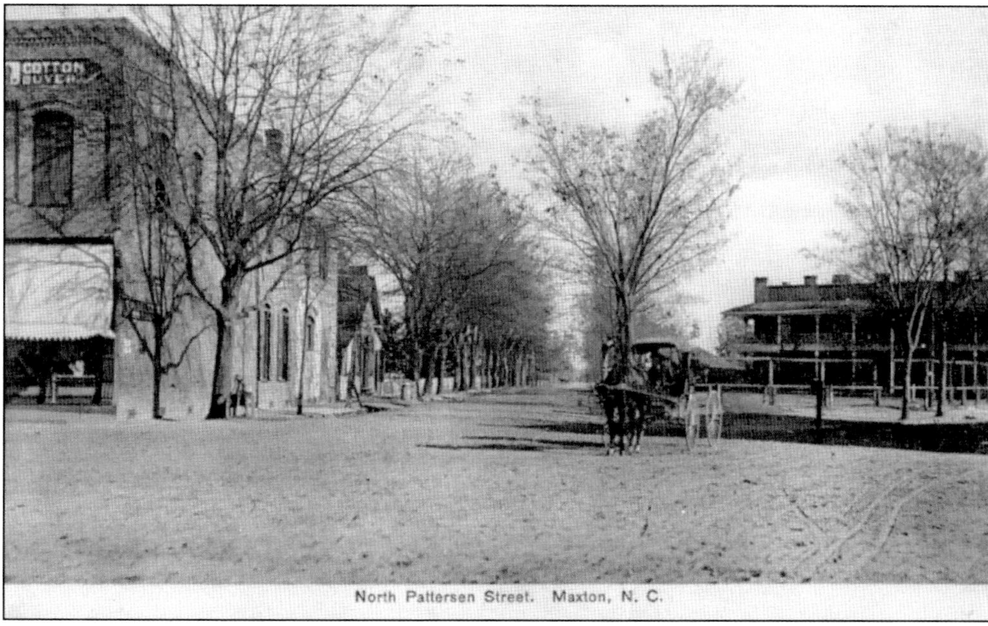

North Patterson Street. This view of Patterson Street was taken before the Patterson Building was built in 1911. The left foreground shows the general merchandise store that would become the J. W. Carter business. Behind it is the Patterson Law Office, along with both of its wings. The 1898 Sanborn Fire Map shows the first room occupied by a cobbler, the center office empty, and the third office belonging to attorney Gilbert Patterson. The center of the postcard shows the Maple Shade Inn.

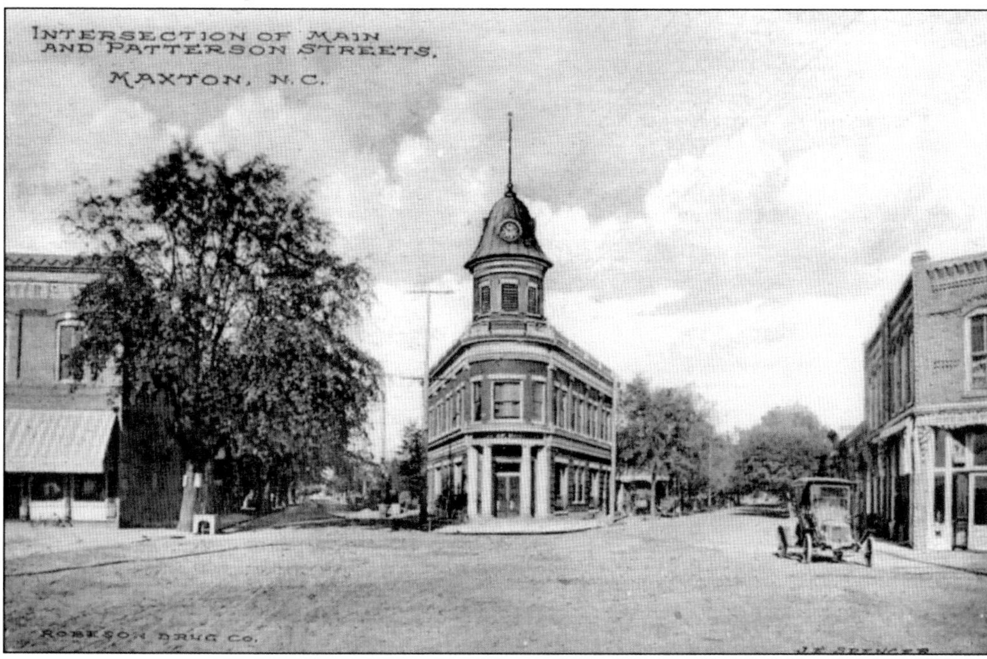

Intersection of Main and Patterson Streets. Shown in the center is the Patterson Building, which was built in 1911 to house the Bank of Robeson. On the left is the J. W. Carter building, and on the right is McNatt's Drug Store.

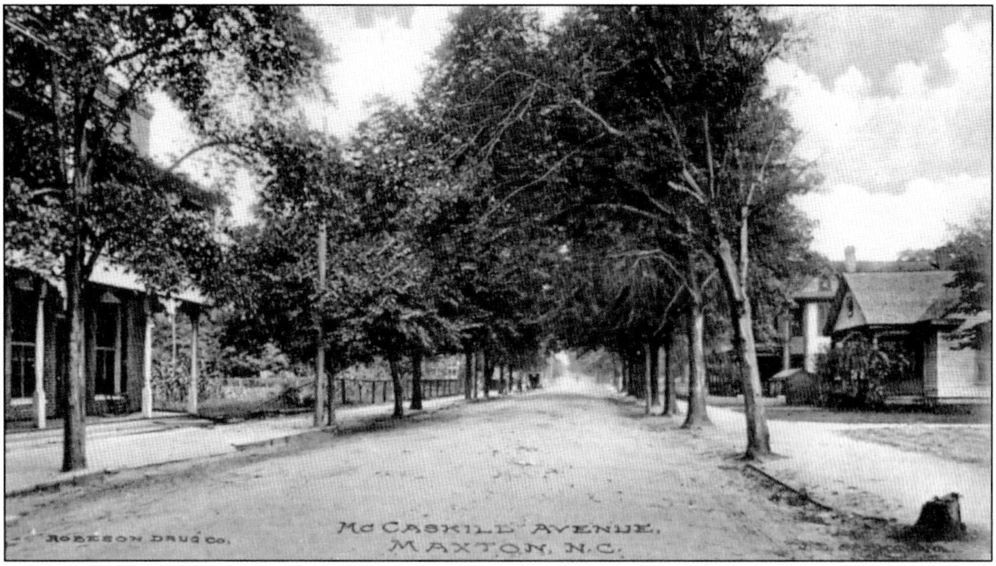

McCaskill Avenue. Once known as Main Street, it was renamed in honor of the McCaskill family, who built large homes in the second block of the street. Maxton was incorporated in 1874 as Shoe Hill. Judge Thomas A. McNeill, of the Seventh Judicial District, drew the charter, and the first mayor was Franklin Henderson, a Civil War veteran. The town next had the names of Tilden, after an 1876 Democratic candidate for U.S. president, and Quhele, Gaelic for narrow part of the stream. The name was changed back to Shoe Hill in 1881. In 1887, Capt. William Black and William Jackson Currie, town commissioners, made the suggestion to rename the town Mack's Town to honor the Scottish settlers to the area. The idea caught on, and the name was shortened to Maxton.

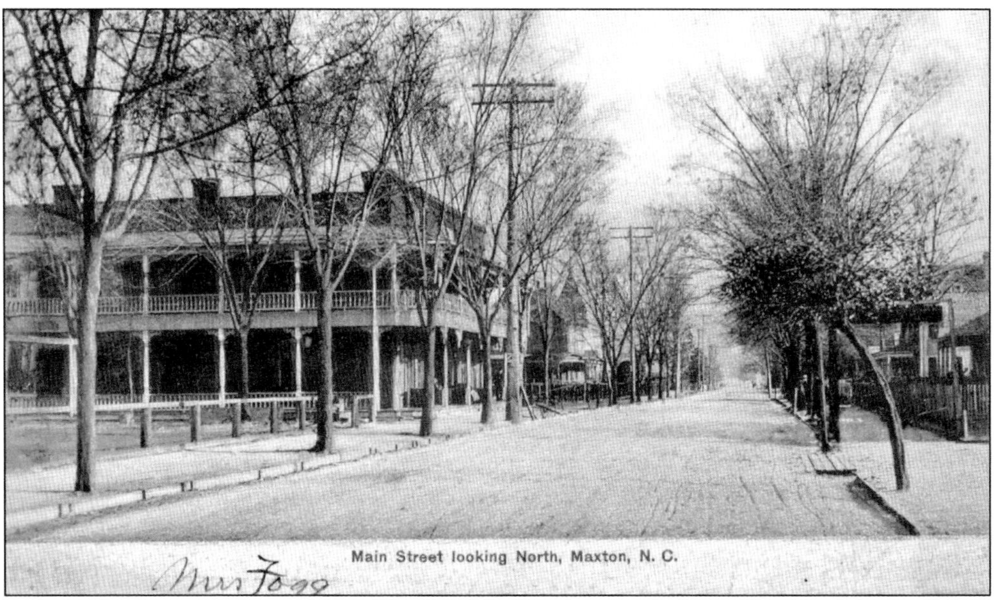

Main Street Looking North. In the left foreground is the Maple Shade Inn, which is known for its hospitality; farther down, on the next block, is the McRae House, a local hotel that served the many visitors to Maxton. Across from the inn is the beginning of the residential section of Main Street.

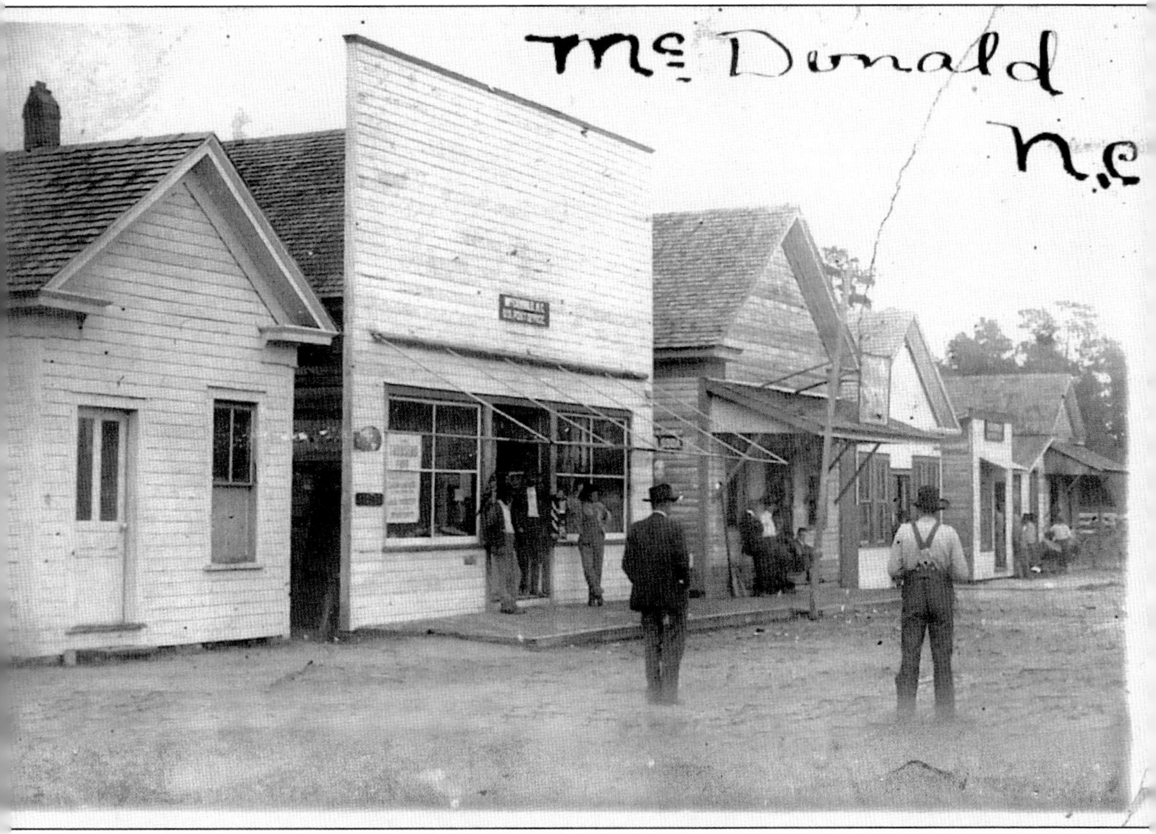

MAIN STREET MCDONALD. When looking at this wonderful postcard of main street McDonald, you feel as though you have stepped into the Old West. The town grew up on the lands of Richard Townsend. The post office opened in 1900 with James L. Townsend as postmaster. The town was officially incorporated in 1911 and had a population of 120 in 1920. McDonald is said to have been named for P. K. McDonald who operated a turpentine distillery nearby. In the early 1900s, the town consisted of a school, a hardware store, telegraph office, post office, and cotton gins. This postcard was sent from Elrod on December 29, 1914. (Courtesy Mutt McCoy.)

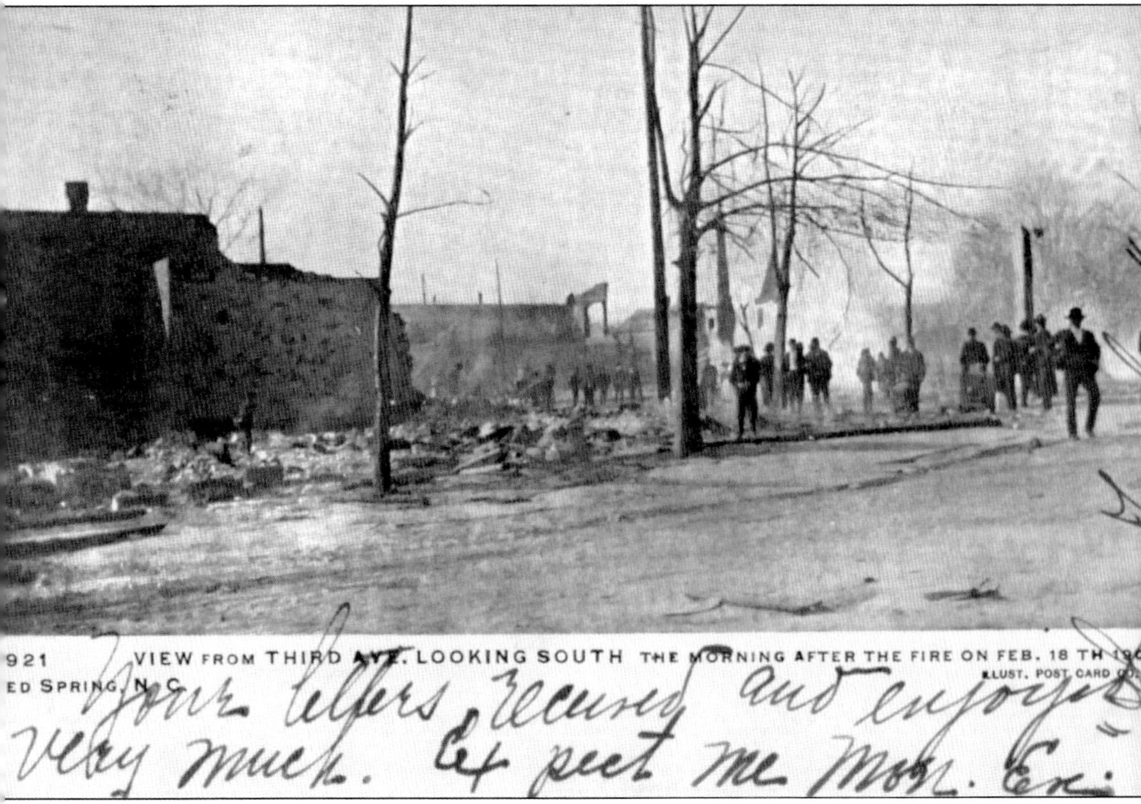

MORNING AFTER. In 1906, a large portion of downtown Red Springs was destroyed by a devastating fire. This scene shows Main Street, looking north, on February 18, 1906, the morning after the fire. The Cape Fear and Yadkin Railroad was laid through this area in June 1884, at which time a post office opened under the name Dora. In 1885, Hamilton McMillan introduced a bill in the North Carolina General Assembly to change the name of the area to Red Springs. The name came from the rust-colored sediment of the local waters that was caused by iron and sulphur. The local waters had been a mecca to visitors for their beneficial qualities for years. Red Springs was officially incorporated in 1887 with "Red" Hector McNeill as mayor. McNeill was the grandson of "Sailor" Hector McNeill, who received a royal land grant on March 11, 1775, for a large portion of Red Springs.

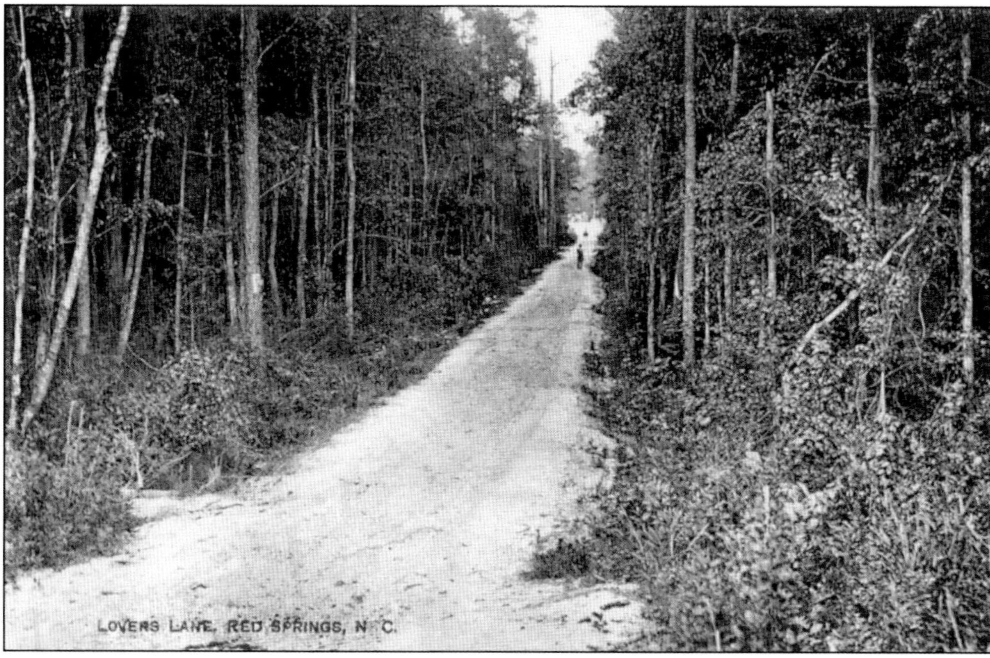

LOVER'S LANE. While most lover's lanes remain a secret to the general public, this one in Red Springs was advertised on a postcard.

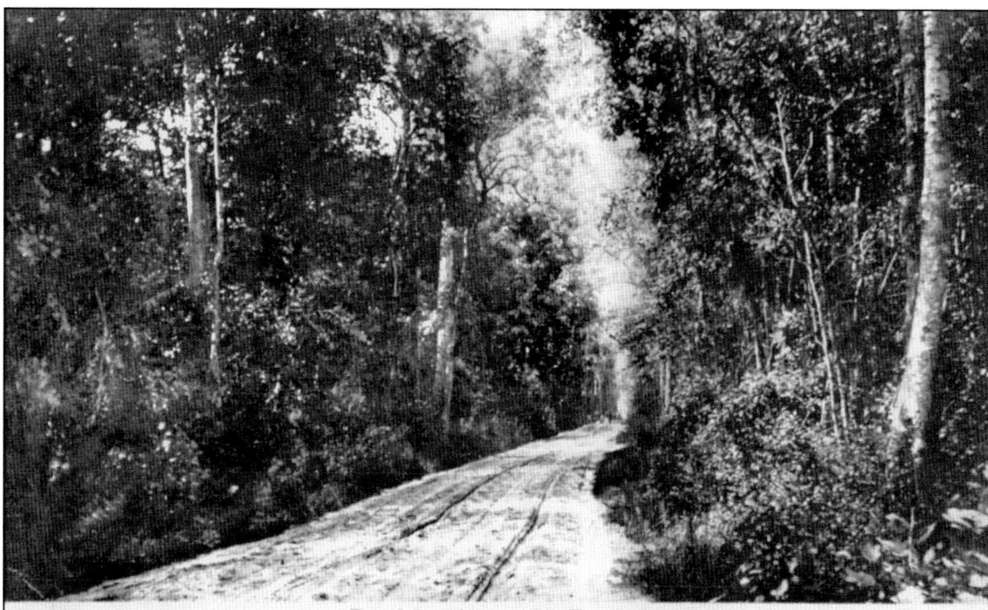

ROAD LEADING TO ST. PAULS. The road referred to in this postcard is likely either the Lumberton to St. Pauls road, now Highway 301, or the Red Springs to St. Pauls road, now the Great Marsh Church Road.

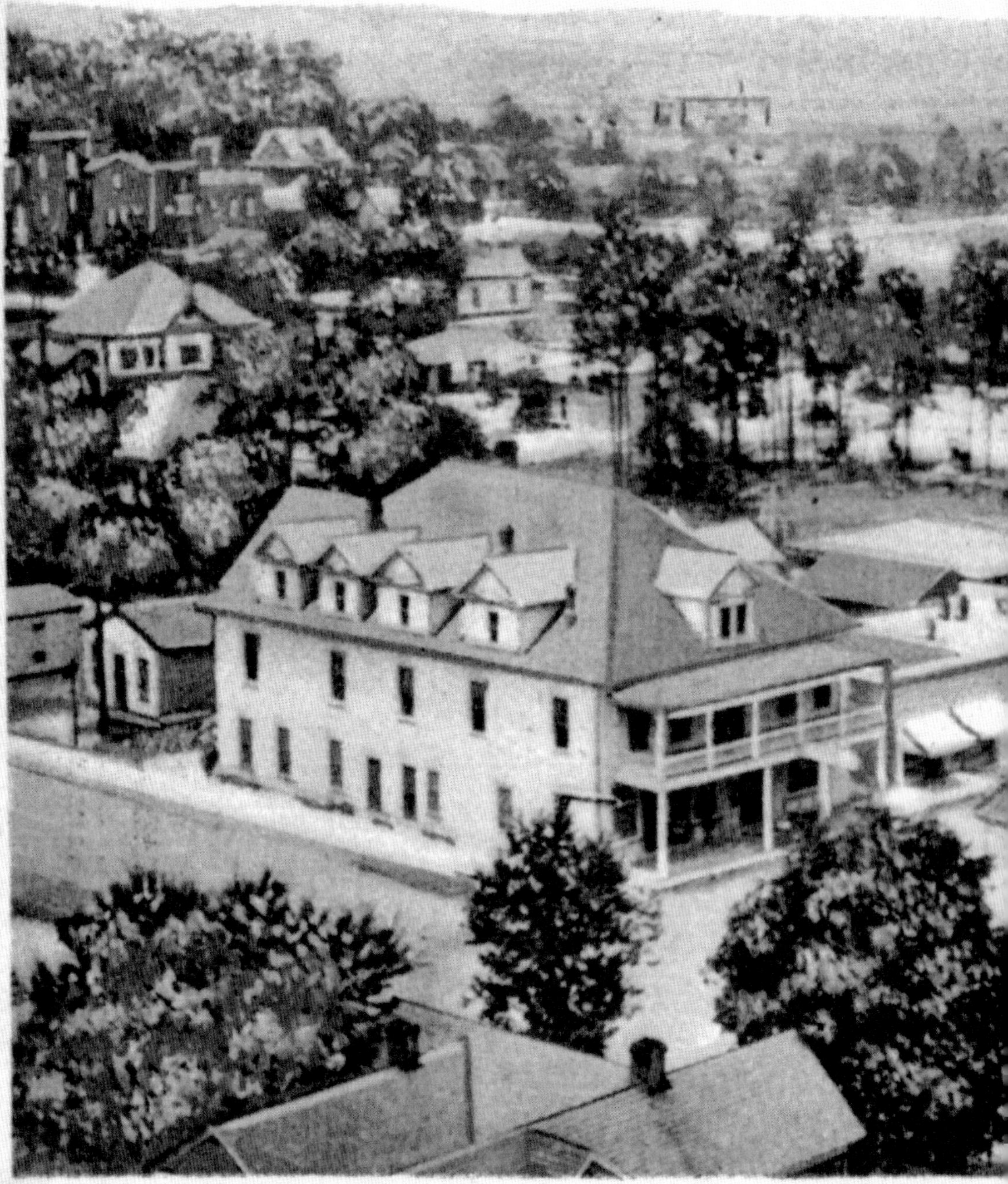

A VIEW FROM THE AIR; ST. PAULS, N. C.

VIEW FROM THE AIR. This aerial drawing of St. Pauls provides a bird's-eye-view of the central portion of downtown St. Pauls. The large, three-story, wood-framed building in the center foreground was the hotel; it was originally located on the northern end of that block but was

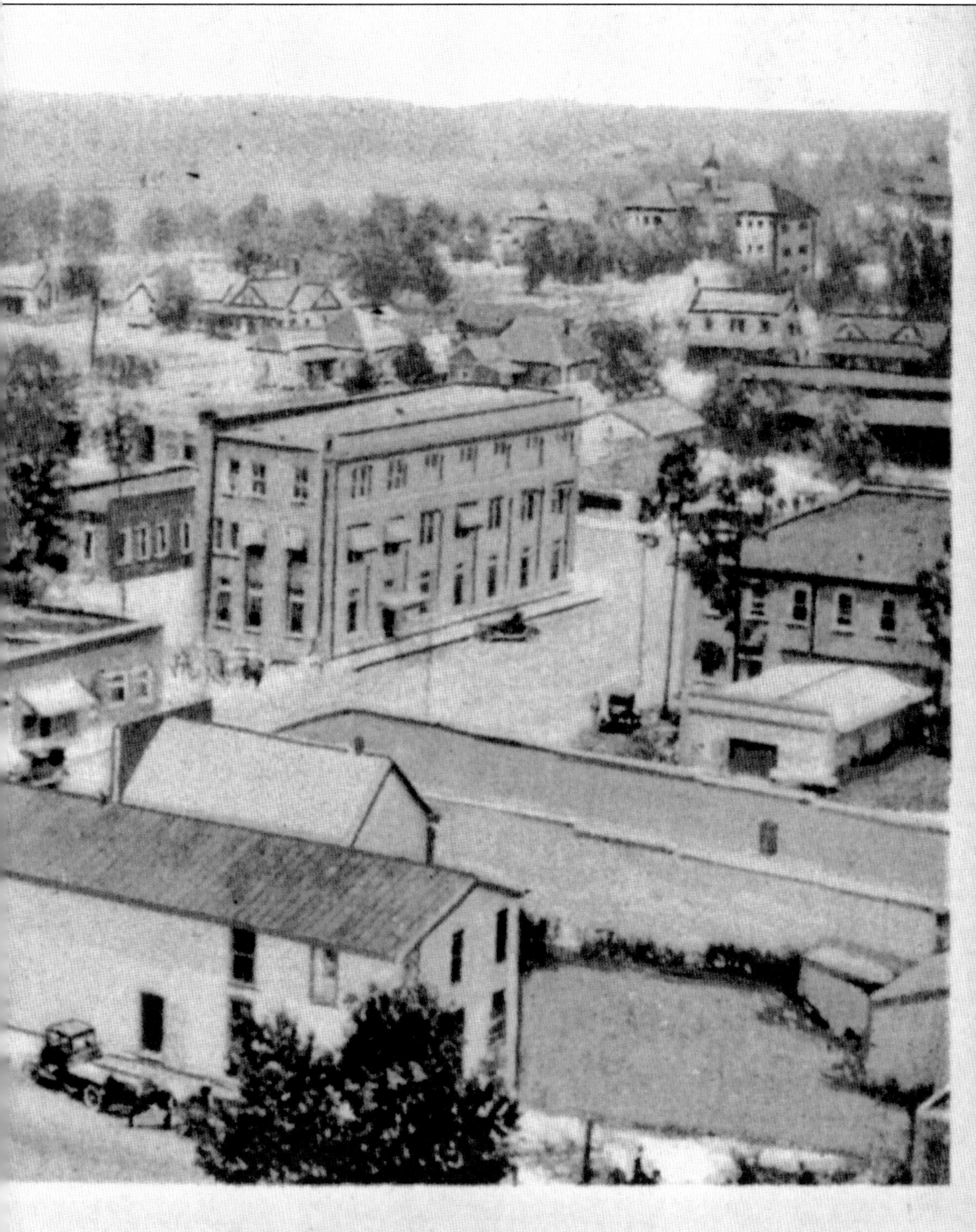

moved in 1911 to make way for the Bank of St. Pauls. In front of the hotel is the ice and fuel company, and behind that was the location of Joe McNeill's gristmill and blacksmith shop. The roof of McNeill's house can be seen in the lower-left foreground.

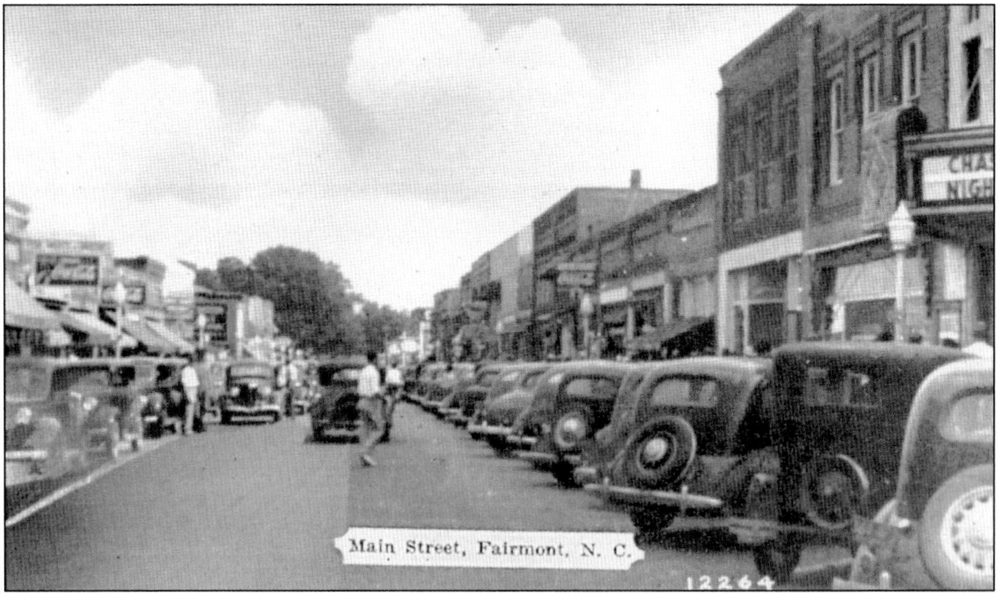

MAIN STREET FAIRMONT. The town of Fairmont, first known as Ashpole and incorporated in 1899 as Union City, began when the Southeastern Railroad was laid. The first town lots were sold in 1899. The name was changed to Fairmont in 1907.

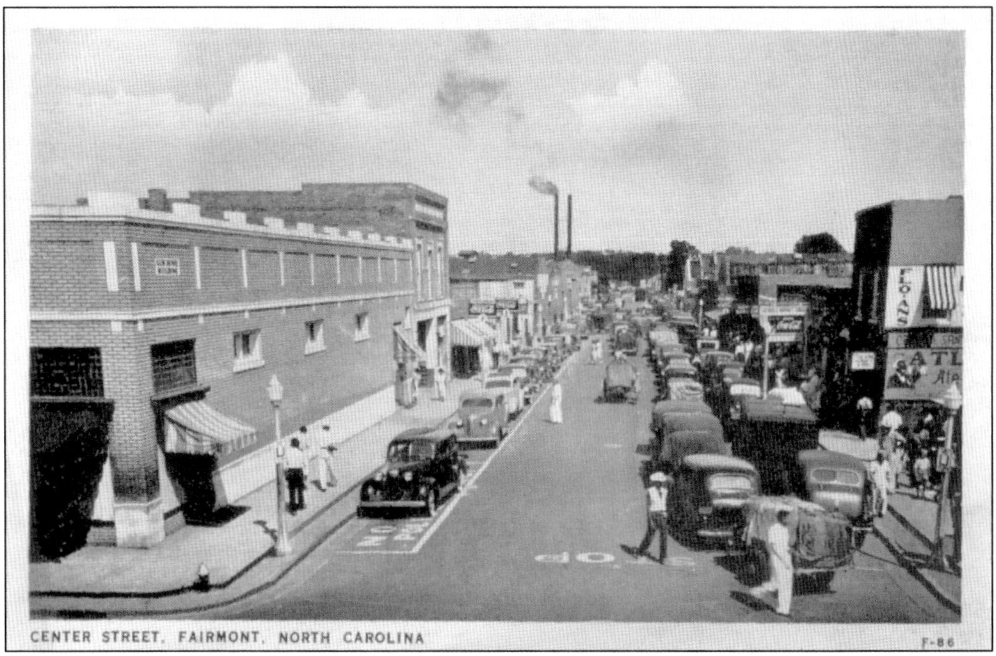

MAIN STREET FAIRMONT. Fairmont, known as the tobacco capital of the county, opened its first tobacco warehouse in 1899. The year 1978 marked 79 years of Fairmont's tobacco markets. At that time, they boasted 24 modern warehouses and eight pack houses that were shipping a million pounds of tobacco a day. They held the world's largest flue-cured tobacco market by population. In 1919, they sold 6,998,393 pounds of tobacco at an average price of $26.34 per pound, and, by 1978, they sold 33,950,792 pounds at an average price of $137.60 per pound. The depression hit the market hard; 1931 found the average price of tobacco at $11.47.

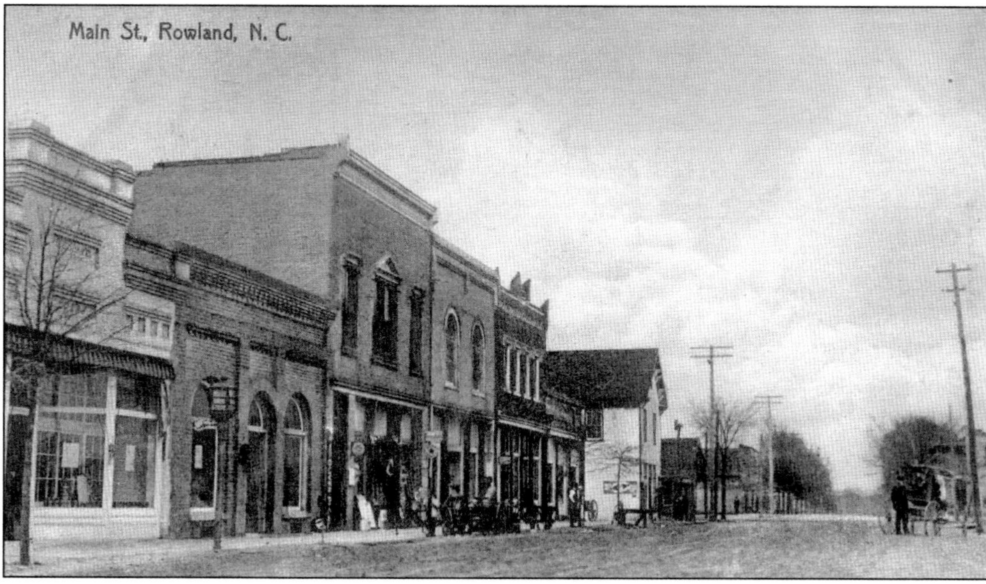

MAIN STREET ROWLAND. The town of Rowland grew up around the Atlantic Coast Railroad that was built in the area in 1888. The town was incorporated in 1899 with Milton Lytch as mayor. The first building in town was a wooden frame, in which R. S. Bond operated a general store. The post office was established November 1888; Charles H. Wyche was the first postmaster. Rowland was named for Col. Alfred Rowland, a member of Congress. The town's nickname, Town of 1,000 Friends, came when the 1940 census showed its population at 999. (Courtesy Rev. James Burt MacLeod and Suzie MacLeod Dedrick.)

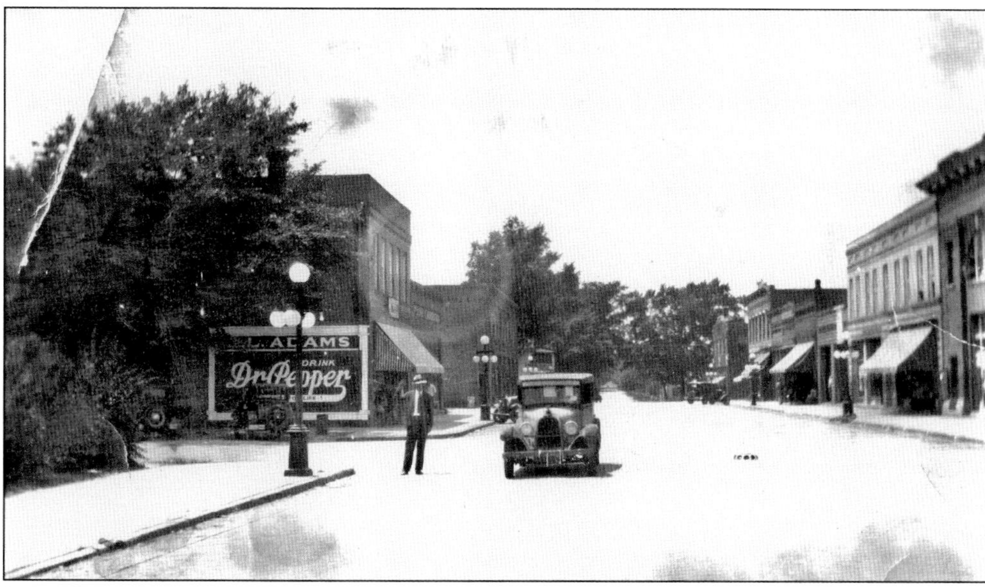

MAIN STREET ROWLAND. The wide streets of Rowland are lined with beautiful brick buildings. The town of Rowland grew up along the North and South Carolina state line and prospered because of businessmen like L. Z. Hedgepeth, William W. McCormick, Graham McKinnon, and, especially, Allen Edens. Edens was referred to as "one of the best businessmen Robeson County has produced" by Robert C. Lawrence in his 1939 book *The State of Robeson.* (Courtesy John and Betty Edens.)

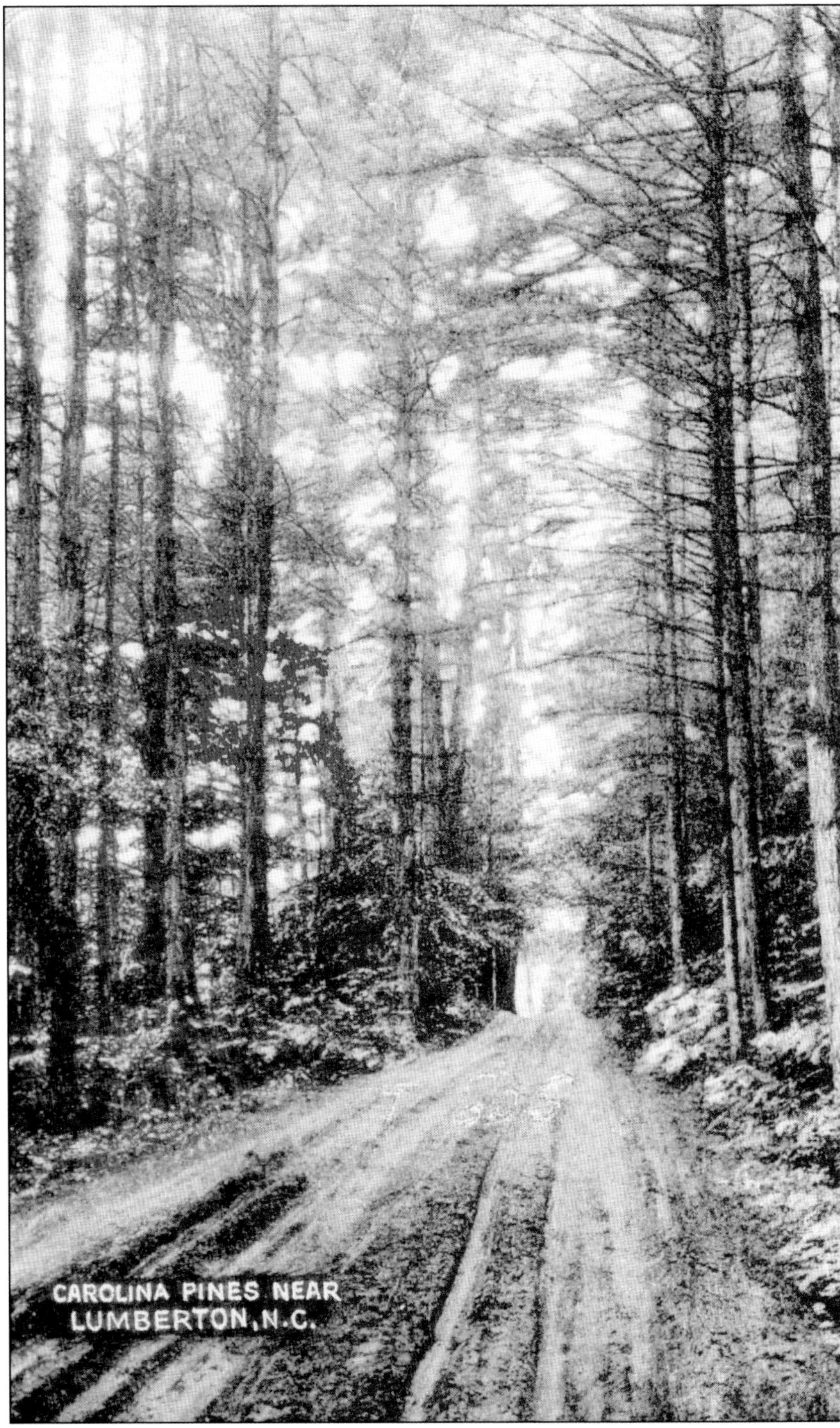

CAROLINA PINES. The lumber industry was an important factor in early growth of Robeson County. In 1884, engineer John McDuffie gave an estimate that the county contained 864 million feet of longleaf pine and 2 million feet of shortleaf pine. This was in spite of all the sawmills that had been operating in the county. (Courtesy Paul Valenti and Carla Baxley.)

Two

WATER AND RAILS

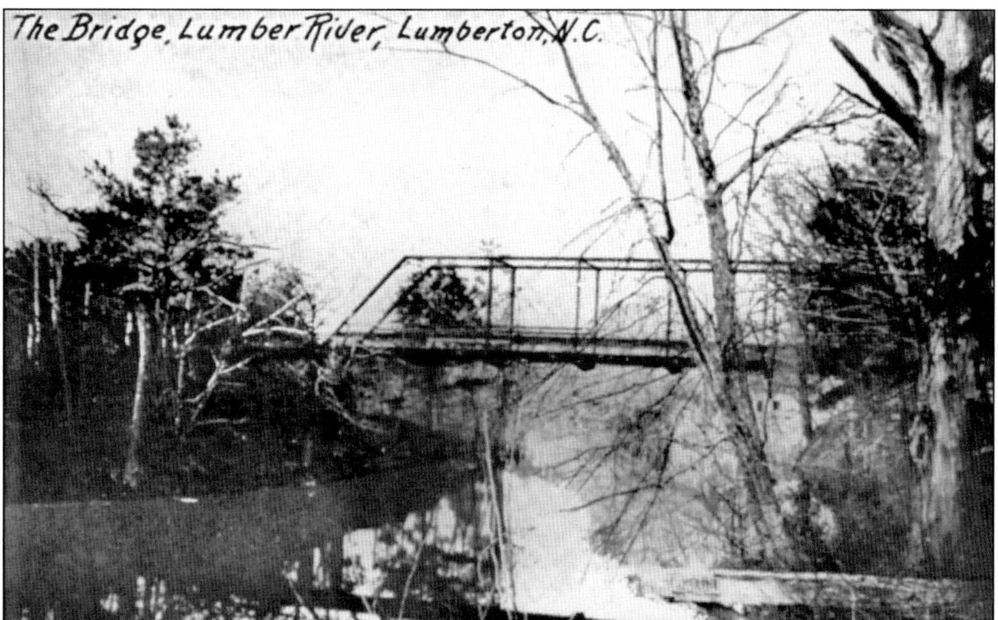

IRON BRIDGE. This wonderful iron bridge, typical of those installed in the early 1900s, was located over the Lumber River just outside of Lumberton and near the Robeson County Health Department.

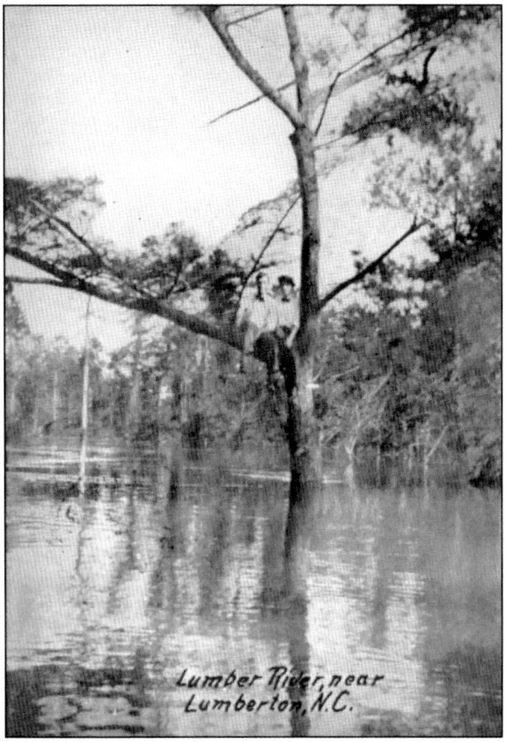

LUMBER RIVER. According to poet John Charles McNeill (1874–1907), the Native American name of Lumbee was originally used for the river and comes from a Native American word that means black water. Early European surveyors and settlers called it Drowning Creek; it appears in Colonial records of 1749. Legislative action in 1809 changed the name to Lumber River, most likely because of the river's heavy use by the lumber industry.

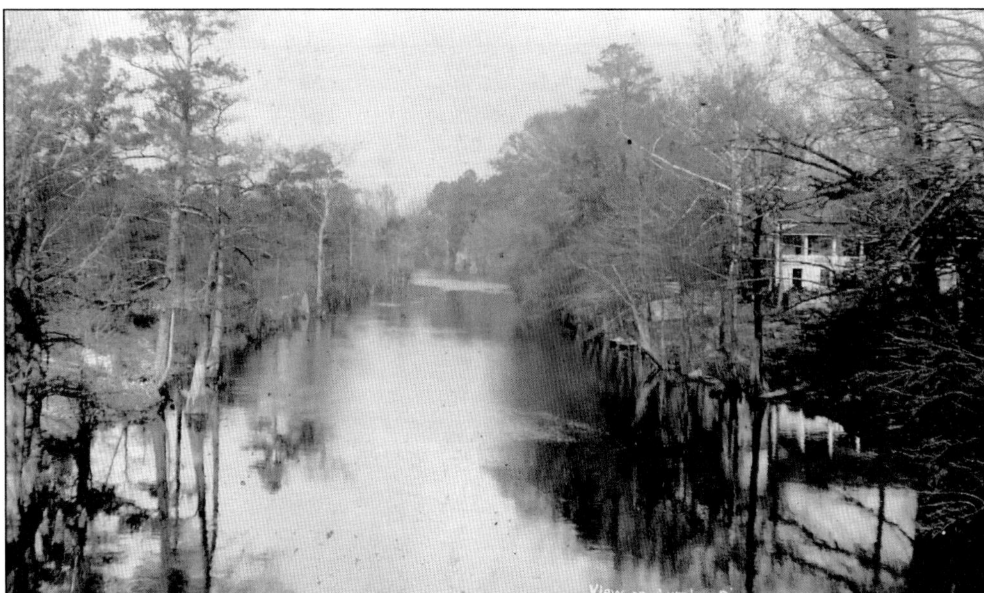

LUMBER RIVER. In the late 18th and 19th centuries, the lumbering and naval stores industries were very important to the region, and the river was a vital route for transporting the products of these industries. One-hundred-foot logs were rafted downriver in the late 18th century to Georgetown, South Carolina. Lumberton itself was an important turpentine and timber town. Unfortunately no standing structure related to these industries has been found that could be considered of historic value. (Courtesy Rev. James Burt MacLeod and Suzie MacLeod Dedrick.)

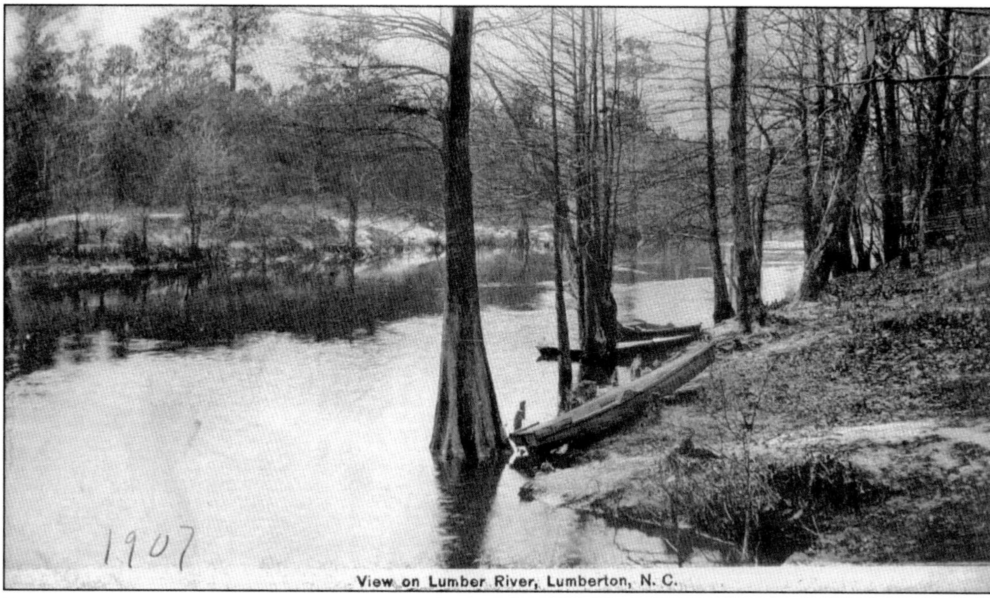

LUMBER RIVER. A quote about the Lumber River appeared in John Charles McNeill's *Argus*: "writing about the Lumber River, to a man who has spent his summers in dalliance with her, is like writing about his sweetheart. She is coquettish, as subject to change, as teasing as any girl that goes; and no human angel ever possessed more variable hues and tints and shadows in her misty eyes than this unconscious flirt."

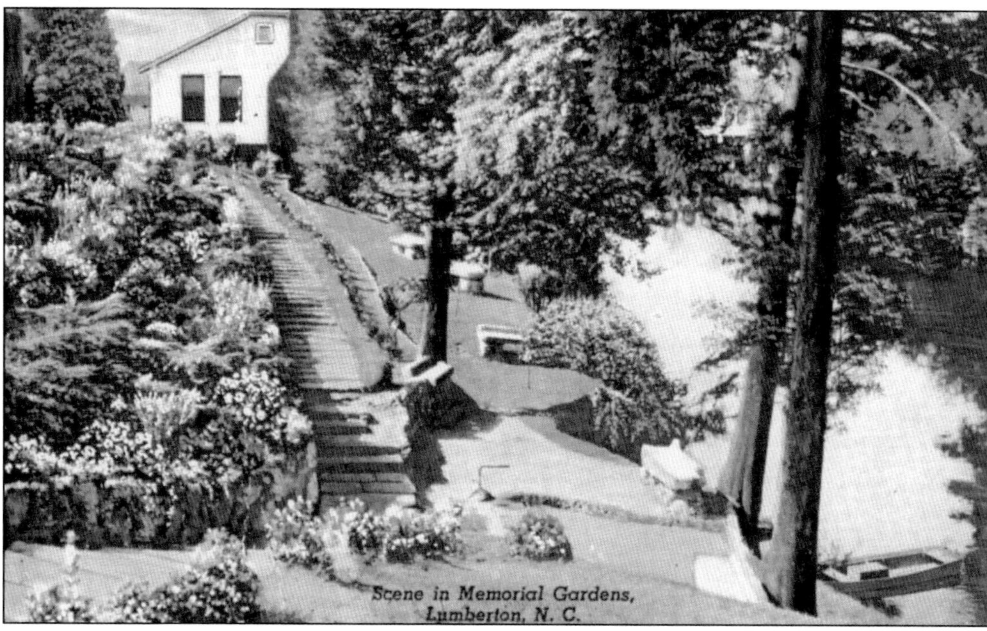

MEMORIAL GARDENS. For years, one of Lumberton's beautiful spots was the memorial gardens, which were located where Third Street connects with Water Street. Located at the top of the garden was the American Legion hut. The 48-by-100-foot wooden edifice was built in 1932 for the American Legion Post #42; the building was remolded over the years. The garden was one of the favorite projects of Kate Britt Biggs, local historian and genealogist. Years ago the landscape was changed and many of the plantings removed.

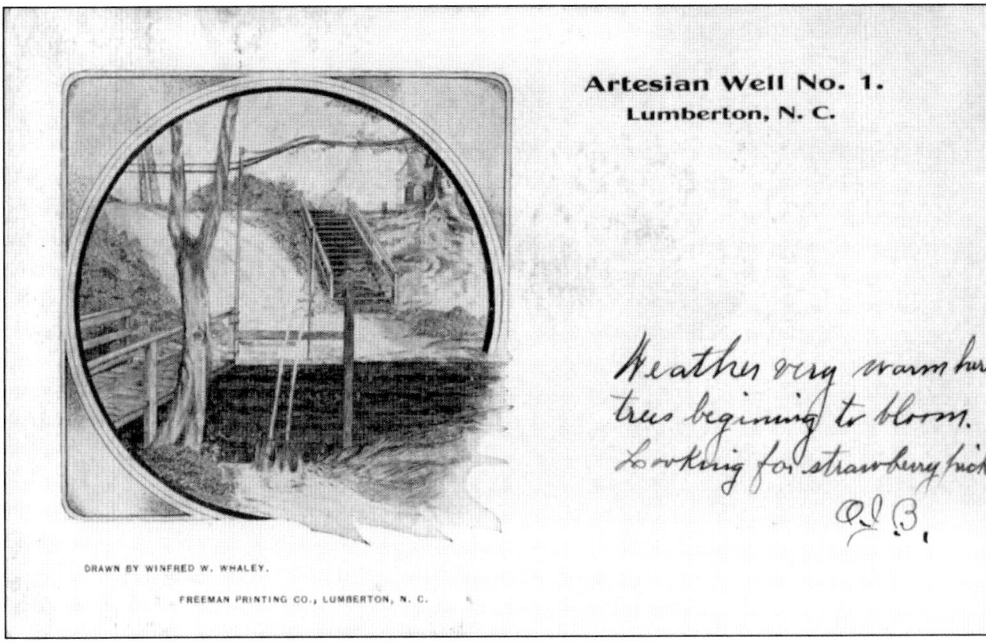

ARTESIAN WELL NO. 1. Lumberton's artesian wells were bored in between 1896 and 1897, when attorney E. K. Proctor Jr. was mayor.

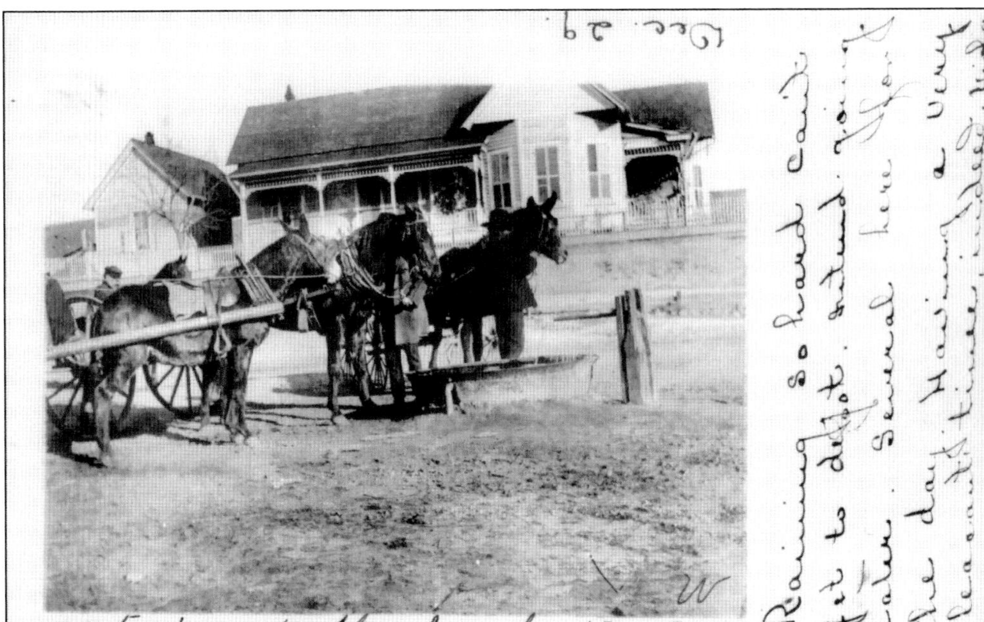

ARTESIAN WELL ELM STREET. This artesian well was located beside the home of Robert D. Caldwell and was later converted into a sunken garden that separated his house from that of his son-in-law and daughter, Dr. and Mrs. Horace Baker Sr. (Courtesy Carolina Collection, UNC-Chapel Hill.)

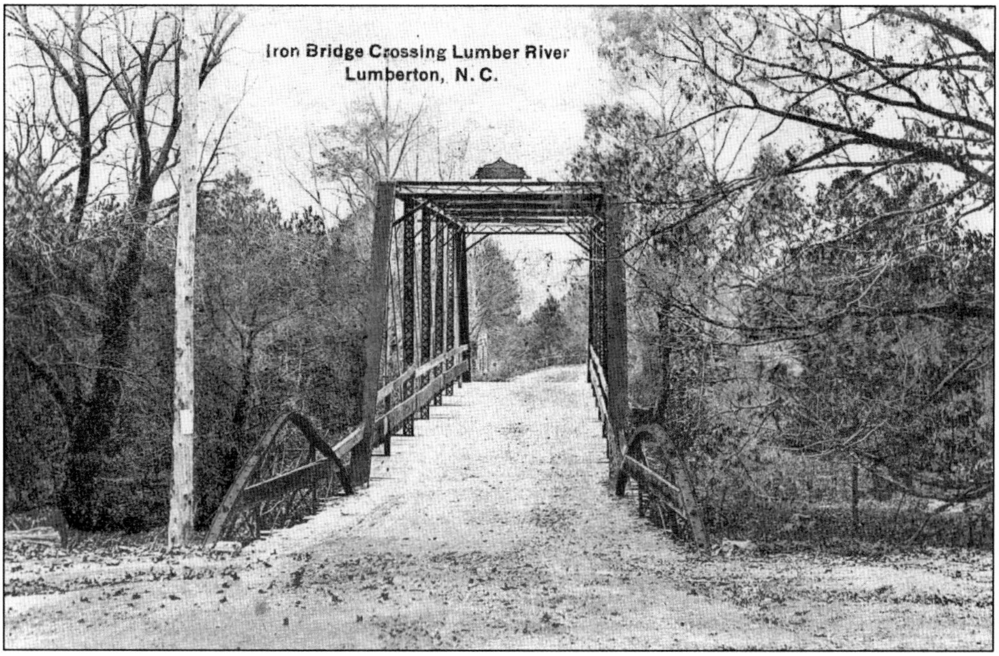

IRON BRIDGE CROSSING LUMBER RIVER. The iron bridge, known as McNeill's Bridge, was removed when the road was enlarged around 2002. It was near this site in 1984 that Paul Valenti found a Native American canoe dating to 930 AD. The canoe is housed at the Native American Resource Center at UNC Pembroke.

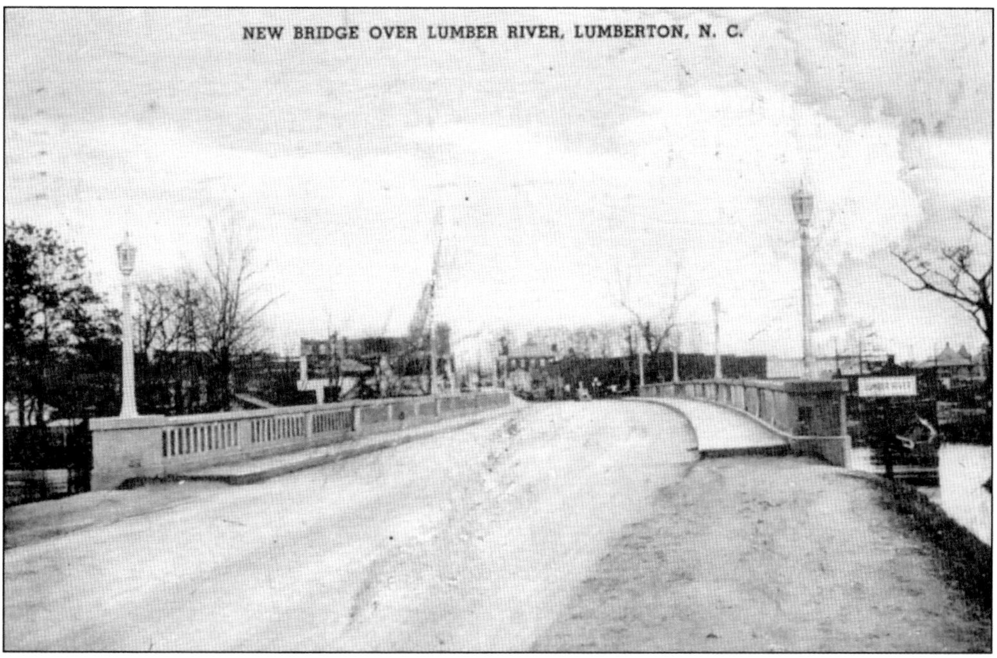

NEW BRIDGE OVER LUMBER RIVER. This bridge crosses the Lumber River at Lumberton's Second Street. In the background, Lumberton's town hall can be seen, as well as the freight building of the Virginia Carolina Southern Railroad that now houses the Robeson County History Museum.

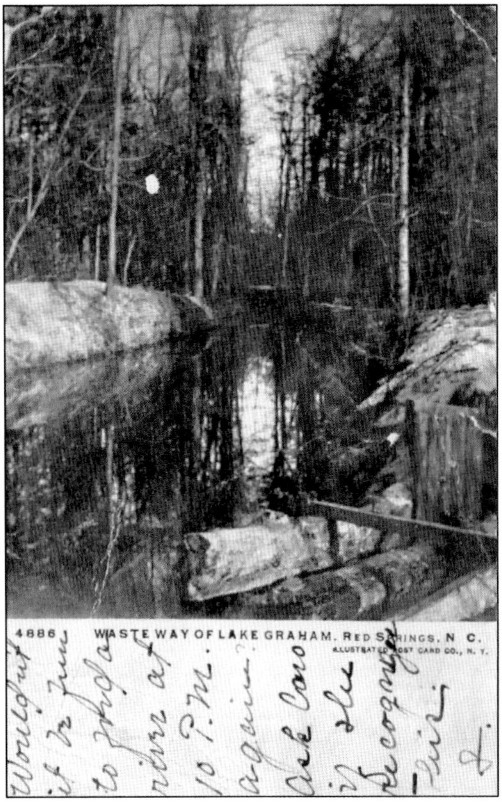

LAKE GRAHAM. This view shows the waste way as it pours into beautiful Lake Graham, located outside of Red Springs.

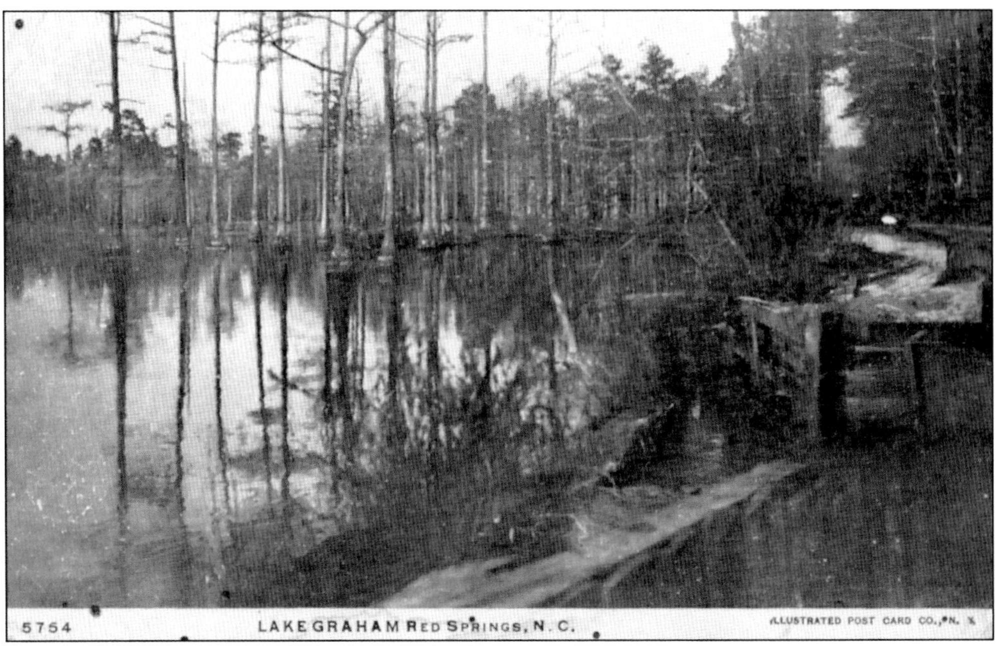

LAKE GRAHAM. Typical of many lakes and ponds in Robeson County, Lake Graham features a wonderful stand of cypress trees.

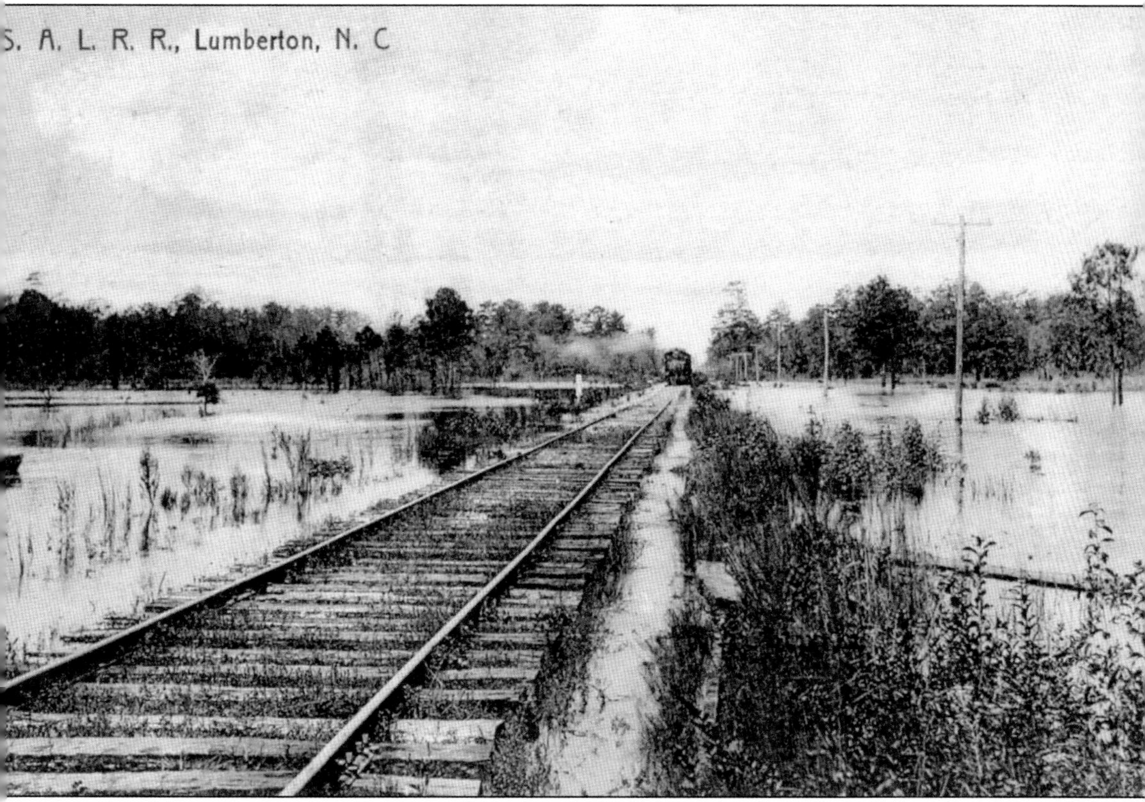

SEABOARD AIR LINE RAILROAD. The first railroad to come to Robeson County was the Wilmington & Charlotte Railroad. In April 1873, it was reorganized as the Carolina Central Railway Company. In 1900, they were merged into the Seaboard Air Line. This postcard shows a section of the railroad, outside of Lumberton, traveling through one of the many swamps.

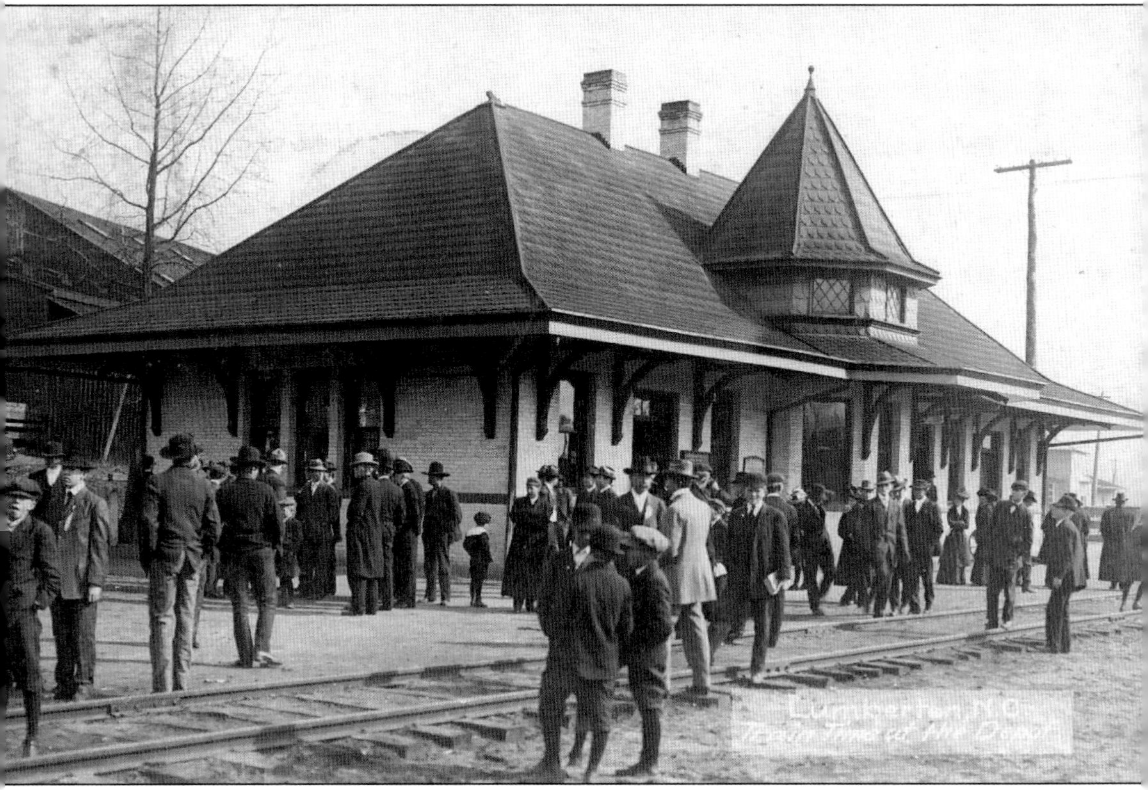

SEABOARD AIR LINE. Shown here is a large crowd gathered at the Lumberton Depot of the Seaboard Air Line Railway. In 1946, a new company was formed, Seaboard Air Line Railroad Company, and in 1967, it merged with Atlantic Coast Line Railroad to form the Seaboard Coast Line Railroad. In the early 1980s, the Seaboard Coast Line Railroad formed a partnership with many other railroads called "The Family Lines System." These partners eventually merged to become known as the Seaboard System Railroad. Finally in the late 1980s, the Seaboard System Railroad merged with the Chessie System Railroad to become what is known today as CSX Transportation. (Courtesy Rev. James Burt MacLeod and Suzie MacLeod Dedrick.)

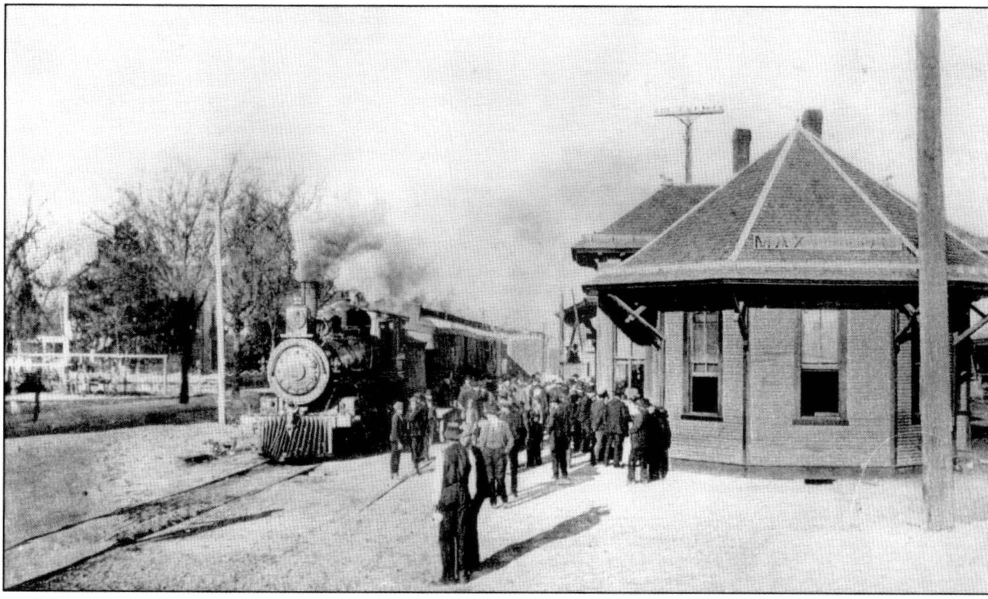

MAXTON STATION. The rails of the Wilmington & Charlotte Railroad arrived at Shoe Heel (now Maxton) on April 17, 1861, but rail construction was stopped due to the War Between the States in August 1861. This railroad operated the first sleeper cars through Maxton in May 1875, and they continued until 1930 when they were taken off the line. The railroad reorganized under the name Carolina Central Railroad in 1873 and merged with Seaboard Air Line in 1900. Special Passenger trains were operated in and out of the Laurinburg-Maxton Air Base over the Seaboard.

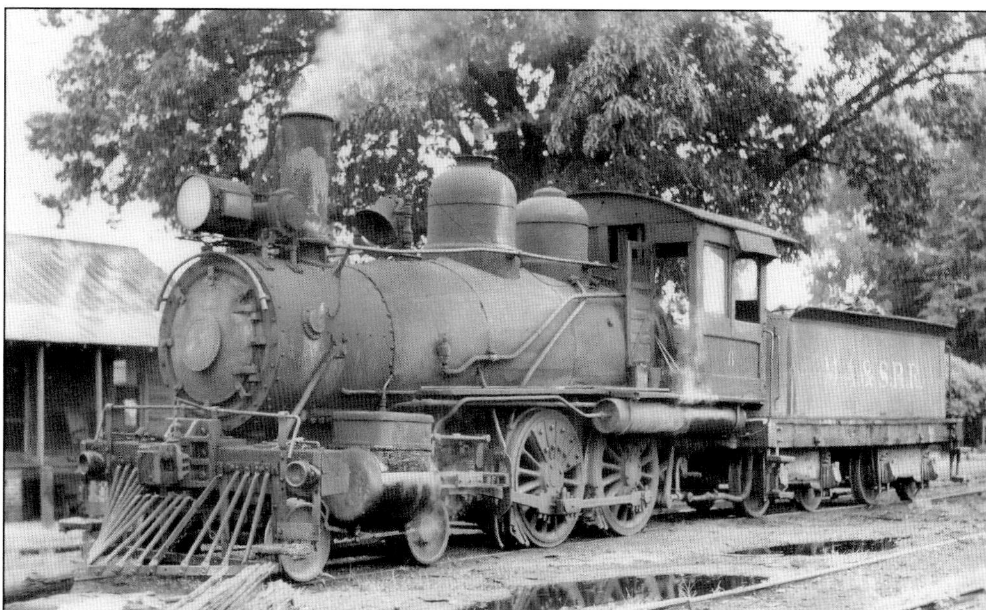

MAXTON ALMA RAILROAD. The Maxton, Alma, and Southbound Railroad Company was incorporated on February 21, 1911. This railroad was largely an industrial line that primarily served the Alma Lumber Company. The line was abandoned on August 13, 1937; pictured here is engine #6.

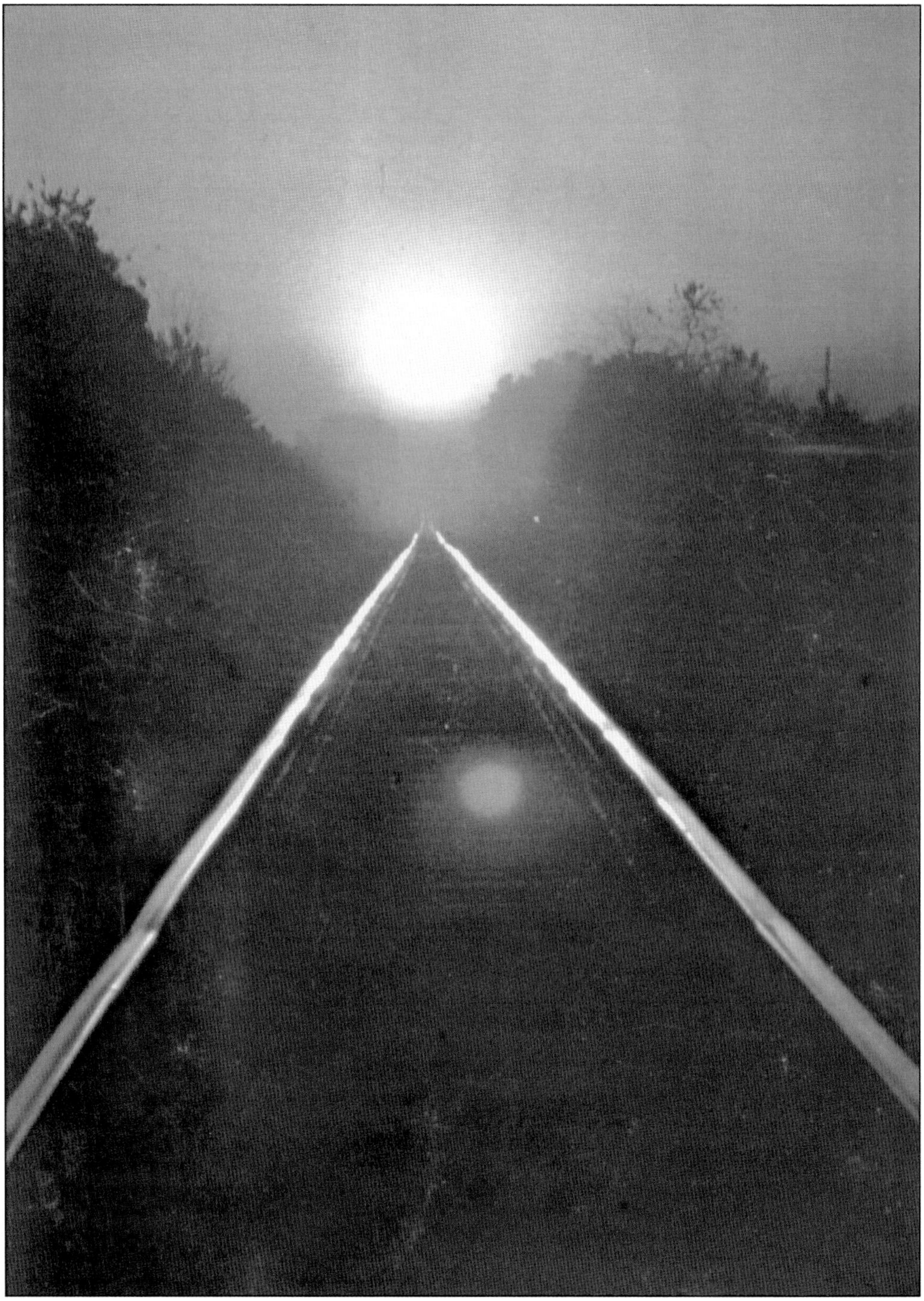

STRAIGHTLINE AT ALMA. This postcard of an autumn sunrise shows a section or railroad between Alma and Maxton. This section is part of the longest stretch of straight railroad track in the United States, which runs between Wilmington and Old Hundred in Scotland County. The Wilmington, Charlotte and Rutherfordton Railroad laid 78.86 miles of straight tracks through pine forests and swamps.

Three

Agriculture, Industry, and Business

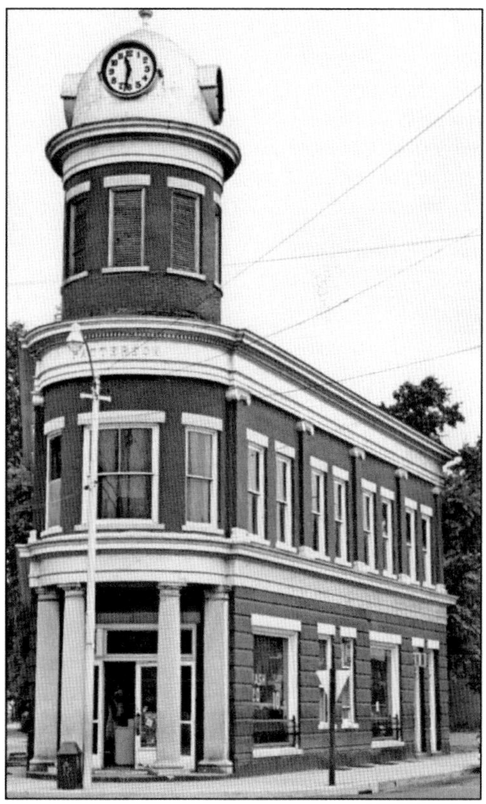

Patterson Building. Built in 1911 by J. A. "Archie" Patterson to house the Bank of Robeson, this flat-iron-shaped Renaissance Revival building was modeled after the famous flat-iron building in New York. The building did not have the clock tower when it was first built; the local citizens raised funds to add the clock, which is now the best known landmark in town. The main floor of the building later housed the post office before being converted to a laundromat. The town purchased the building in the late 1990s and began to look for funds to refurbish the building. Preservation Maxton, with a grant from Clara McLean (former executive of McLean Trucking and Sea-Land), stepped forward with $500,000 to return the building to its former glory.

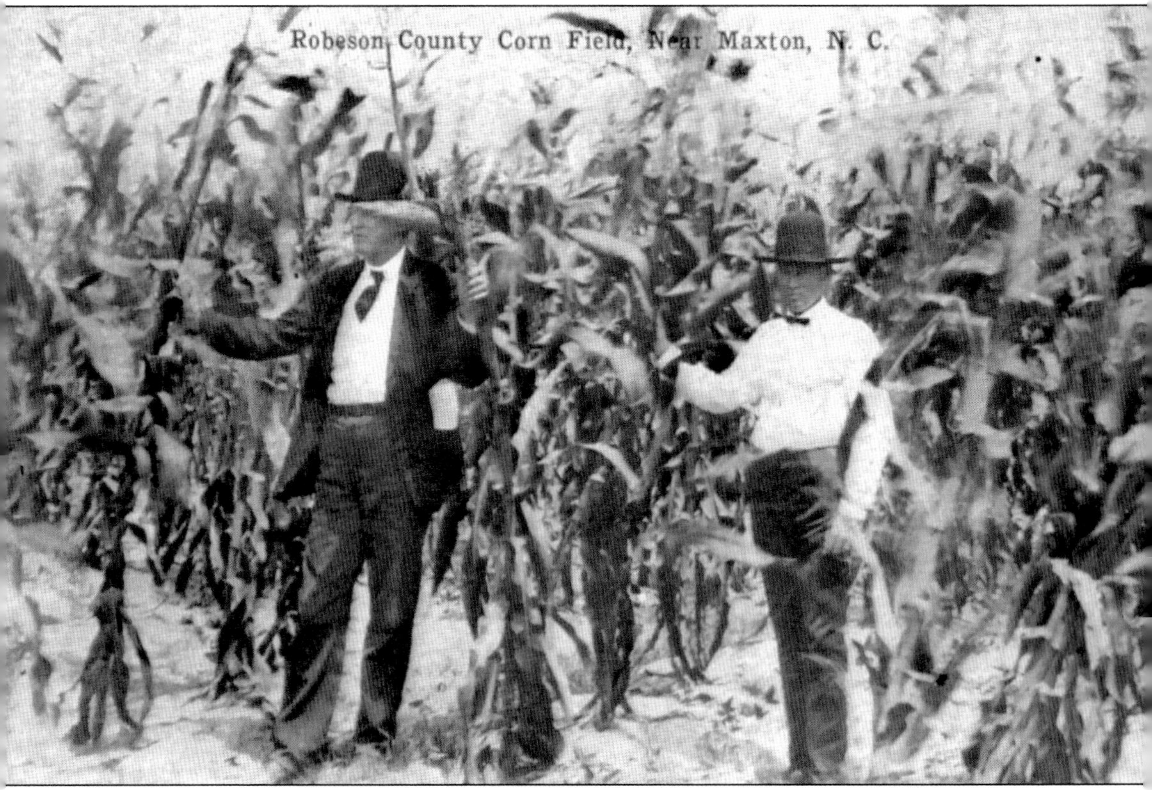

CORNFIELD. Farming has always been an important mainstay of Robeson County's economy and contributed largely to the general prosperity of Maxton. By the early 1900s, farmers were progressive and using most of the modern implements. In addition to corn, the Maxton section of the county grew cotton, wheat, oats, rye, potatoes, melons, and cantaloupes. Capt. A. J. "Sandy" McKinnon played a large role in the production of melons and cantaloupes in the county, and in 1904, he grew 75 railroad cars of them. McKinnon planted 16 acres of cantaloupes in 1904, which netted 2,600 crates and a profit of $3,800. He also experimented with the cultivation of asparagus.

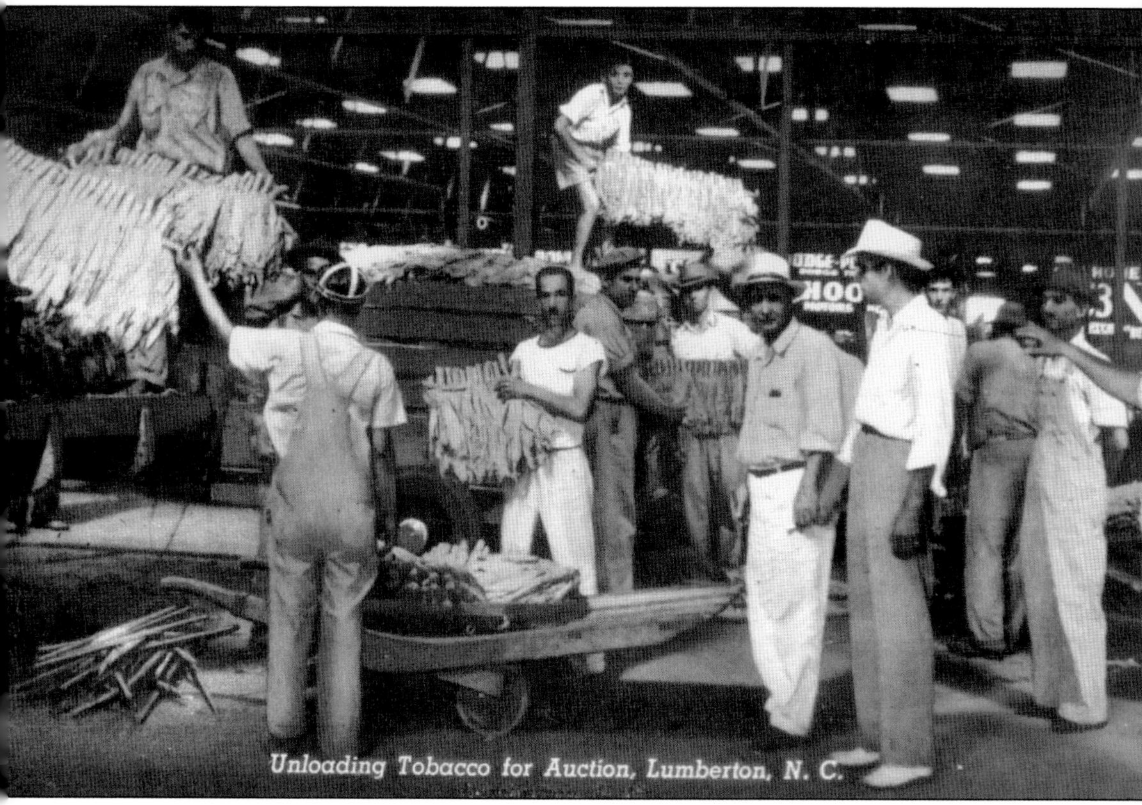

Tobacco Warehouse. At one time, Lumberton boasted 10 tobacco warehouses that drew large crowds during the season from August to November. Tobacco was a rare sight in 1895, but by the early 1900s, it was a major crop in the county. Tobacco production was 17,250.454 pounds in 1935 and by 1944 had grown to 32,751,381 pounds that sold at the market for $14,130,271.98. During the 1940s, Robeson County was the second largest grower of bright leaf flue-cured tobacco in North Carolina. Many of the old tobacco warehouses have vanished from the landscape. The Cooperative Warehouse was destroyed by fire in 1992, and the Star Warehouse was torn down in 1994.

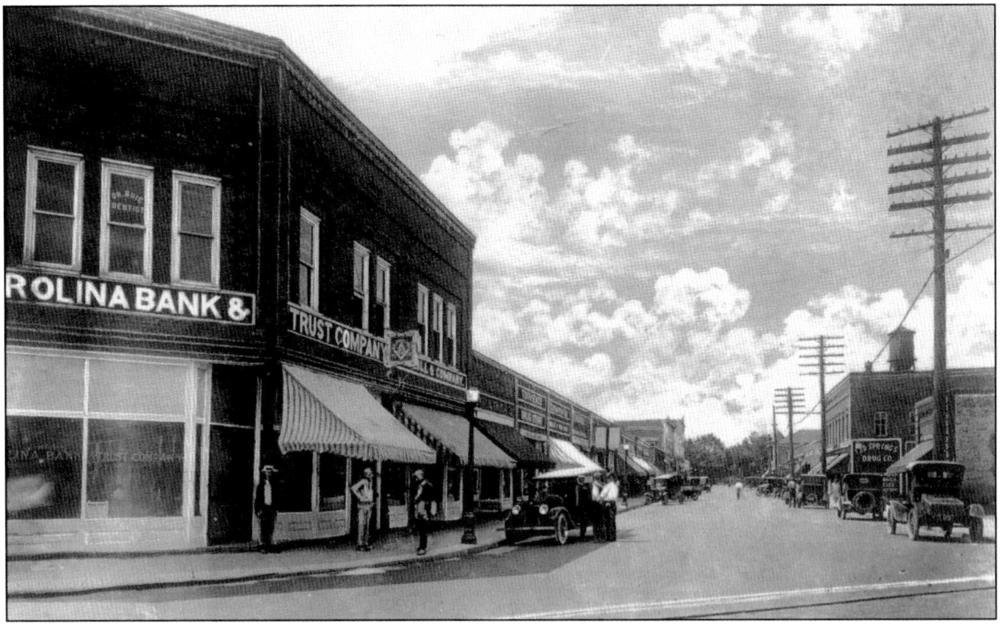

Carolina Bank. The Carolina Bank and Trust Company, pictured above, had A. B. Pearsall serving as its president. Also on the board were J. S. Jones, R. W. Livermore, George H. Hall, B. W. Townsend, A. T. McCallum, J. G. Williams, Dr. Luther McMillan, W. F. Williams, and Hiram Grantham. (Courtesy Carolina Collection, UNC-Chapel Hill.)

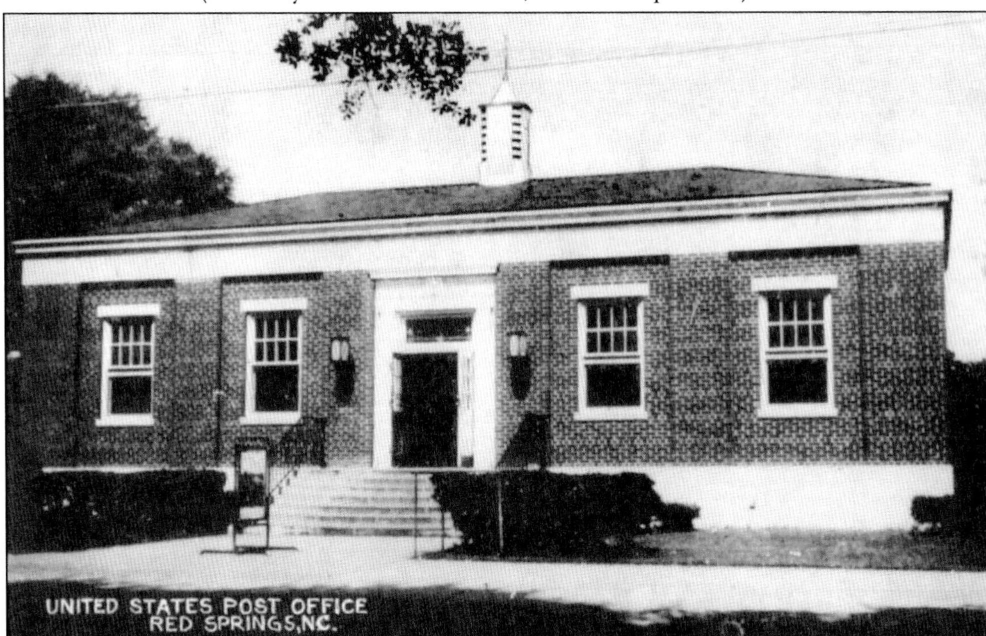

Post Office. The Red Springs Post Office was built as part of the depression-era WPA program. It still maintains many of its original features including beautiful brass window booths and woodwork. The most outstanding feature is the mural painted as part of the WPA Artist Program. It contains three panels: the Scottish settlers being greeted by the Native Americans, the American Revolutionary Battle of Raft Swamp, and an agricultural scene.

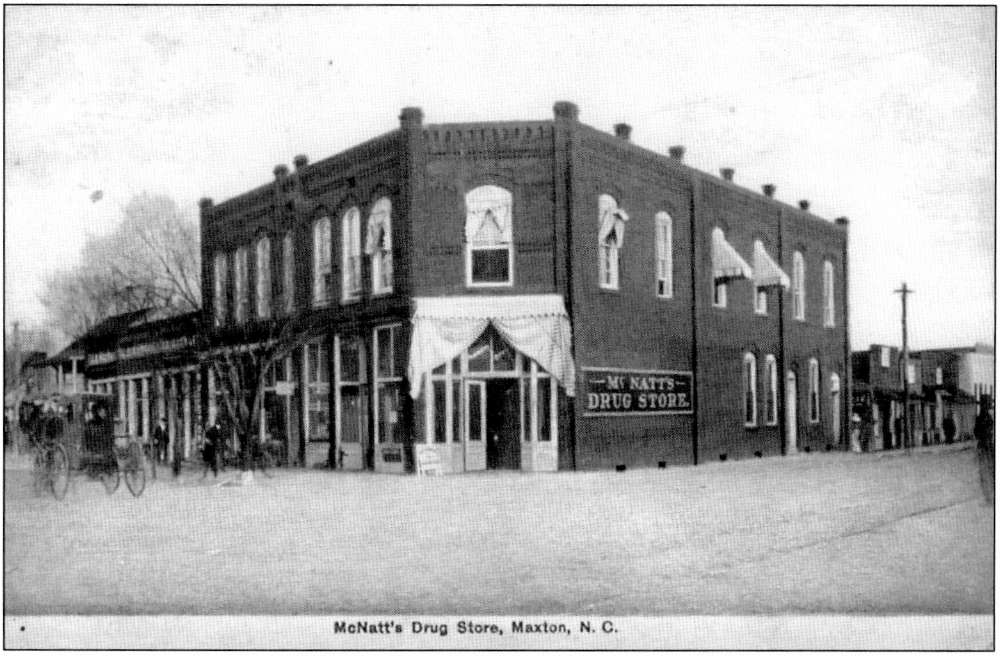

McNATT'S DRUG STORE. Dr. Henry Wise McNatt was born in Parkton and graduated from the University of Maryland in 1881. He began to practice in Maxton in 1885 and continued until his death in 1910. He was married to the former Jessie McRae, and they had no children.

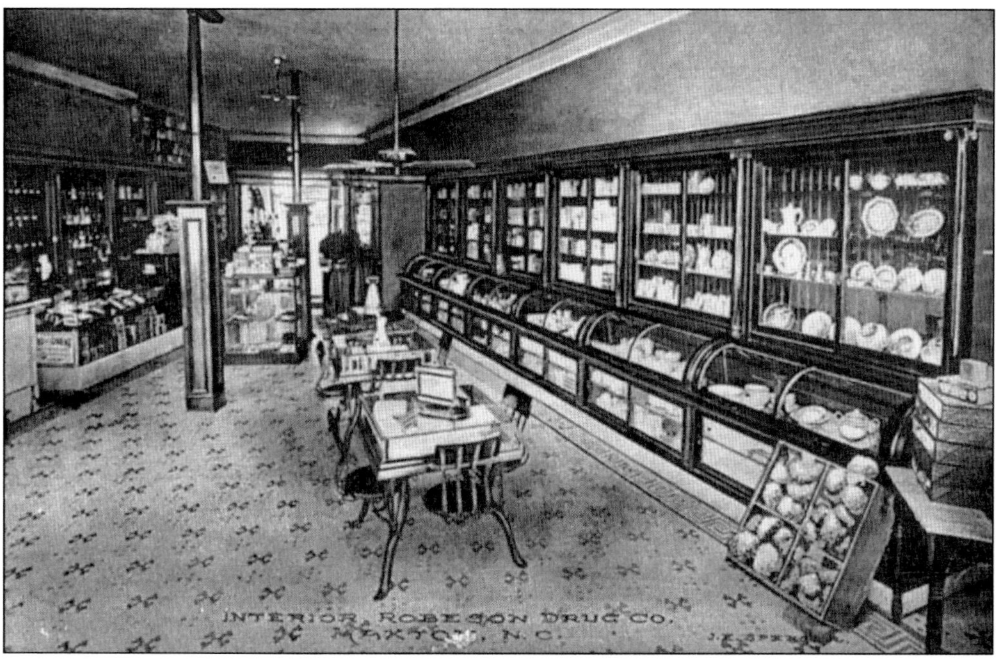

ROBESON DRUG COMPANY. The Robeson Drug Company was located in downtown Maxton and sold a wide array of items in addition to medicines.

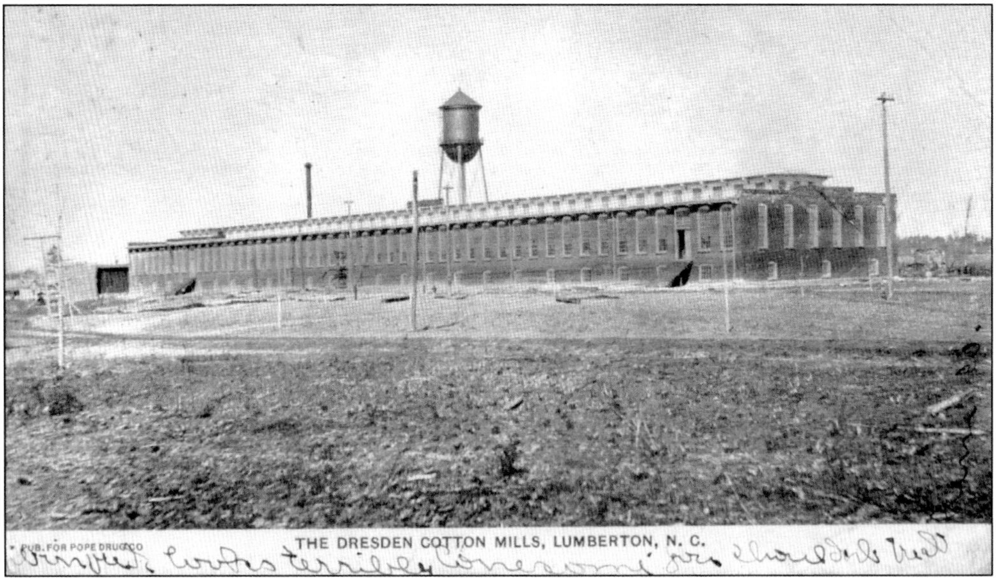

DRESDEN COTTON MILLS. The Dresden Cotton Mill was organized in 1896 on the Seaboard Airline Railroad in East Lumberton. The 75-acre tract included the mill, 54 tenant houses, and a large two-story brick flat that contained eight apartments with four rooms each. Each dwelling has its own artesian well. The children attended school at the schoolhouse located at the Lumberton Cotton Mill. The hall of the school also served the community as a place for religious services and entertainment. Officers were R. D. Caldwell (president), A. W. McLean (vice president), H. B. Jennings (secretary treasurer), and F. R. Gray (assistant treasurer).

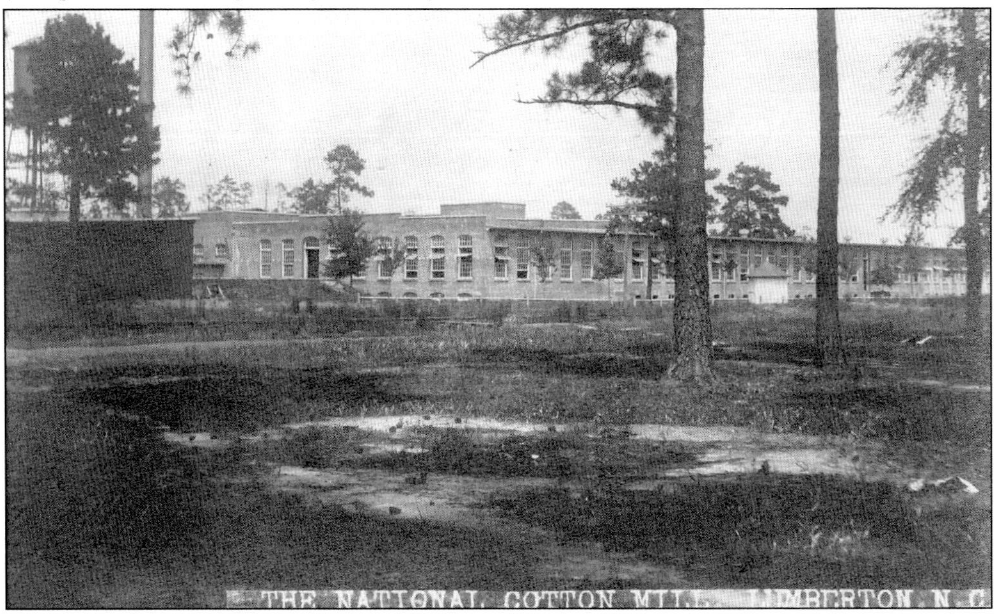

NATIONAL COTTON MILL. Organized in 1906, the National Cotton Mill was located a half-mile from the Lumber River on the Seaboard Airline Railroad, one and one-half miles west of Lumberton. The mill operated 6,240 spindles of knitting yarns in white and colors. The officers were George B. McLeod (president), R. C. Lawrence (vice president), A. P. McAllister (secretary treasurer), and J. W. Kanser (superintendent).

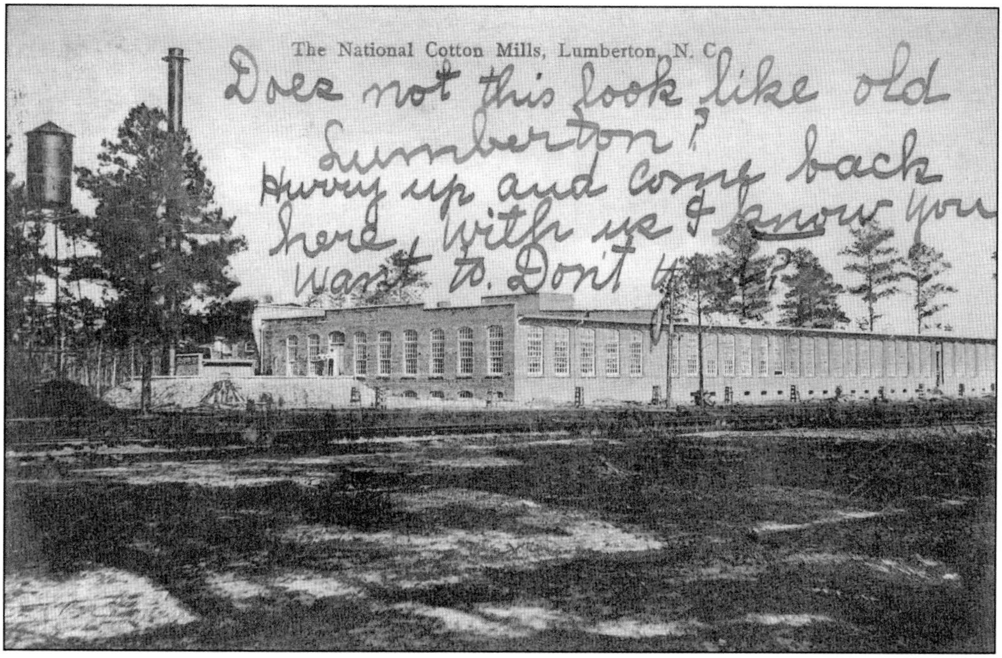

NATIONAL COTTON MILLS. The mill owners operated a school on the property that the children were encouraged to attend. The owners also sponsored religious services and entertainment for the young people.

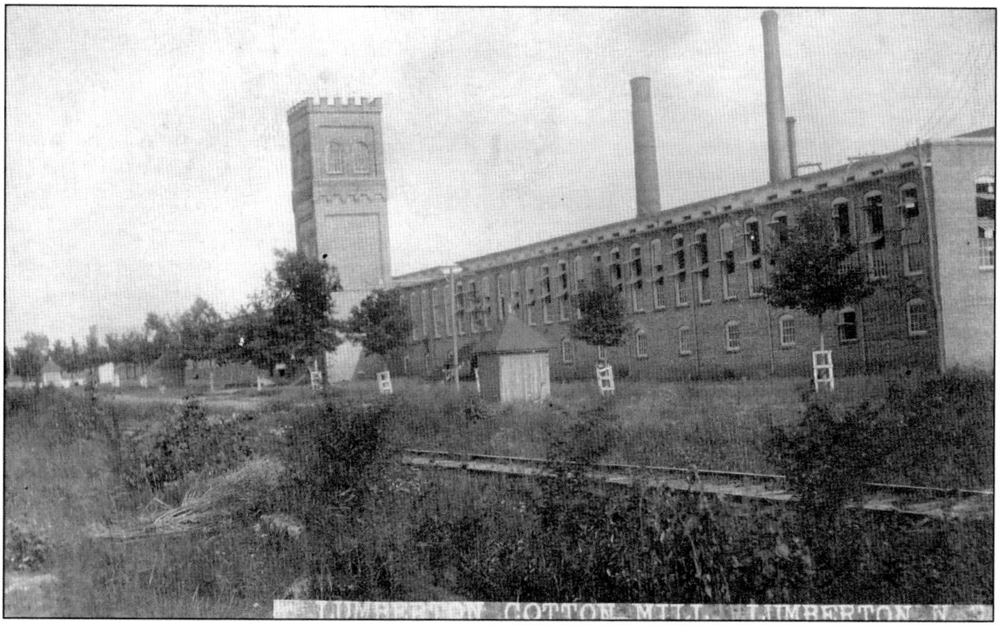

LUMBERTON COTTON MILL. The Lumberton Cotton Mill was incorporated in 1900 with capital stock valued at $70,000. It was located in East Lumberton on the Seaboard Airline Railroad. The property covered 250 acres with the mill buildings, company store, public school, and 175 cottages. The main building was one-story, brick, 75-feet-by-250-feet, and had 5,000 spindles. S. J. Webb was the mill superintendent. Officers were R. D. Caldwell (president), A. W. McLean (vice president), H. B. Jennings (secretary treasurer), and F. R. Gray (assistant treasurer).

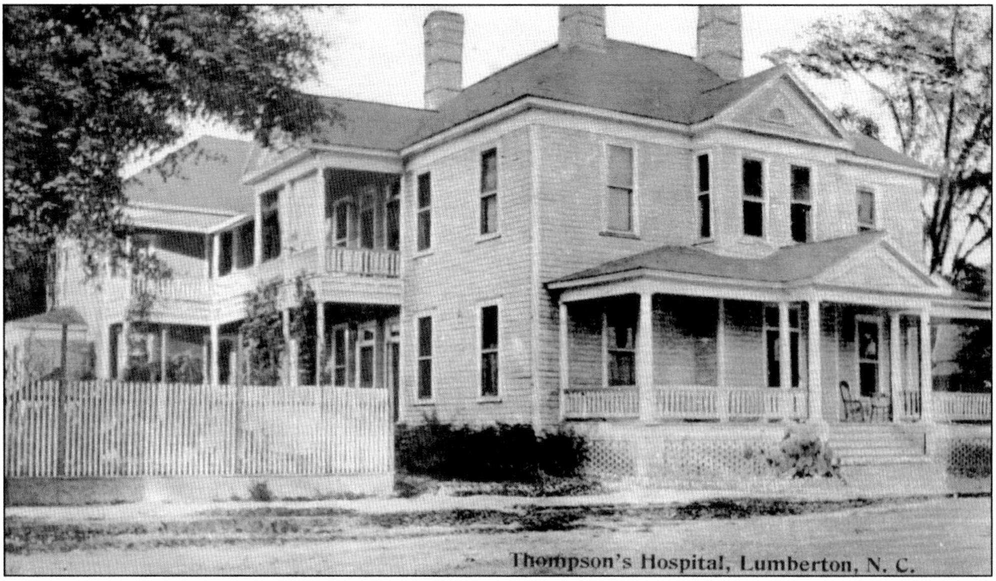

THOMPSON HOSPITAL. The Thompson Hospital was organized in 1905 by Dr. Neill Archie Thompson Sr., Dr. Richard Gregory Rozier, and R. C. Lawrence. It was located in a house built by Solomon Bennett on the northwest corner of Pine and Fourth Streets. An advertisement for the hospital in a 1910 special edition of the *News and Observer* stated that the hospital cared for all classes of surgical, gynecological, and non-contagious medical patients; they had superior operating rooms and two large wards for colored patients. The Thompson family lived in the hospital building.

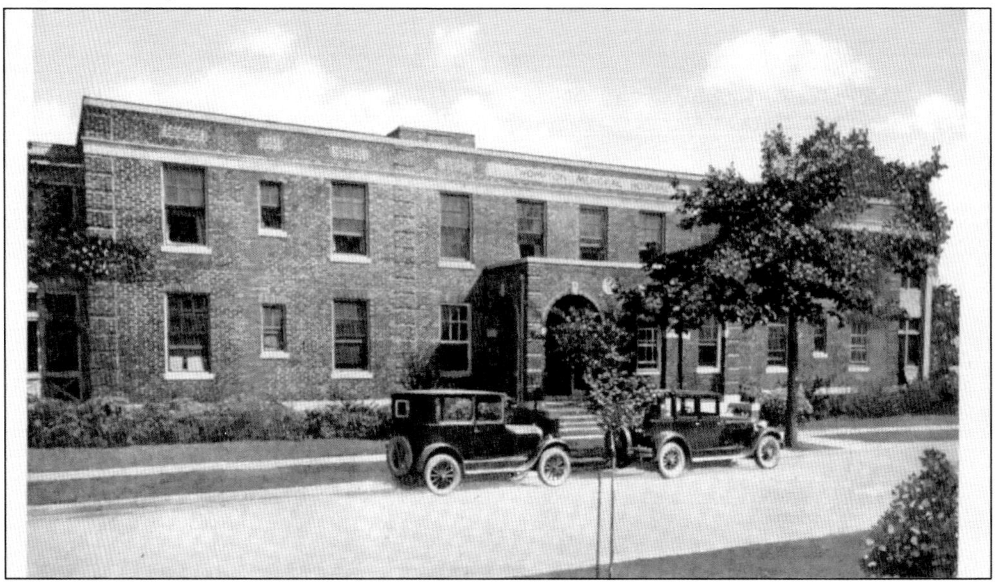

THOMPSON MEMORIAL HOSPITAL. Dr. Thompson was killed in 1922 while crossing Fayetteville Street. Under the leadership of Dr. Thomas C. Johnson, a new hospital was built on the northeast corner of Cedar and Fifth Streets in 1926. The construction was done by Thomas Matthew Burney, son of William and Elmira Cain Burney. The building was completed and equipped for $100,000 and housed 40 patient beds, an elevator, and x-ray department. This building is currently the Lumberton Municipal building.

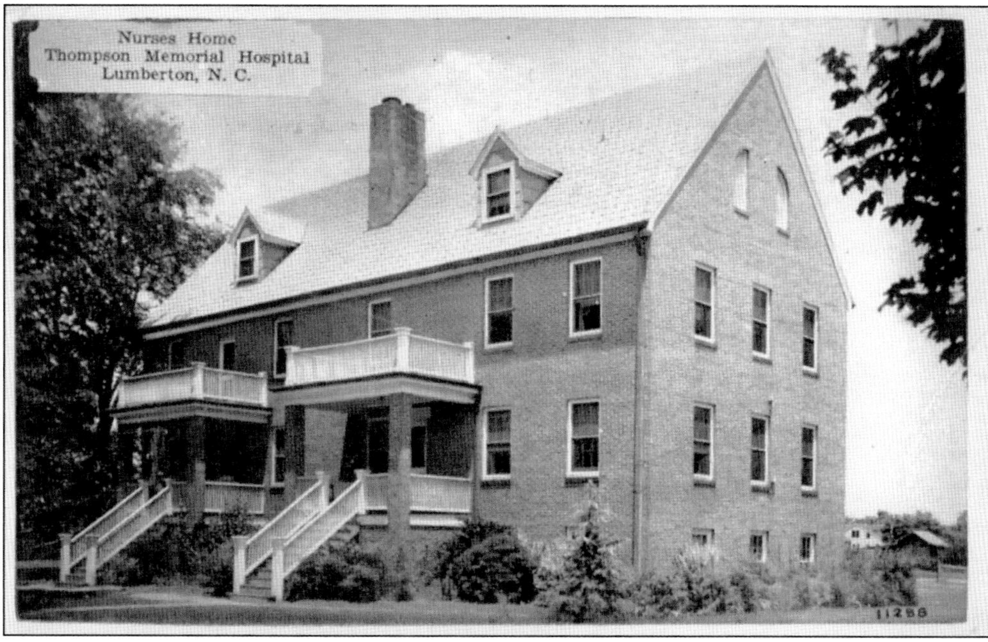

NURSES HOME. The Thompson Memorial Hospital operated a nursing school on the grounds of the hospital.

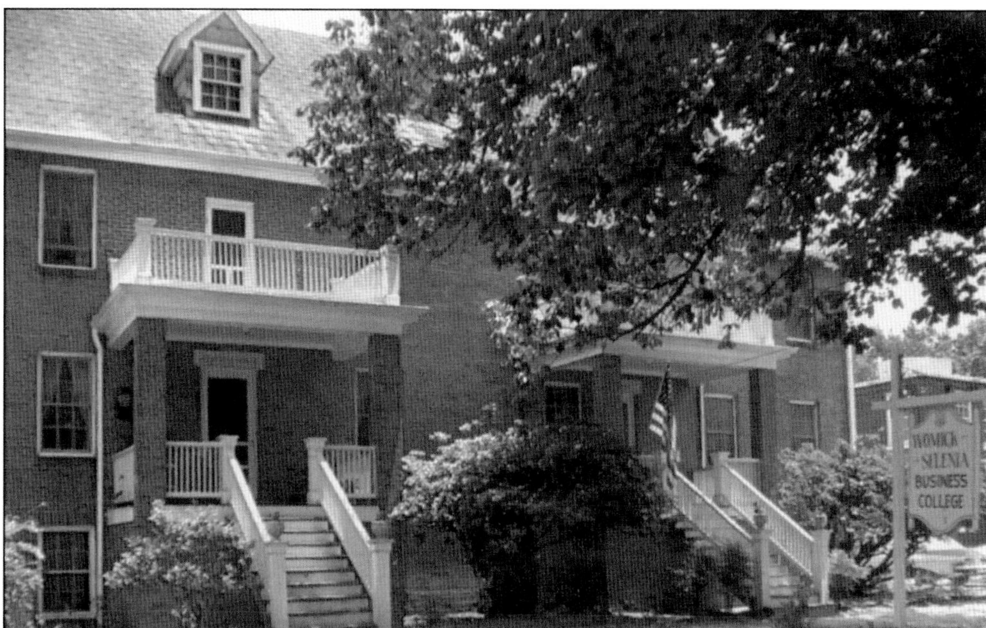

WOMICK-SELENIA BUSINESS COLLEGE. Located in the former Nurses Home of the Thompson Hospital, the Womick-Selenia Business College was established in 1956. It offered complete business training, including general office in 48 weeks, stenographic in 36 weeks, junior accounting in 48 weeks, secretarial in 48 weeks, and business administration in 72 weeks.

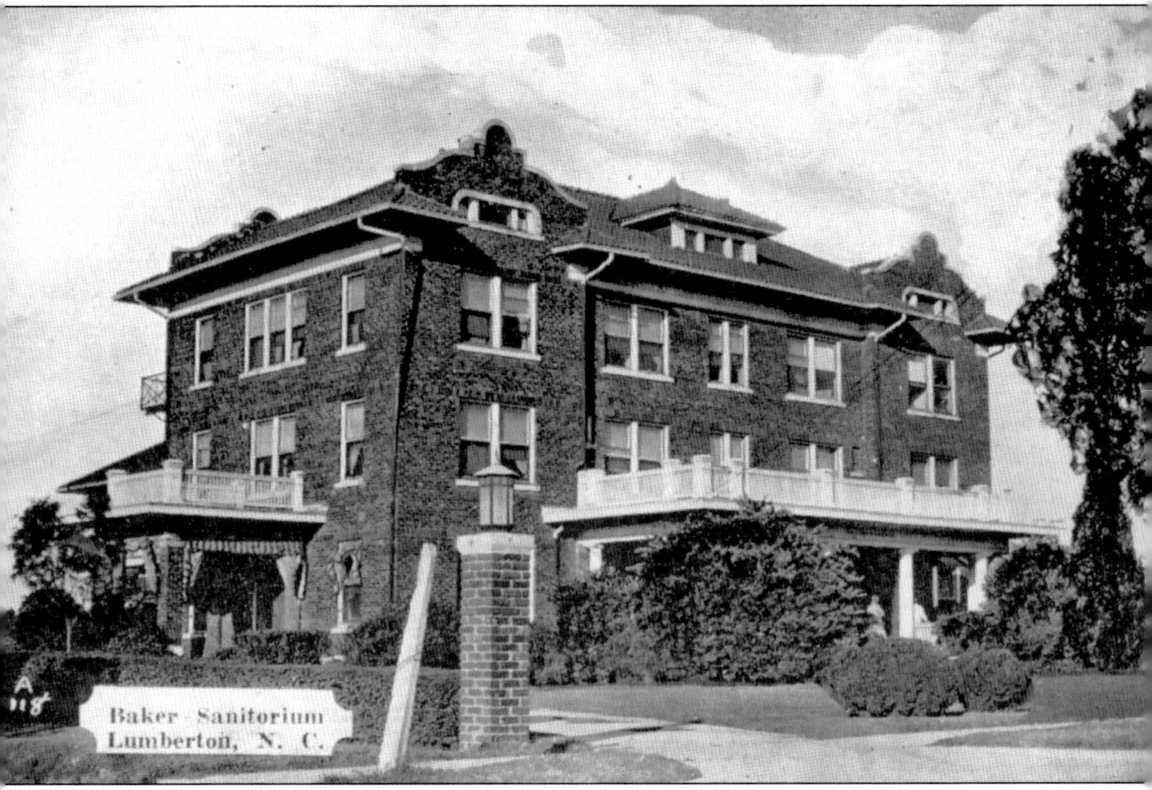

BAKER SANITARIUM. The Baker Sanatorium opened in January 1921; the 75-bed facility was located on North Chestnut Street. The building was constructed by Thomas Matthew Burney and William Moody Burney, under the auspices of Burney Brothers Construction Company. They were the sons of William and Elmira Cain Burney. Construction was in the Burney blood; their father had constructed the Luther H. Caldwell House, and each had a son who went into the construction business. An advertisement in the October 7, 1920, issue of *The Robesonian* was seeking six trim carpenters to work on the hospital at the rate of 75¢ per hour. This hospital was the dream of Dr. Horace Baker and his wife, the former Annie Ruth Caldwell. Mrs. Baker's father, R. D. Caldwell, was instrumental in planning the hospital. The hospital took care of medical, surgical, and obstetric-gynecological cases. The building was purchased by the In the Duke Endowment in the 1930s and became a community hospital. When Dr. Baker died in 1945, the sanatorium merged with the Thompson Hospital, which was also under the Duke Endowment. (Courtesy Paul Valenti and Carla Baxley.)

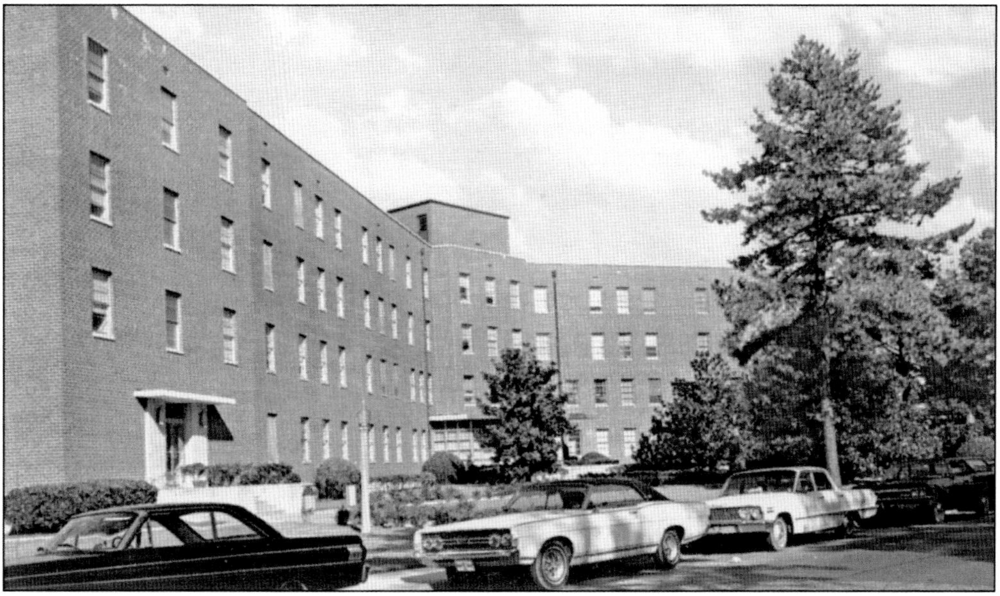

SOUTHEASTERN HOSPITAL. The Baker-Thompson Memorial Hospital performed surgical procedures at the Baker site, while medical, pediatric, and obstetric cases went to the Thompson facility. The trustees decided that one new hospital could better serve the needs of Robeson County. The result was the Robeson County Memorial Hospital, now Southeastern Regional Medical Center. A new building was completed in 1953 on a 10-acre site between Rowland and Elm Streets in North Lumberton.

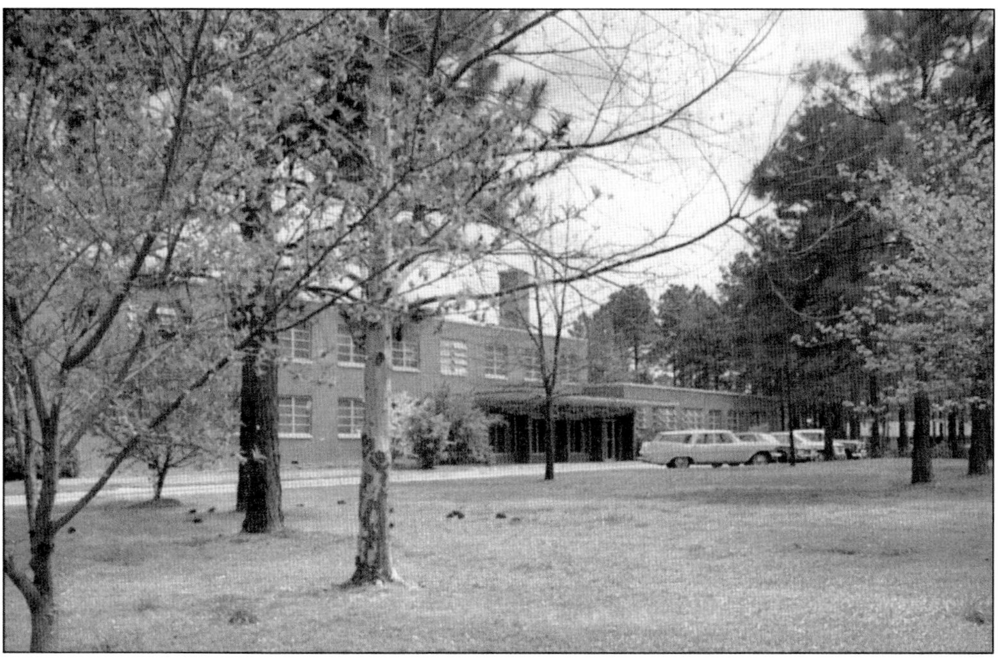

NURSES HOME. Southeastern General Hospital provided the McRae Nurses Home for the training of its nursing staff. The nurses home was completed in 1954.

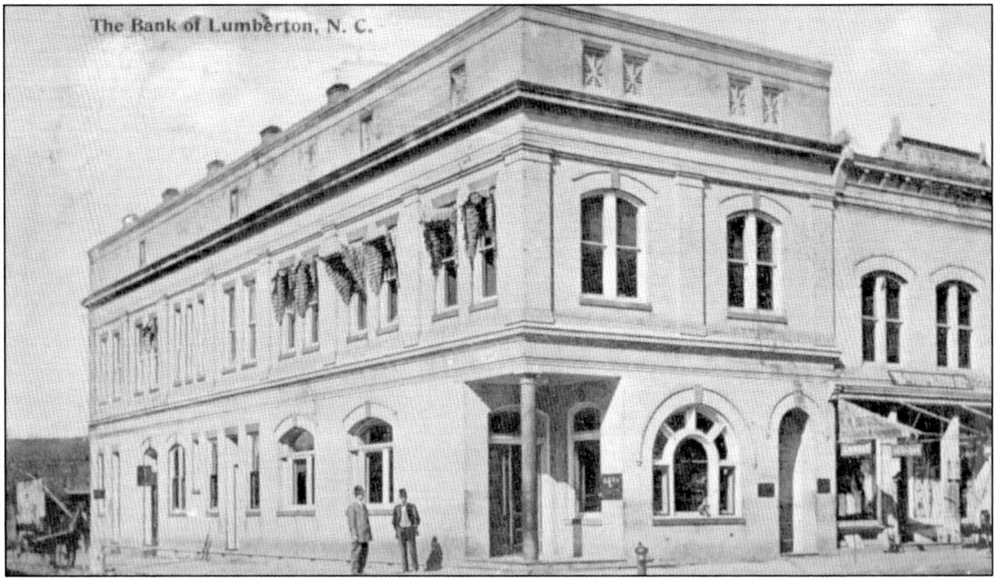

BANK OF LUMBERTON. The Bank of Lumberton was organized in 1896; this was the first bank in Robeson County. The first president was T. A. McNeill, who resigned after six months. A. W. McLean was then elected and served until his death in 1935, at which point A. E. White became president. Located in the building behind the bank was the K. M. Biggs store, which was owned by Kenneth Murchison Biggs. Biggs opened in 1903 after receiving a loan from A. W. McLean. In 1924, Biggs moved farther down Elm Street into the building occupied by House of Quality Pawnshop. (Courtesy Rev. James Burt MacLeod and Suzie MacLeod Dedrick.)

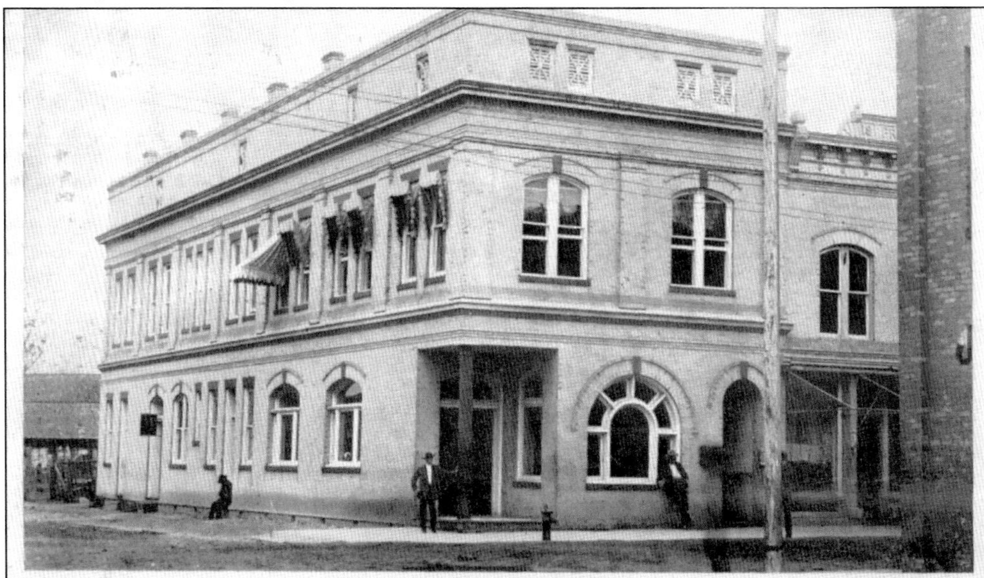

BANK OF LUMBERTON. In 1910, an advertisement appeared in a special edition of the *News and Observer* for the Bank of Lumberton. The advertisement stated that the bank had never lost one penny on any loan. Their officers were A. W. McLean (president), A. E. White (vice president), C. B. Townsend (active vice president), R. D. Caldwell (vice president), A. T. McLean (assistant cashier), and A. W. Peace (cashier).

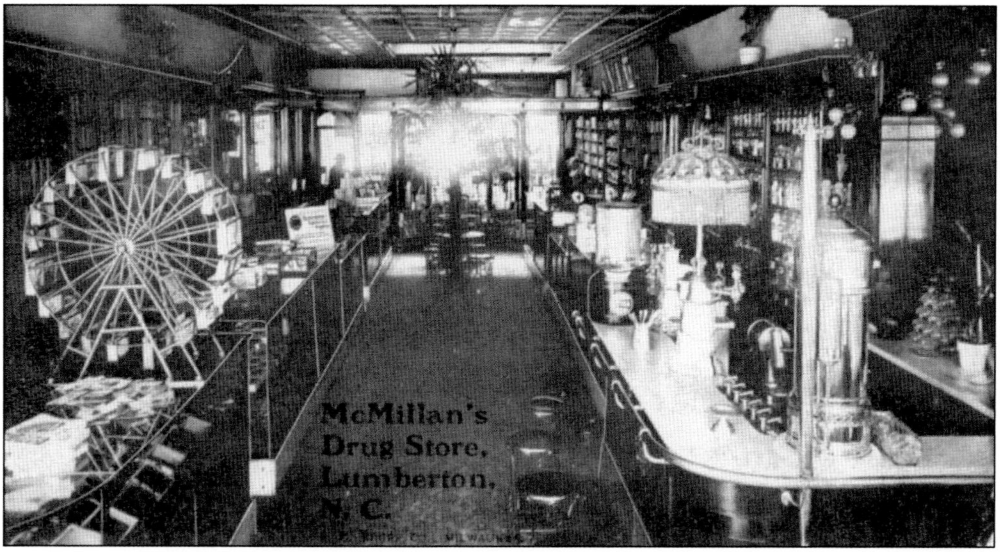

McMillan's Drug Store. Dr. John Duncan McMillian Sr. was born near Parkton on September 11, 1850, to Daniel and Isabella McMillan. He graduated from the Jefferson Medical College in Philadelphia in 1876. He began practice in Lumberton in 1876 and established McMillan's Drug Store in downtown Lumberton, which was operated by his descendants for over 75 years. He married Sara Ellen McMillan and had a son, John Duncan McMillan Jr. After Sara's death, he married Arabella Rowland and had a daughter, Flora Neill McMillan. (Courtesy Rev. James Burt MacLeod and Suzie MacLeod Dedrick.)

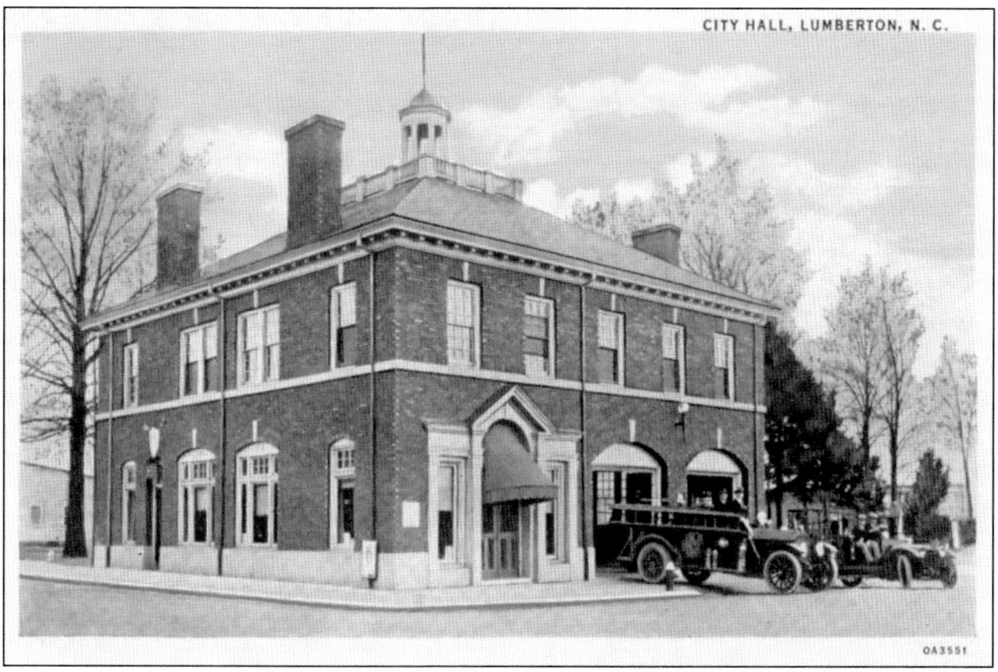

City Hall. This building was built in 1917 by builder William Moody Burney to house the Lumberton City Hall and fire department. It also was the site of the Robeson County Public Library. Fireman Rudolph Lewis spoke fondly of his service to the department and remembers that the Carolina Theatre used to provide two movie tickets a week for each of the fireman.

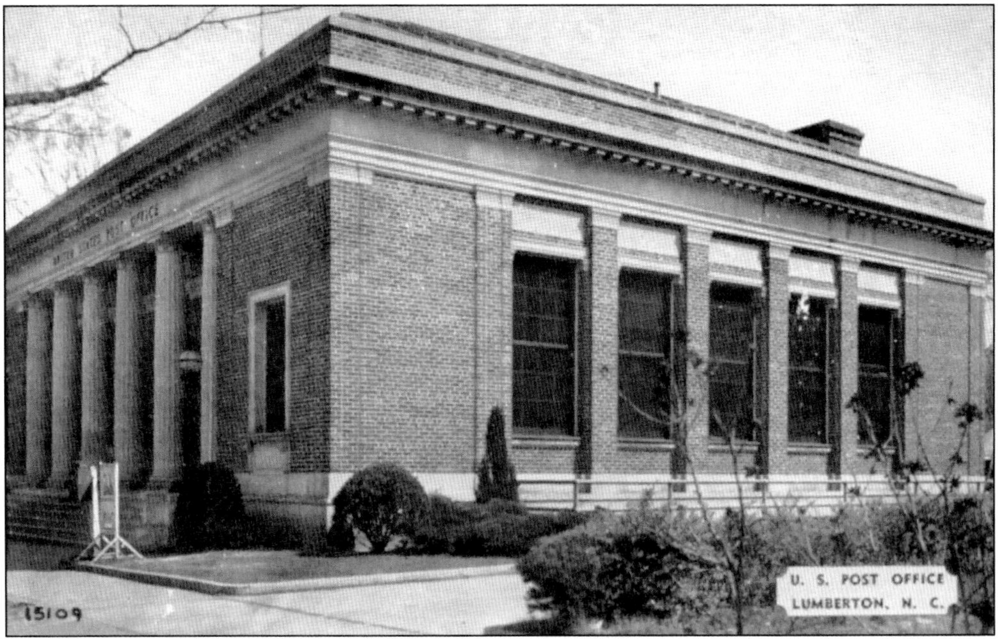

Post Office. This neoclassical Revival building was erected in 1931 at a cost of $75,000 with James A. Wethmore as the supervising architect. For years, the red brick building with granite detailing served as the main Lumberton Post Office. Located on Elm Street, it is now home to the law firm of Musselwhite and Branch.

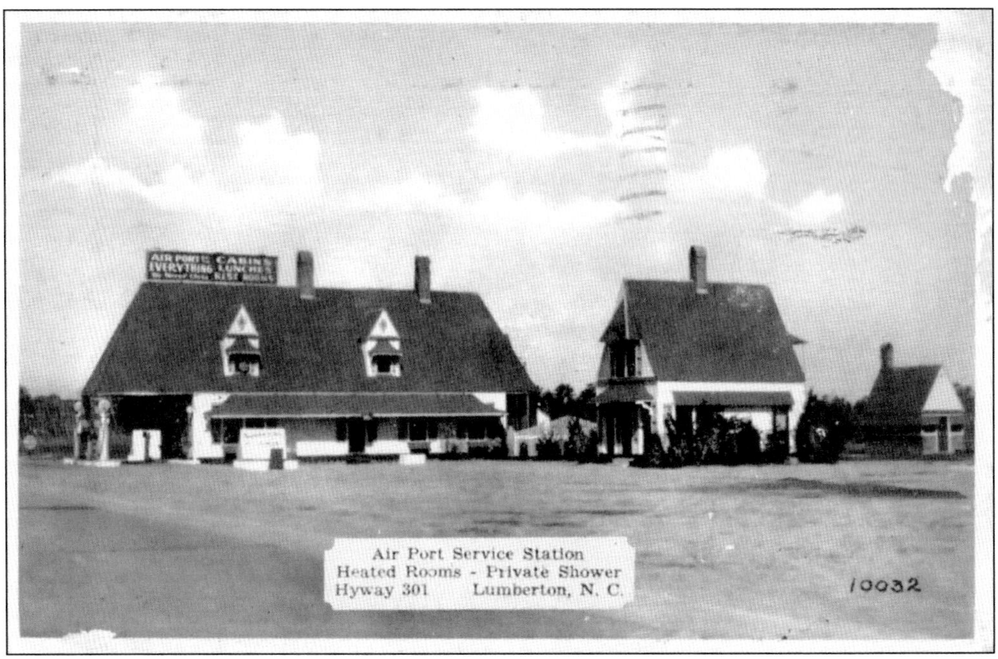

Air Port Service Station. Located on Highway 301 in Lumberton, heated rooms with private showers were available.

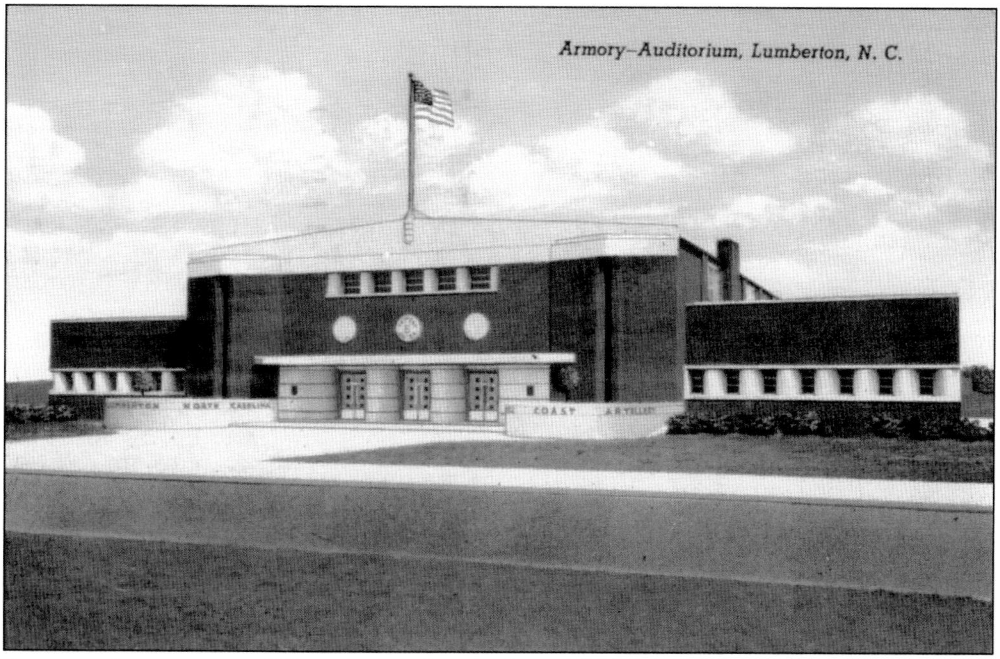

ARMORY AUDITORIUM. When the Lumberton City Armory Auditorium was built in the 1930s, it was one of the most handsome and best equipped buildings of its kind in North Carolina. It was home to the famous Lumberton Coast Artillery Company and the war-time organization Home Guards. It is now the Bill Sapp Recreation Center.

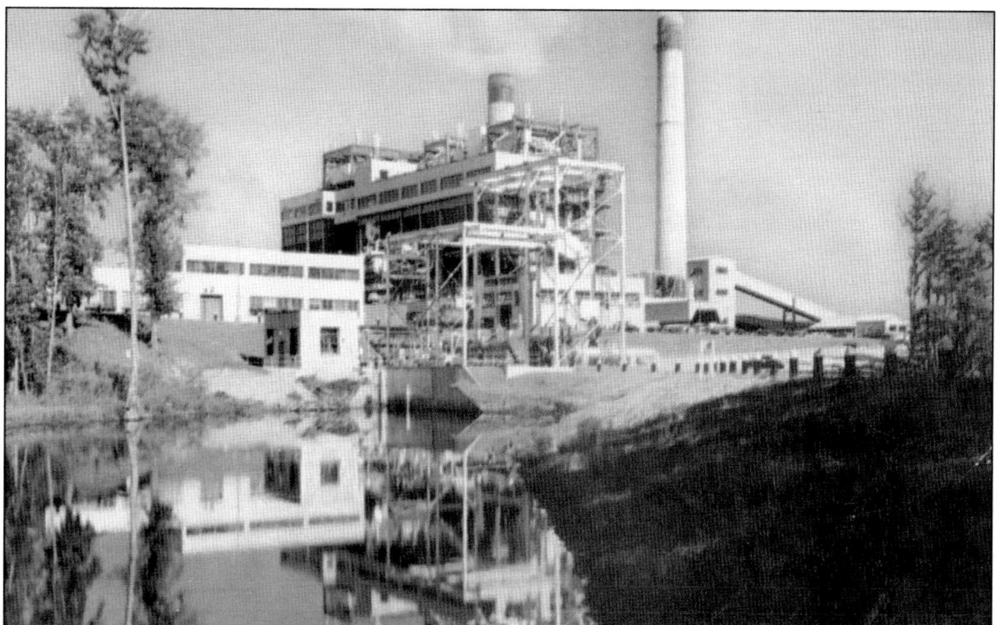

LUMBERTON POWER PLANT. The smoke stacks of this steam-electric generating plant of Carolina Power and Light Company are located above the Lumber River. It was capable of producing one and one-fourth billion kilowatt hours annually.

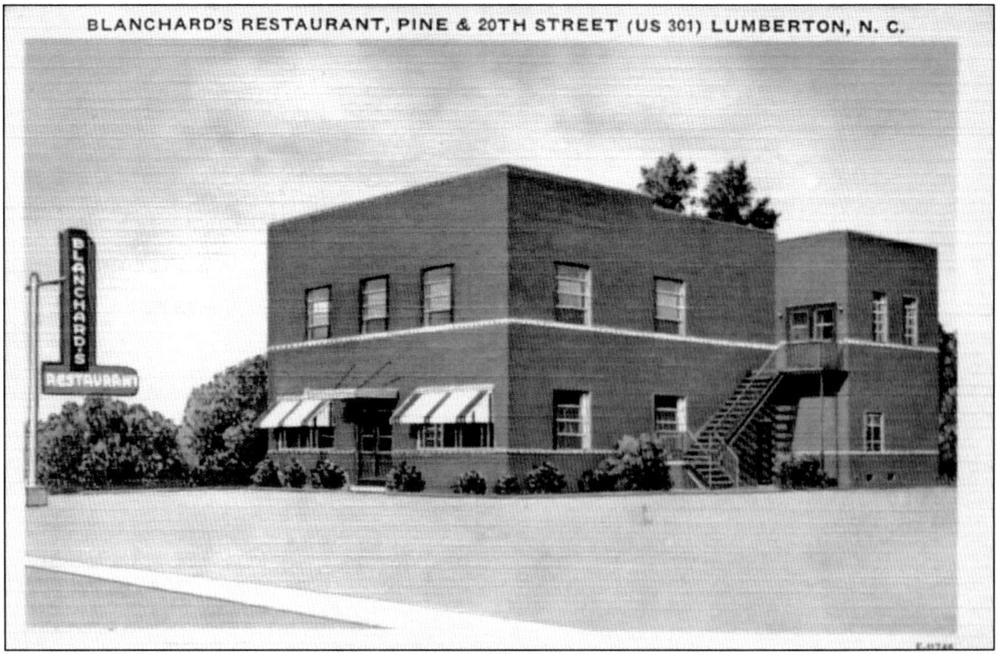

BLANCHARD'S RESTAURANT. This restaurant advertised itself as a source of wonderful food in the heart of tobaccoland. It was located on Highway 301 heading into downtown Lumberton and known for its peanut pie. It is now the site of the Chocolate Moon Restaurant.

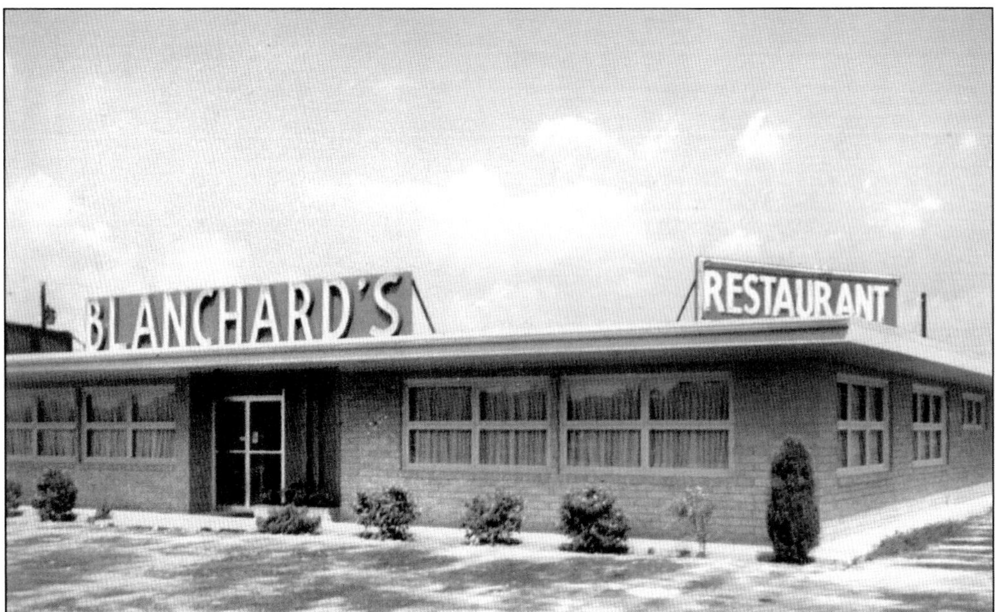

BLANCHARD'S RESTAURANT. Blanchard's Restaurant moved from its in-town location to the outskirts of town to be part of the hotel row. It was located beside the Redwood Motel Lodge and featured two private-party rooms. This is now the site of John's Restaurant, a haven to not only the traveler but also to the citizens of the county.

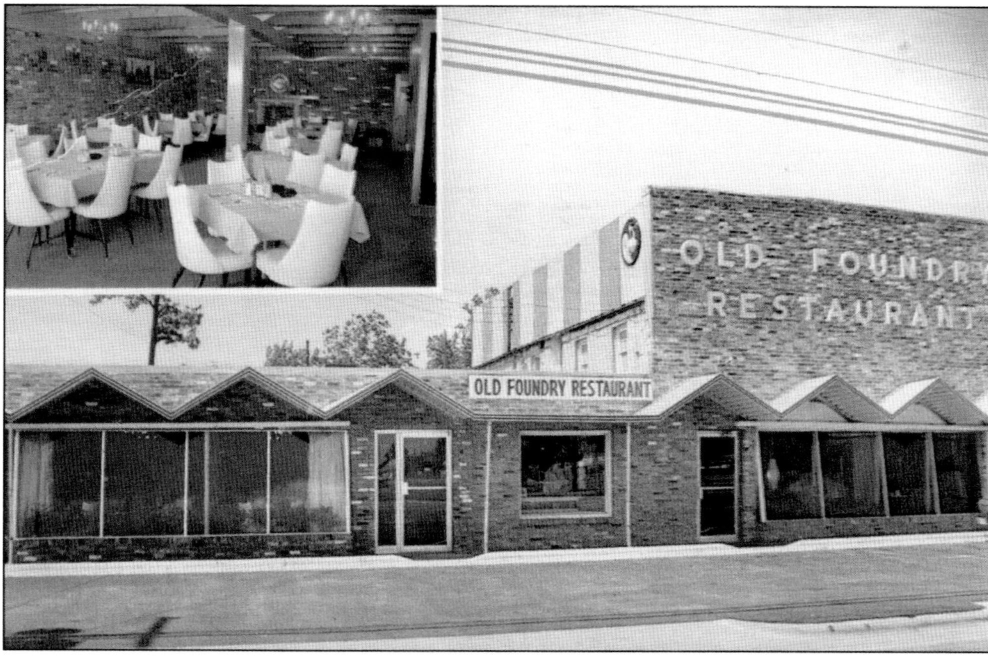

OLD FOUNDRY RESTAURANT. The Old Foundry Restaurant was opened by Hubert, Hilton, and Dobbs Oxendine in 1946 on the site of the Old Iron Foundry. They were located a quarter mile east of the Pembroke exit of Interstate 95 just south of Lumberton.

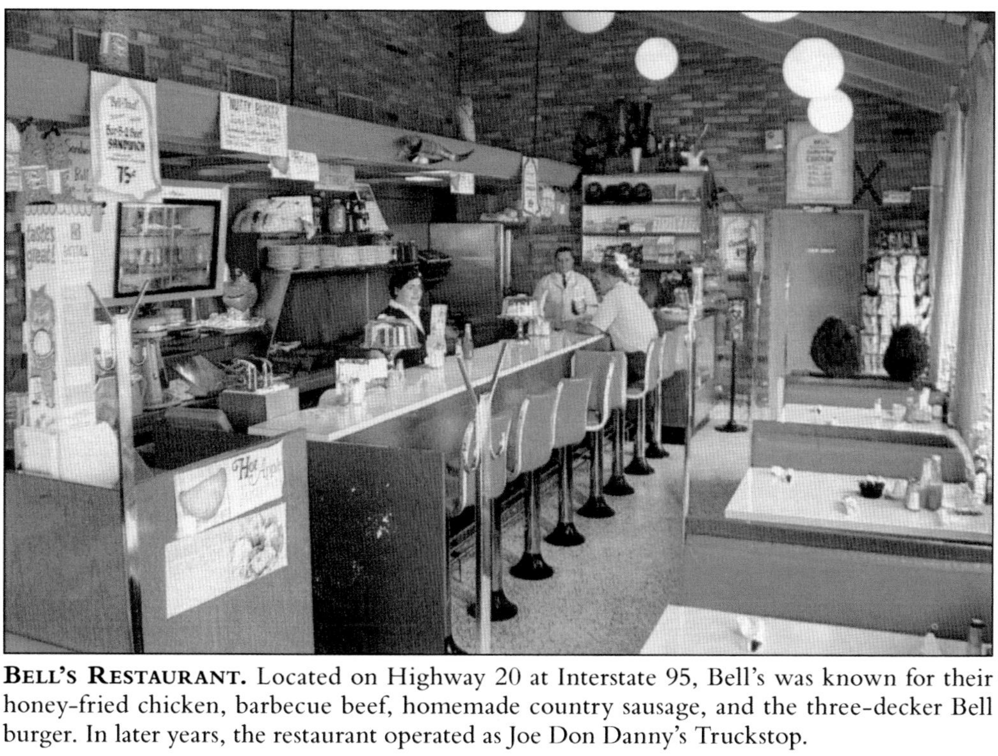

BELL'S RESTAURANT. Located on Highway 20 at Interstate 95, Bell's was known for their honey-fried chicken, barbecue beef, homemade country sausage, and the three-decker Bell burger. In later years, the restaurant operated as Joe Don Danny's Truckstop.

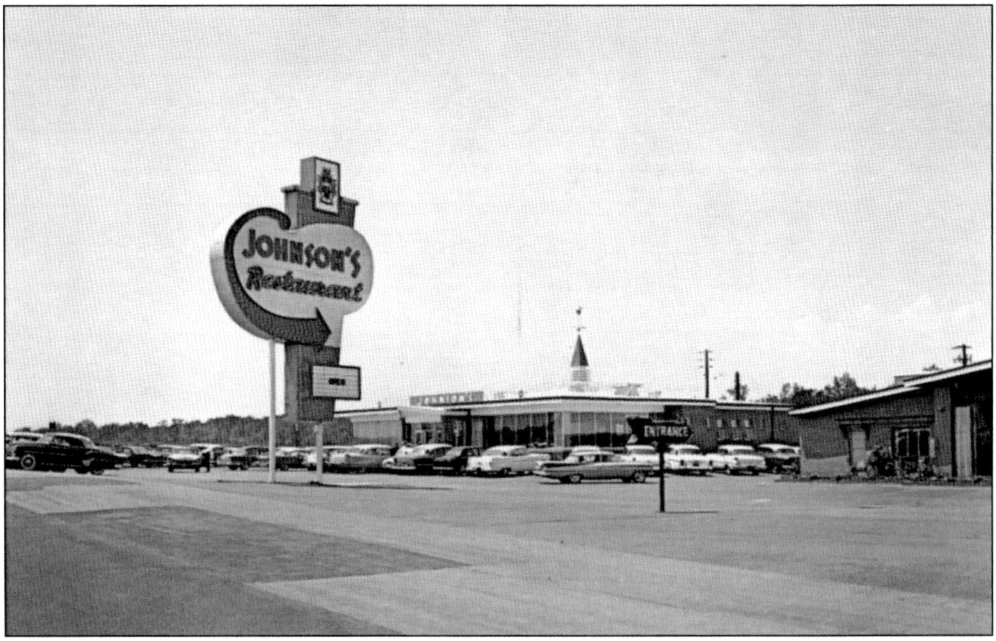

JOHNSON'S RESTAURANT. Located in Lumberton at the intersection of Highways 301 and 211 alongside the Greenbrier Motel, this restaurant was not the usual highway food joint. They offered charcoal steaks, seafood, and Long Island duck in an atmosphere that included soft organ music.

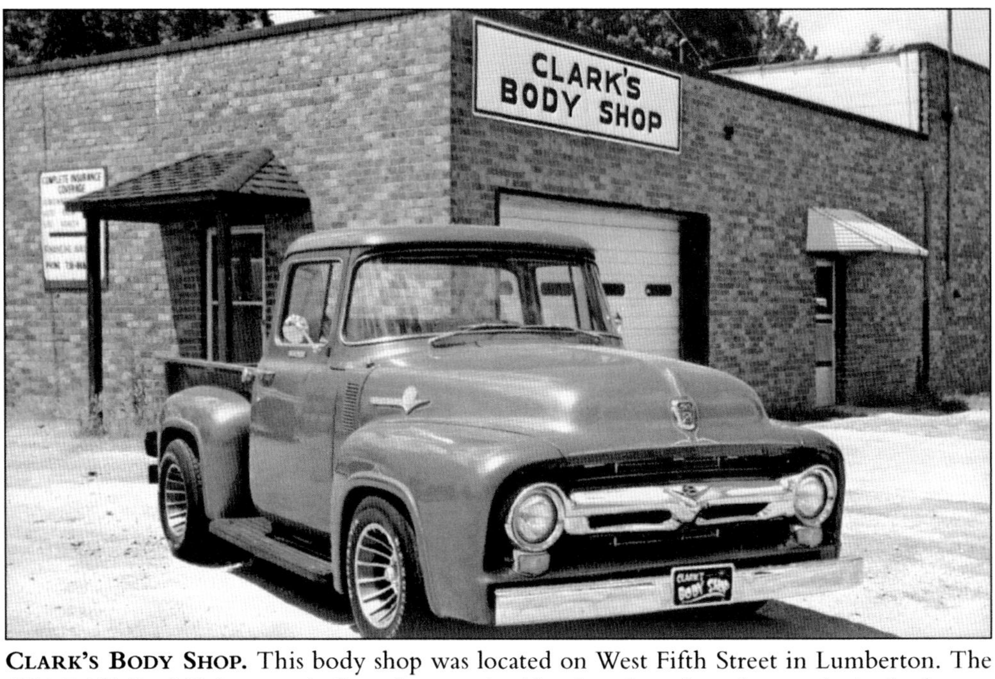

CLARK'S BODY SHOP. This body shop was located on West Fifth Street in Lumberton. The 1956 F-100 Ford Pickup was built and customized by the talented workers at the body shop.

Four

Hotels and Inns

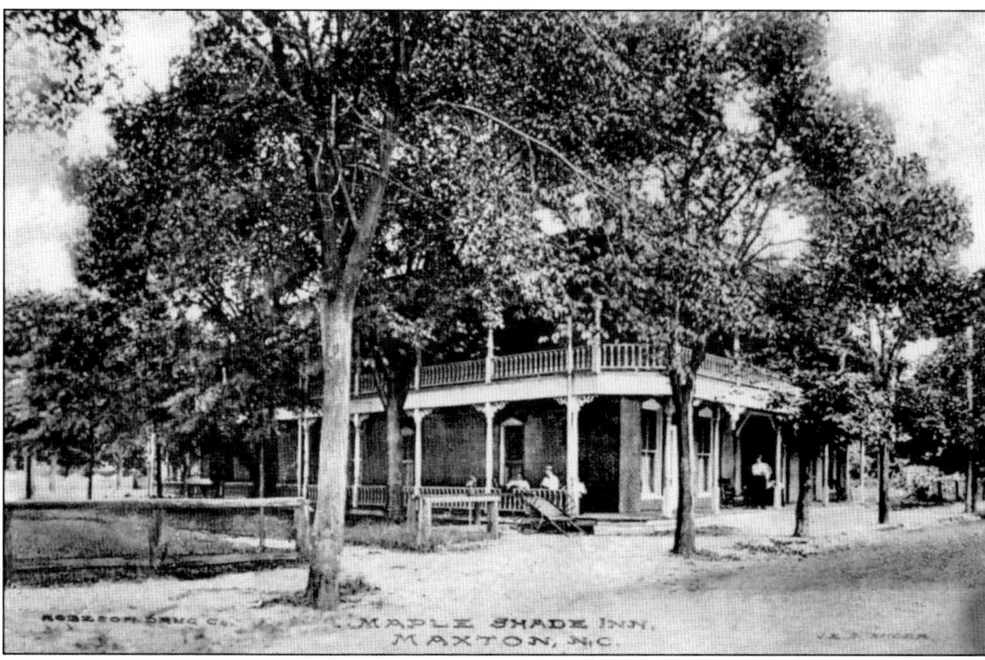

Maple Shade Inn. The Maple Shade Inn was located on Main Street (later McCaskill Avenue) in downtown Maxton.

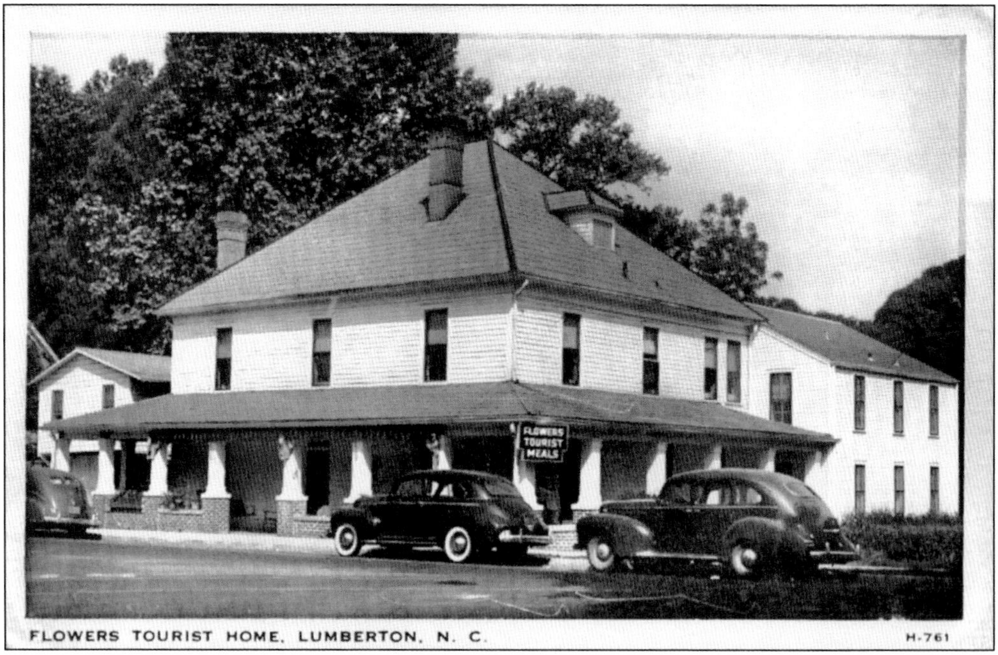

Flowers's Tourist Home. This tourist home was located in downtown Lumberton in what was once a fashionable residential section but is now considered commercial property. It was located across from the depression-era post office that now houses the law firm of Musselwhite and Branch.

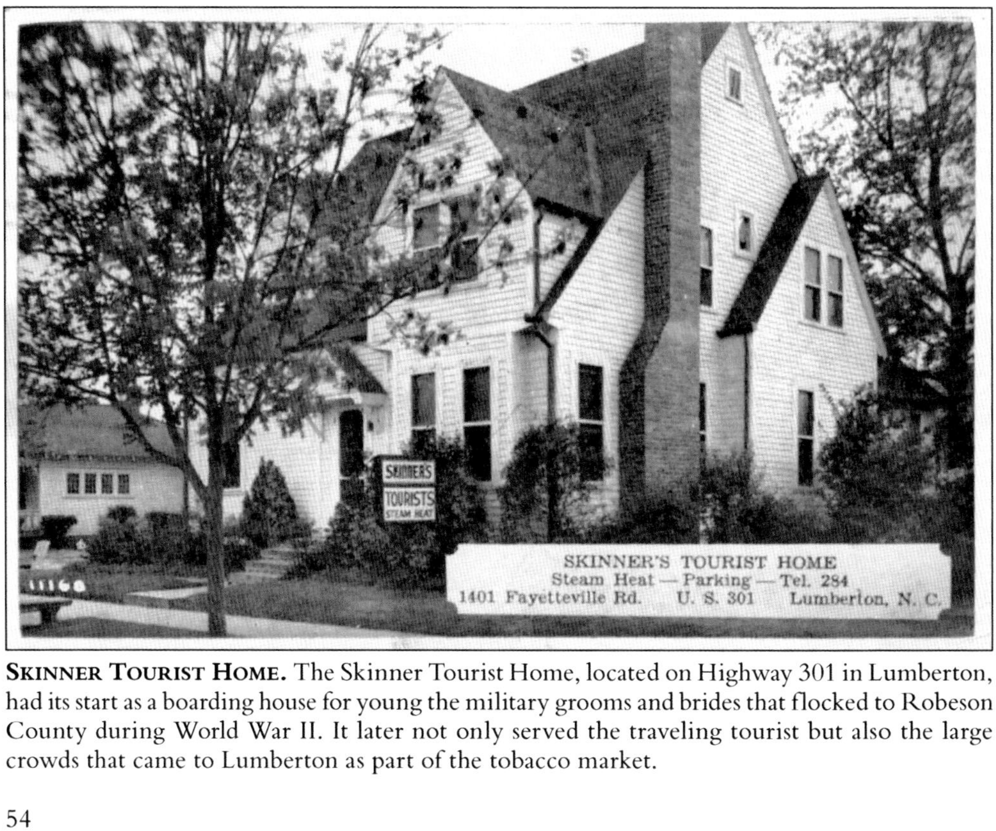

Skinner Tourist Home. The Skinner Tourist Home, located on Highway 301 in Lumberton, had its start as a boarding house for young the military grooms and brides that flocked to Robeson County during World War II. It later not only served the traveling tourist but also the large crowds that came to Lumberton as part of the tobacco market.

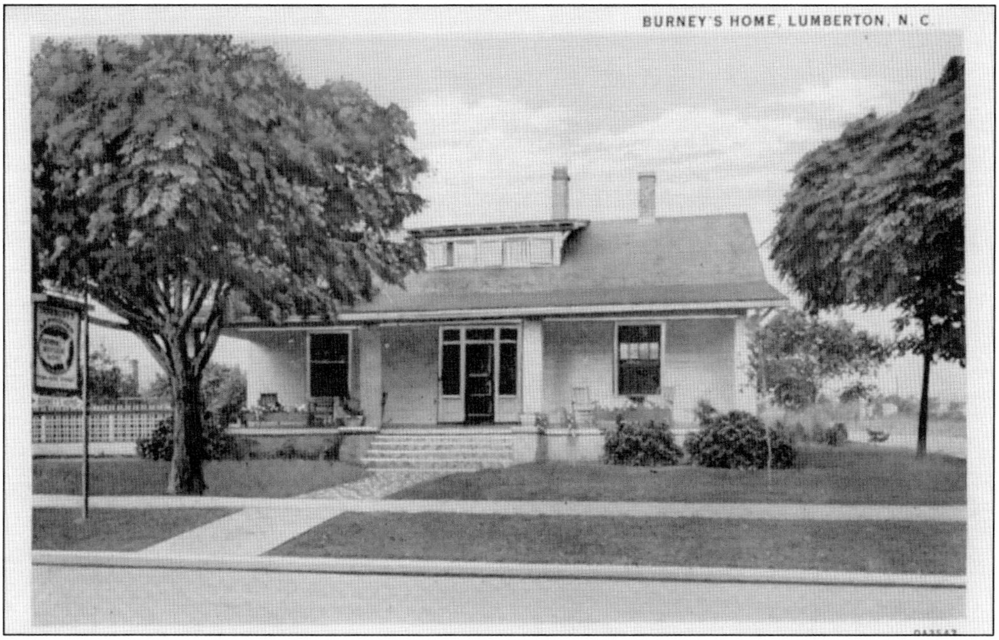

BURNEY'S TOURIST HOME. This bungalow-style home was built by local builder Thomas Matthew Burney in 1916 as a home for him and his wife, Mary Emily "Mollie" Russell. They were parents of Russell Thomas, Mary Pauline "Polly," Doris Elizabeth, Loris Fay, and Cleo. In October 1929, Mollie began operating a tourist home in the house.

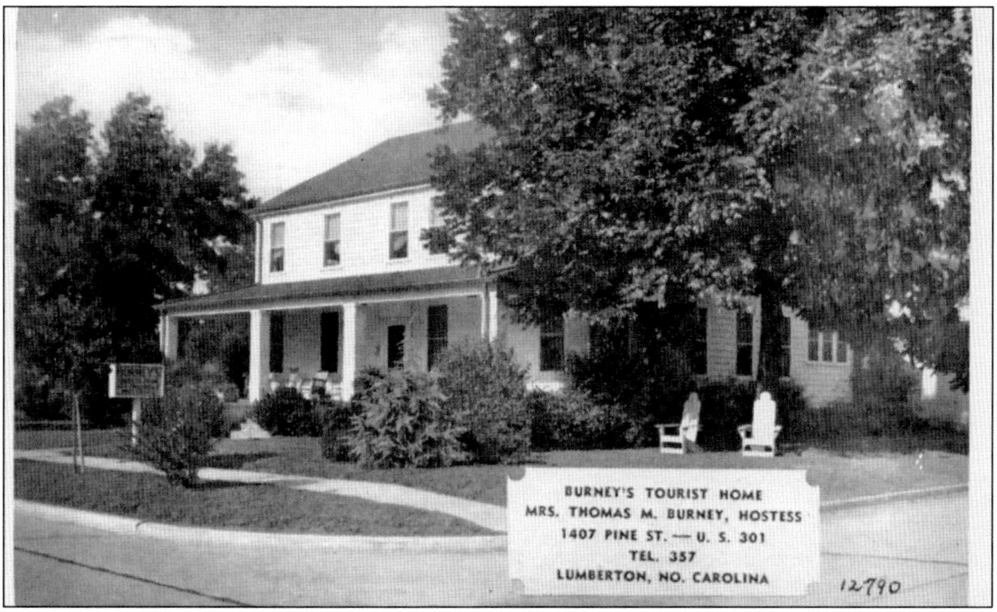

BURNEY'S TOURIST. After his wife had operated the tourist home for eight years in the bungalow house, Thomas Matthew Burney remolded the house into this large two-story home. Mollie Burney operated the home until her death. Afterward her daughter Polly continued its operation. Located on Highway 301 in downtown Lumberton, this tourist home was located on the same block as the Skinner Tourist Home. It was operated by Mrs. Thomas Burney, and during tobacco season, there was never an empty room.

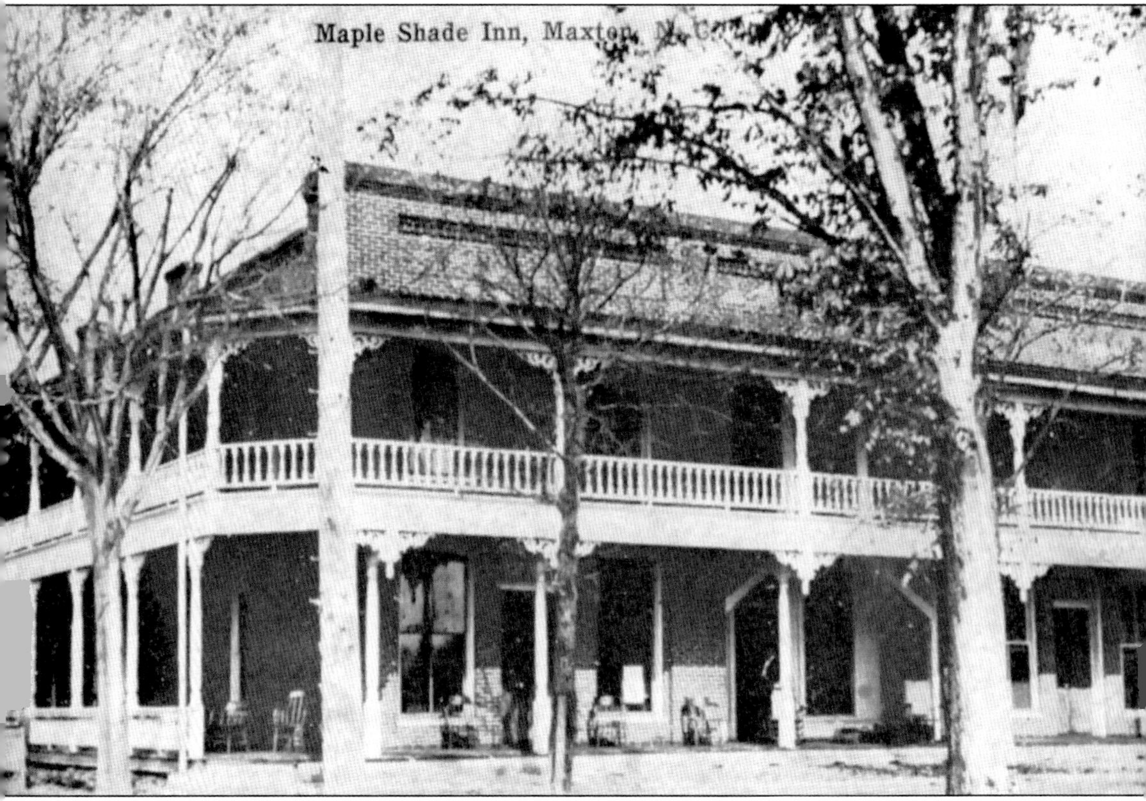

Maple Shade Inn. The Maple Shade Inn served the many travelers that came to Maxton by the three railroads and those who came to visit the girls of Carolina College with true southern hospitality. In a special 1905 issue of the *Lumberton Argus* newspaper, the Maple Shade was reviewed as one of the most thoroughly equipped and modernly conducted hotels in North Carolina; it was supplied with water and electricity. Operated by Mr. and Mrs. J. B. Weatherly, rooms were available for $2 per day or $7 per week. The Maple Shade was known far and near by traveling men who considered that they reached home when they found themselves at the Maple Shade.

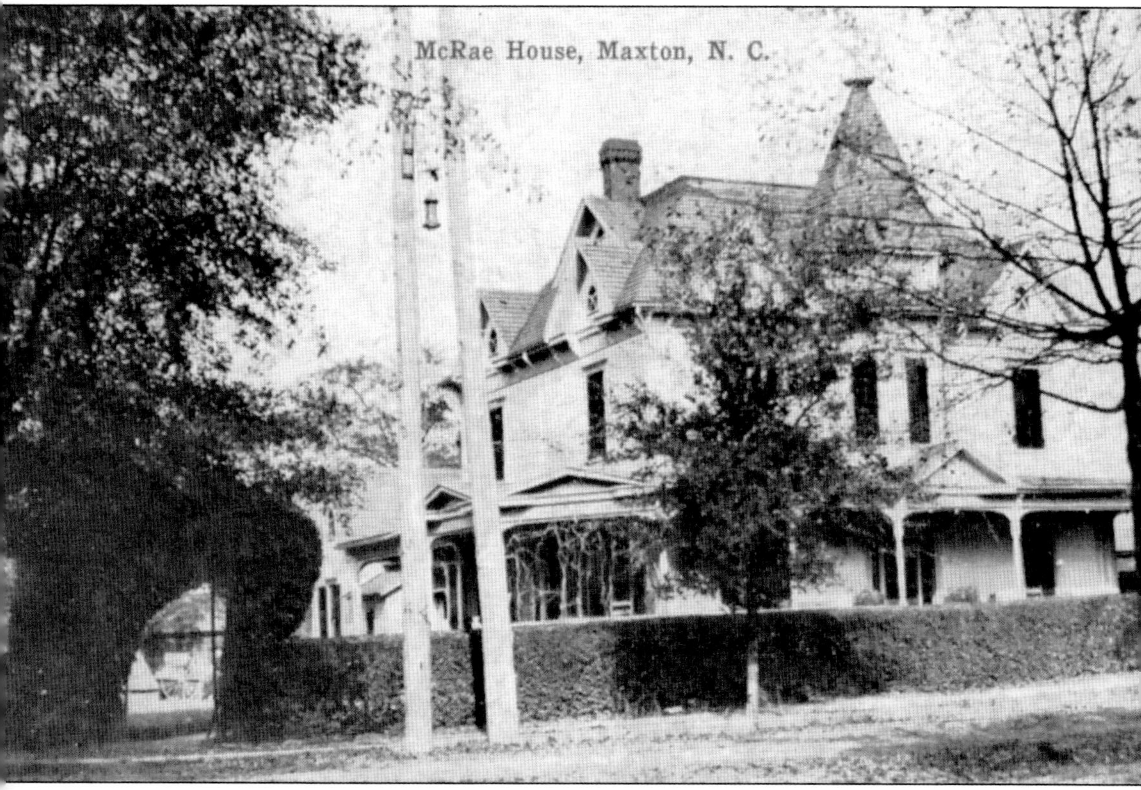

McRAE HOUSE. When the original Maple Shade Inn burned, Sue Kelly McRae (wife of Edward McRae) converted part of this large house and outbuilding into a hotel. She was assisted in operating the hotel by a bachelor brother-in-law, Col. Elijah Fuller McRae. In 1912, she closed the hotel and remodeled the house, turning it from a lovely example of a Victorian home to a simple Colonial Revival house.

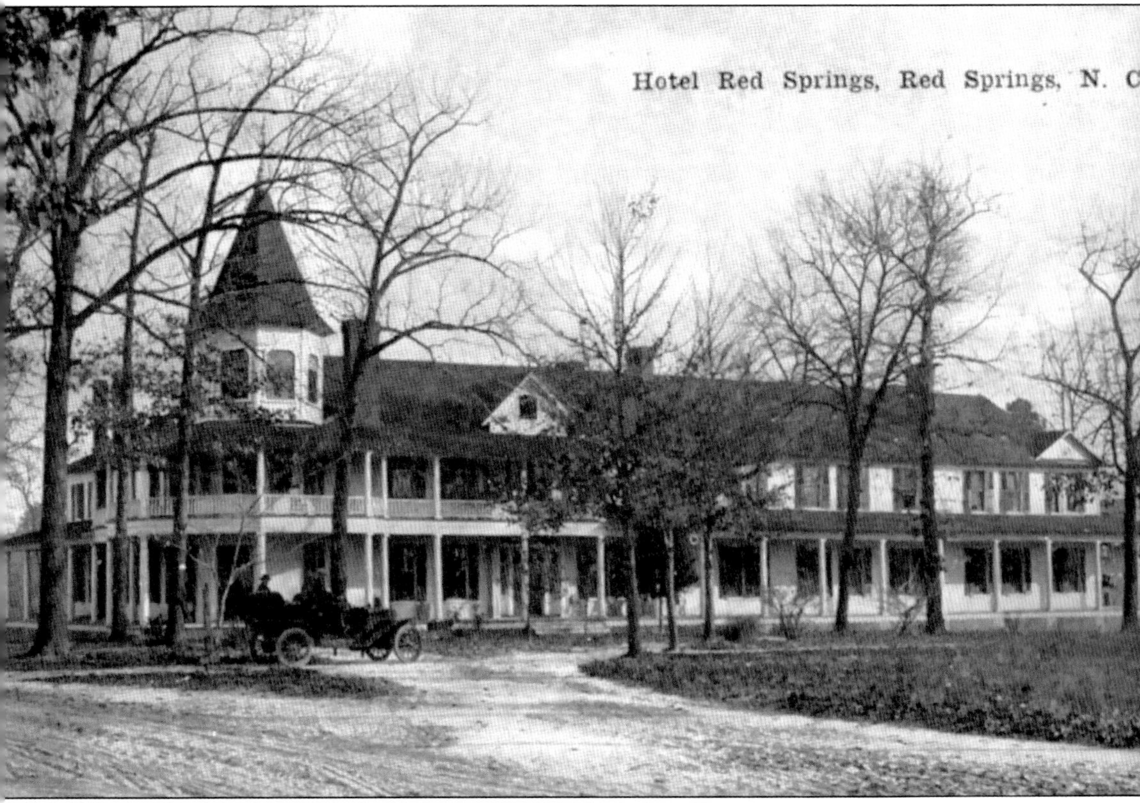

HOTEL RED SPRINGS. This wooden hotel was located in a nine-acre grove. It served not only the visitors of the Southern Presbyterian College but also offered services to those seeking the mineral springs located nearby. The hotel also drew large groups of hunters, who came year after year to hunt in the game-filled woods surrounding Red Springs. The hotel had hunting privileges to over 20,000 acres. It featured hot and cold water in each room with private baths on every floor.

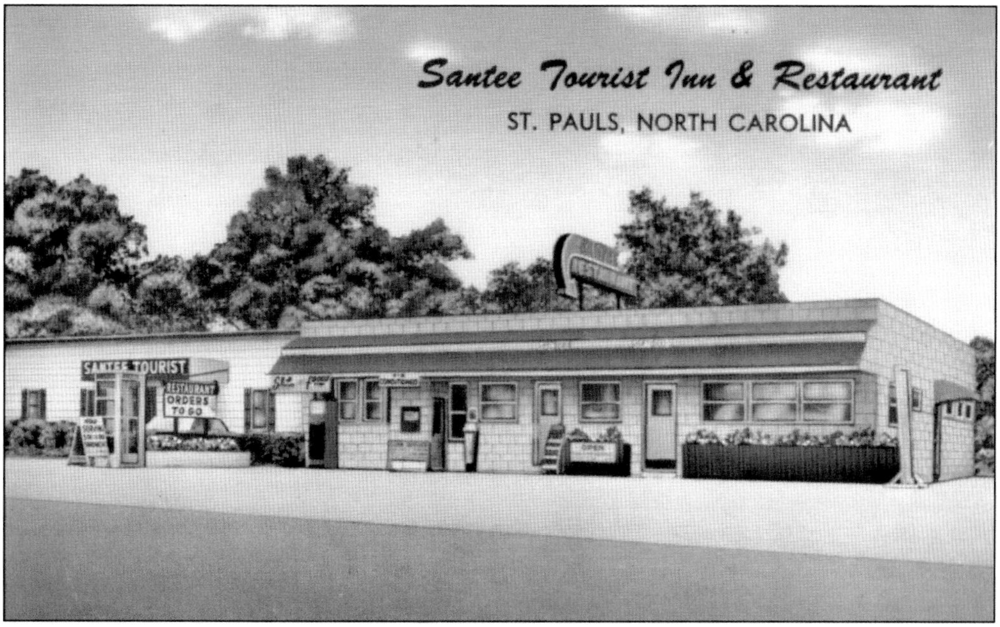

SANTEE TOURIST INN AND RESTAURANT. Located in St. Pauls, 19 miles south of Fayetteville and 14 miles north of Lumberton, this tourist inn was operated until the late 1980s.

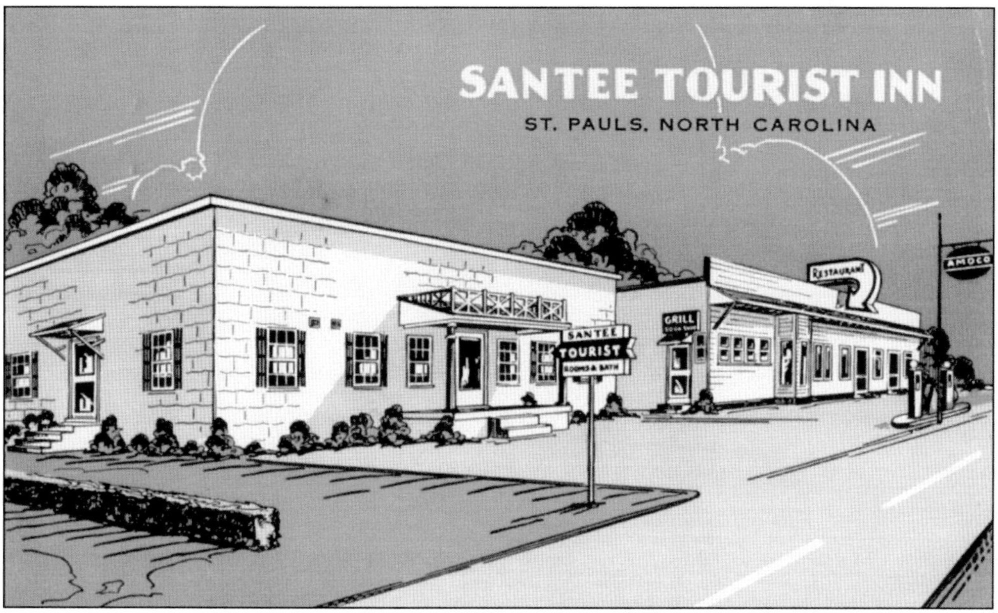

SANTEE TOURIST INN. A favorite story concerning this place was about the restaurant that was known for its fried chicken. Janette Sibbett said that she and her sisters craved the chicken late one night; they climbed out the window of their bedroom and pushed the family car out of the driveway and down the street a block. They then started the car, went to the Santee, and picked up a bucket of chicken to-go. They stopped on the block before their house and pushed the car back into the drive. Crawling back in the window, they quickly ate the chicken and fell asleep. They thought they had managed to get away with their late night trip until they realized, while at school the next day, that they left the bucket of bones under the bed.

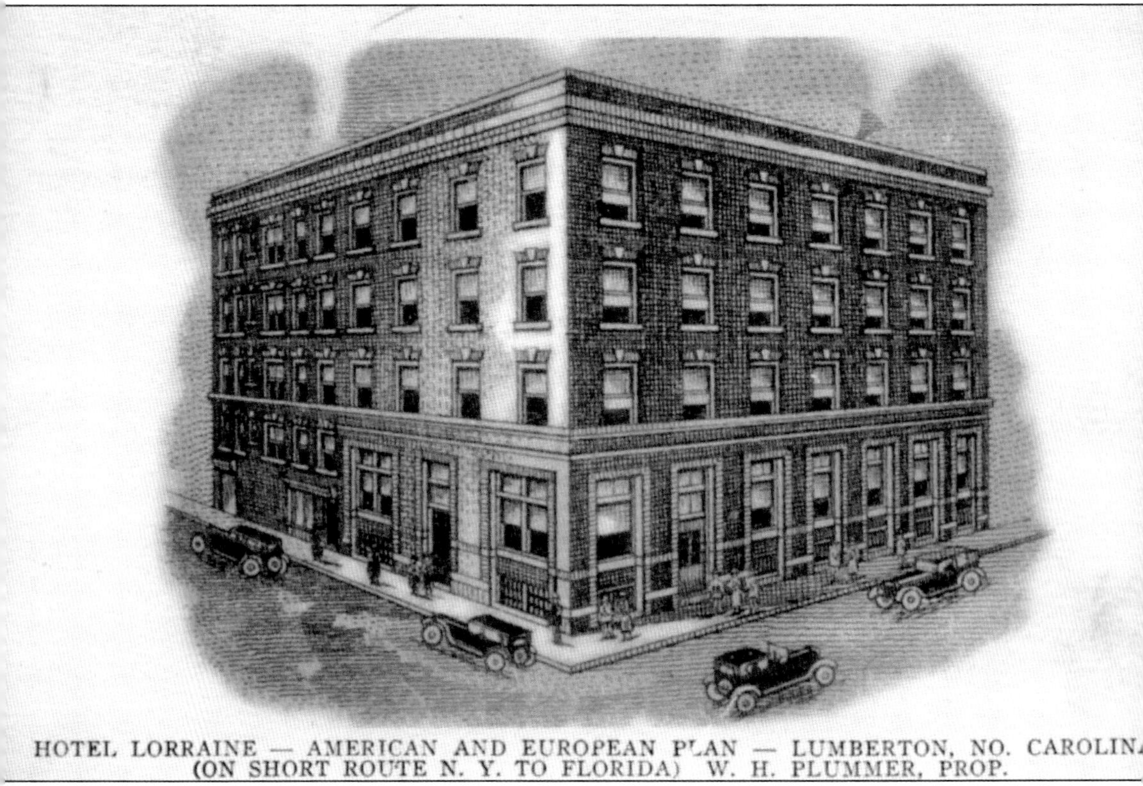

LORRAINE HOTEL. Located in the heart of downtown Lumberton beside the courthouse, this five-story hotel was operated by W. H. Plummer and featured 100 rooms.

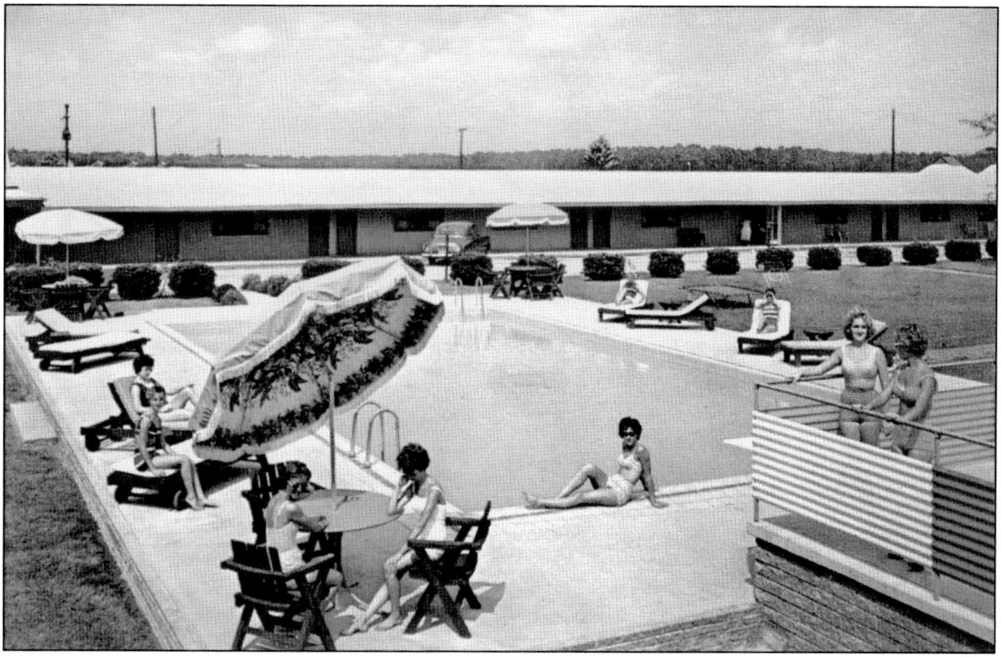

Bathing Beauties. The Redwood Motor Lodge was recommended by Quality Courts, Duncan Hines, and AAA; it had 40 spacious guest rooms that had air conditioning and central heat. Each room also had tile bathrooms with tub and shower, as well as a television and telephone.

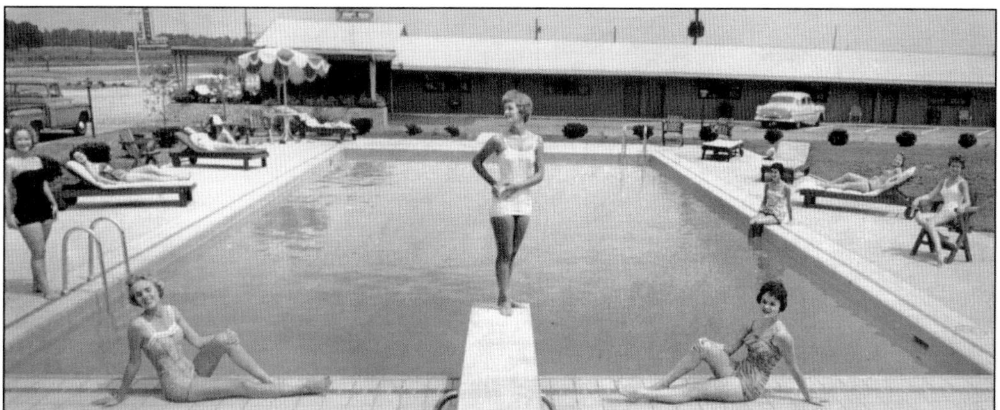

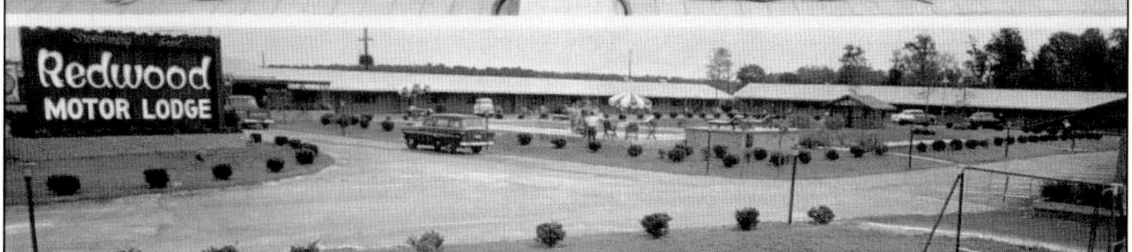

Posing by the Pool. The 50-foot pool served to draw visitors to the Redwood Motor Lodge, located 2 miles north of Lumberton on Highway 301. Located next door was Blanchard's Restaurant. It was owned by Mr. and Mrs. William L. Bauer.

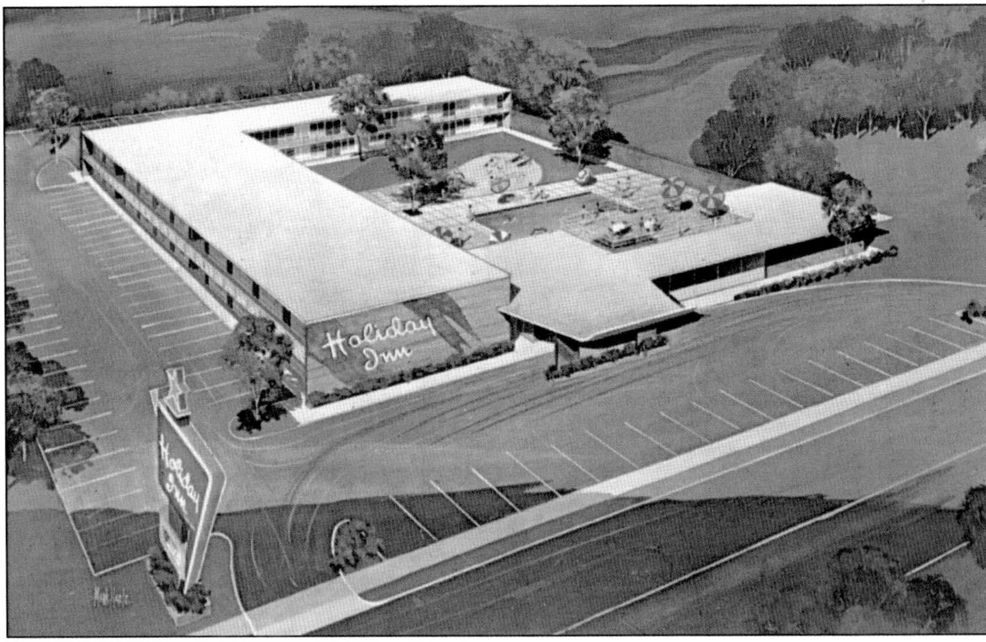

HOLIDAY INN. This Holiday Inn was located on Interstate 95 near Highway 211; it featured a swimming pool that was wonderful to guests tired from the interstate traffic. Next door was the Waffle House, which also attracted large amounts of travelers.

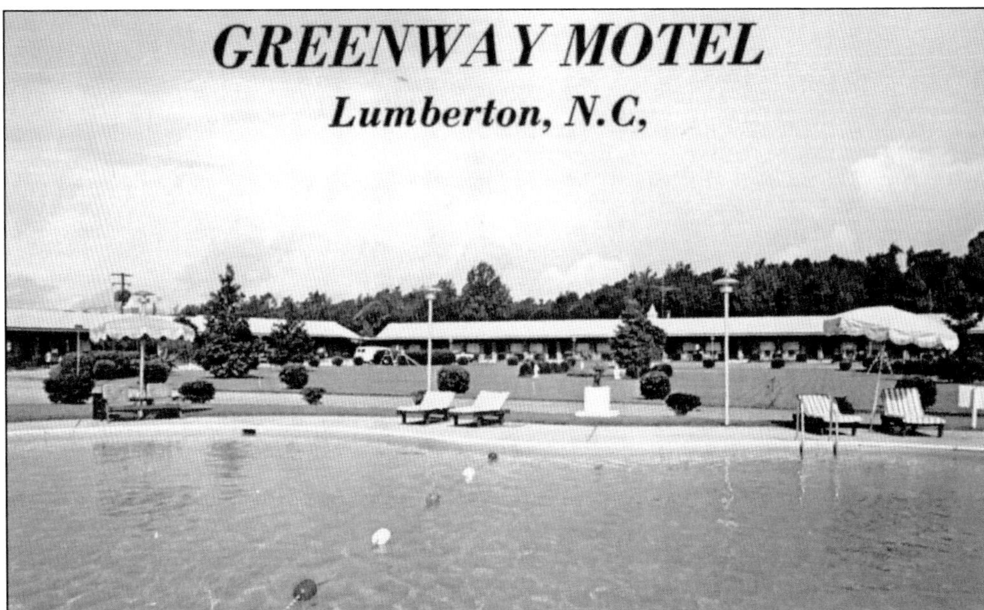

GREENWAY MOTEL. The Greenway Motel was located in Lumberton and served as a favorite resting spot for travelers because of its large inviting pool.

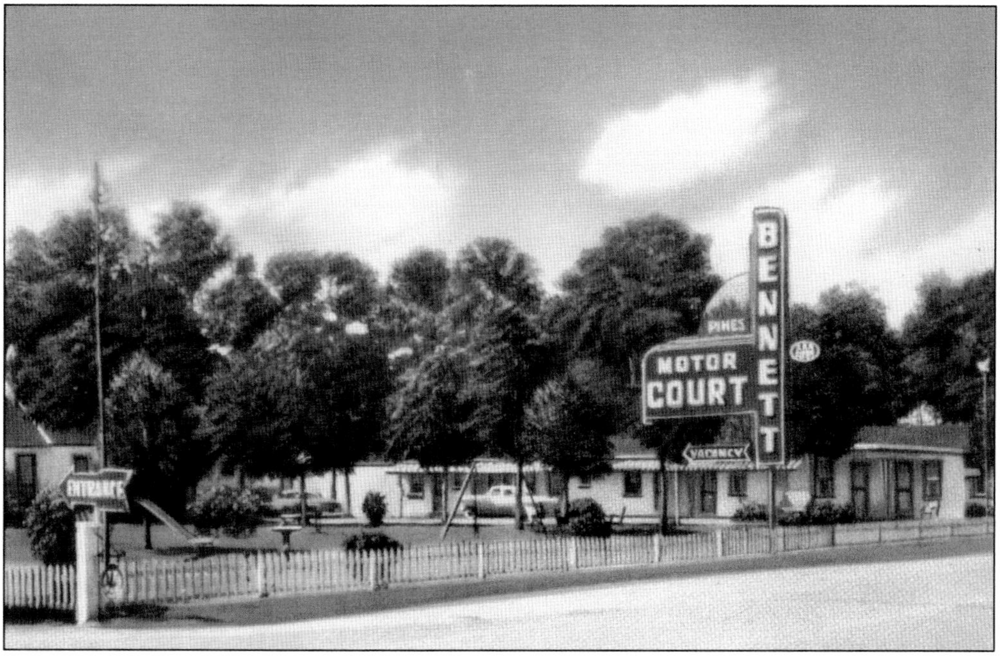

BENNETT MOTOR COURT. Located three miles south of Lumberton on Highway 301, this motor court was owned by Mr. and Mrs. H. G. Branch and managed by Catherine Byrd. It advertises the fact that it had private baths with tubs and showers, a children's playground, and free television.

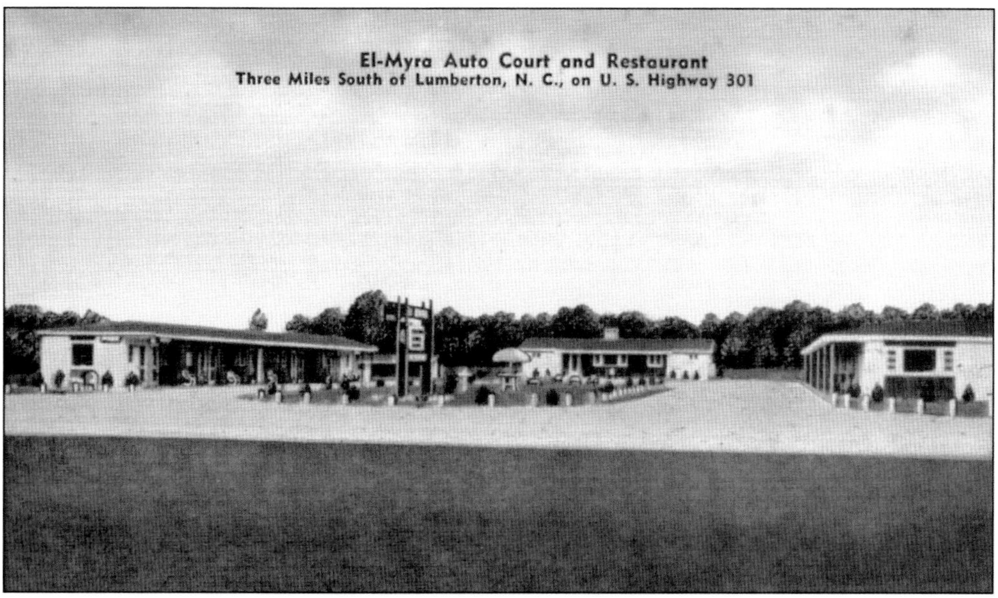

EL-MYRA AUTO COURT. This establishment located on Highway 301, just three miles south of Lumberton, offered the traveler many choices. It consisted of 16 clean and comfortable units with Simmons metal furniture and Beauty Rest beds. Choices included rooms with a shower or a tub and shower and furnace heat or electric heat. Rooms were air conditioned for summer. Games included miniature golf and shuffleboard. The auto court was managed by Mr. and Mrs. O. L. Deese.

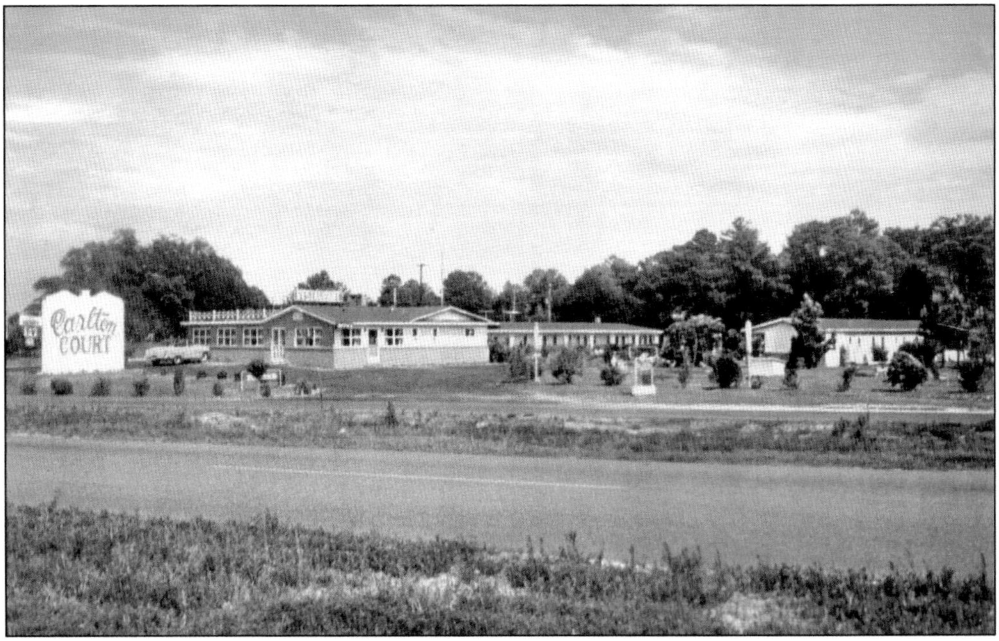

Carlton Court. Located at the intersection of Highway 301 and Highway 74 south of Lumberton, this hotel featured in-room telephones, ceramic tile baths, and air-conditioned rooms with televisions.

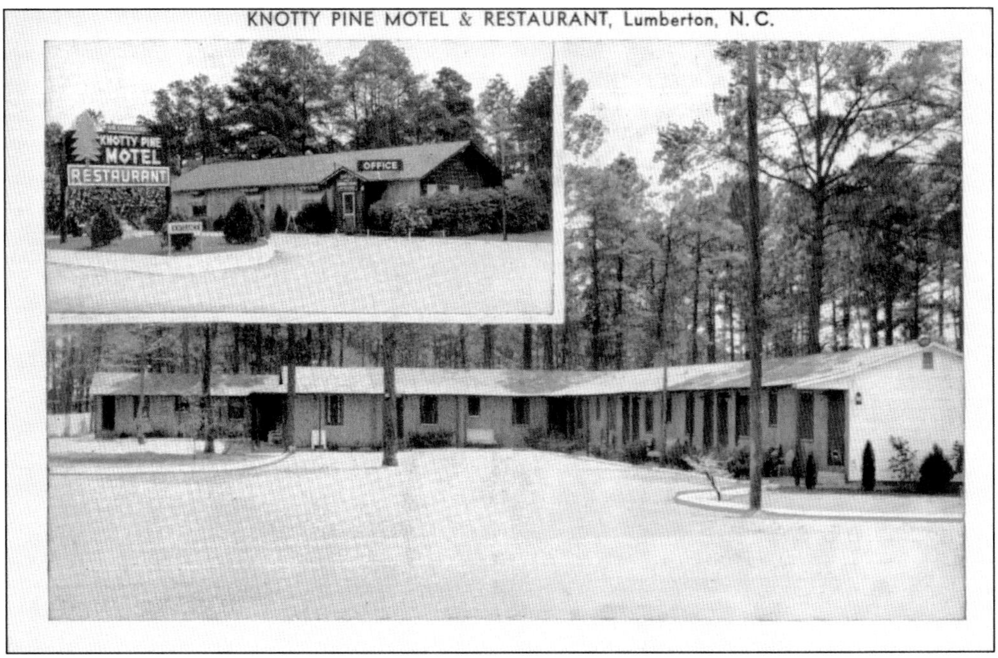

Knotty Pine Motel. This motel had 23 modern rooms with private baths and a dining room serving the finest in foods. It was owned and managed by Mr. and Mrs. William Bauer.

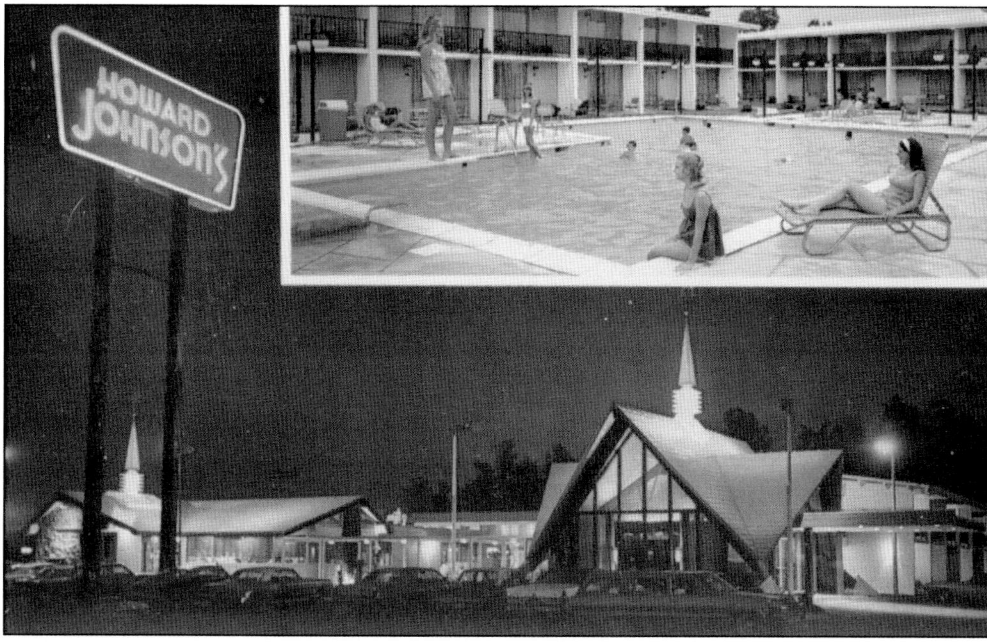

HOWARD JOHNSON. Located on Interstate 95 at Highway 211, this modern motor lodge featured a refreshing pool. Someone noted on the back of this 1975 postcard that their room rate was $17.

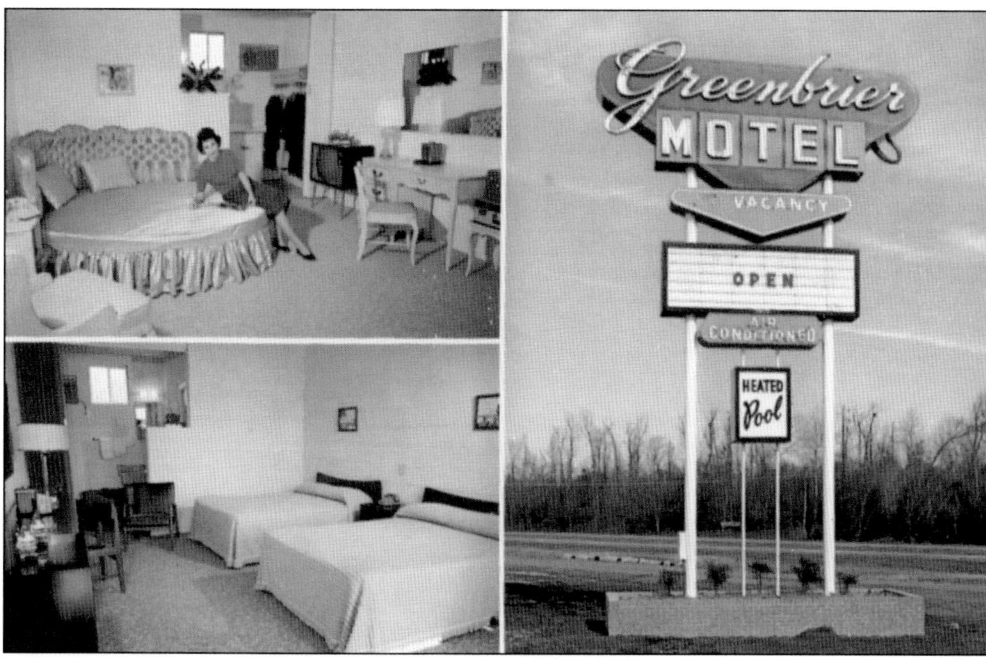

GREENBRIER MOTEL. The Greenbrier promoted itself as the newest and most ultra-modern motel in the Lumberton area. Located on Highway 301, they had 50 units offering travelers comfort in air conditioning, thermo-controlled heating, in-room television, and a heated swimming pool. Johnson's Restaurant was located next door. Their bridal suite offered a circular bed, which they claimed was the talk of the southland.

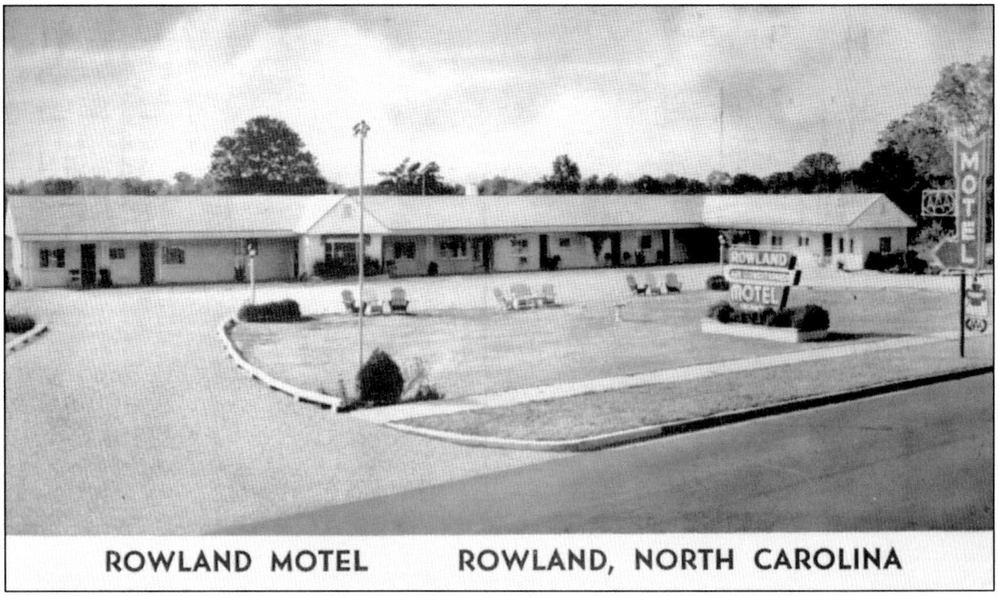

ROWLAND MOTEL. This motel marketed itself as family accommodations located opposite fine restaurants. The rooms were said to be beautifully-decorated with wall-to-wall carpet, tile baths, and room-controlled electric heat and air conditioning. It was located in the heart of Rowland on Highways 301 and 501, owned and managed by Mr. and Mrs. Walter F. Hellmer.

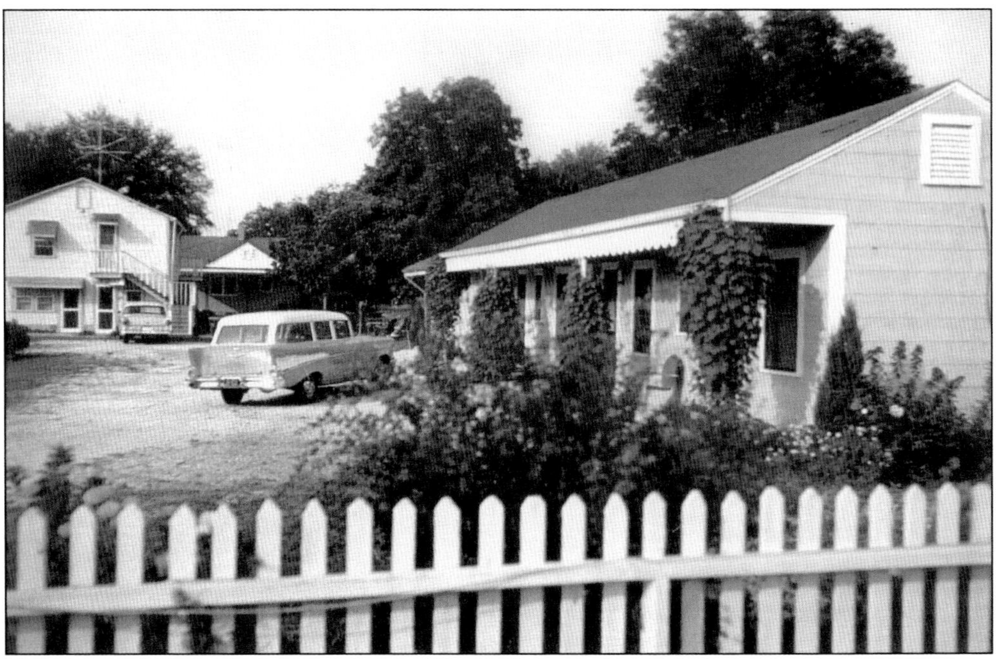

REST-A-WHILE. This Rowland motel was located one and one-half blocks off of Highway 301 and advertised that it had no highway noise. Owned by Mr. and Mrs. J. N. Sinclair, it was meant to be restful and quiet.

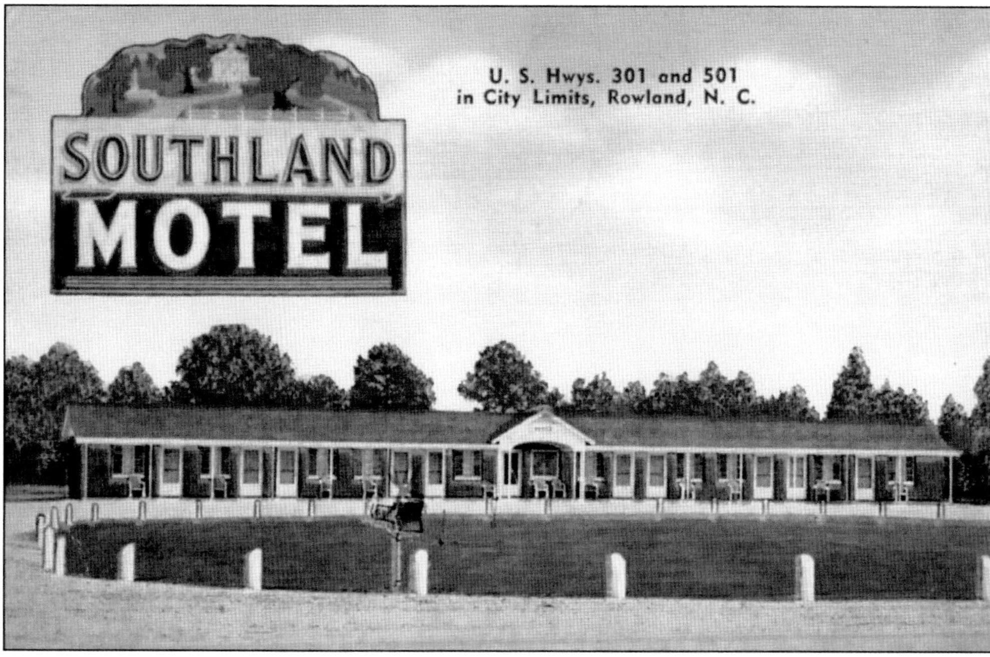

SOUTHLAND MOTEL. In the city limits of Rowland, on Highways 301 and 501, this motel featured home-size tiled bathrooms with tubs and showers. The rooms were furnished with Simmons all-metal furniture.

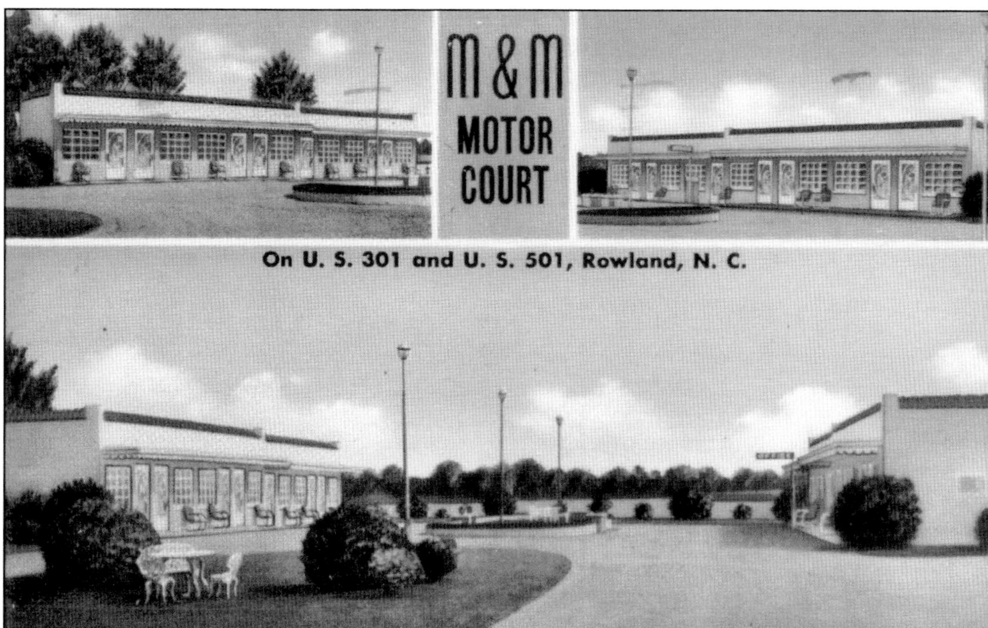

M & M MOTOR COURT. Owned and managed by W. P. McArthur and W. T. McCormic, this site had 14 guest rooms with private baths and individually-controlled heat. Located in the city limits of Rowland, it was at the intersection of Highways 301 and 501.

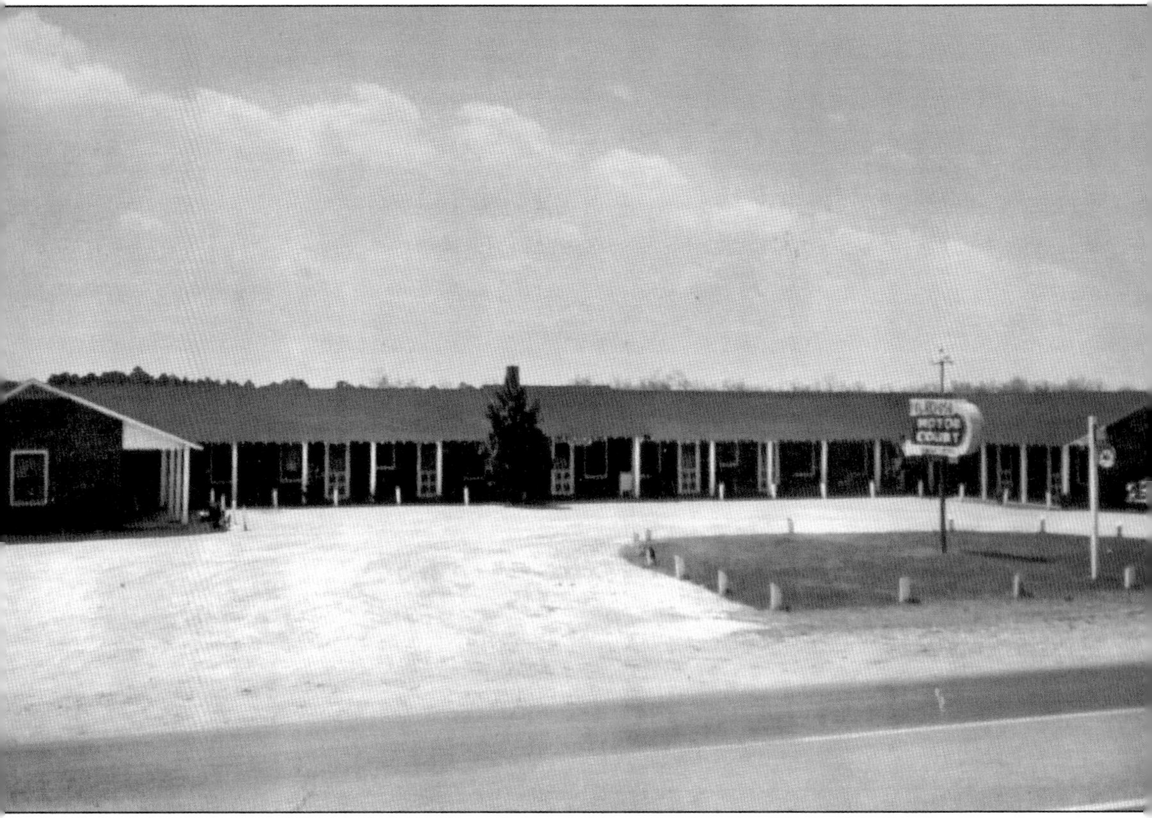

EL REPOSO MOTOR COURT. This modern facility included air-conditioned rooms with tile baths and radiant heat. It was located on Highway 301 at Highway 74, just two and one-half miles south of Lumberton.

Five

Homes

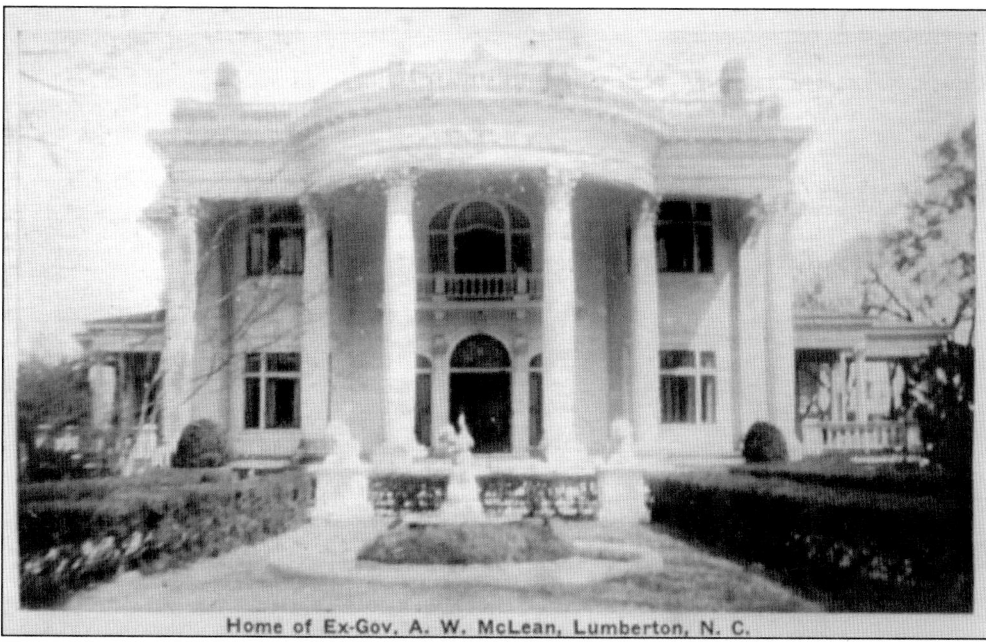

McLean Mansion. This home was built by Angus Wilton McLean and his wife, Margaret French, at the site of her grandfather, Berry Godwin's, home on Chestnut Street. The front of the home was graced by a large, cast-iron fountain featuring a three-foot-tall cherub, a duck, turtles, and frogs. The fountain was donated to Historic Robeson by the children of the McLeans' daughter, Margaret "Bushy" McLean Shepherd.

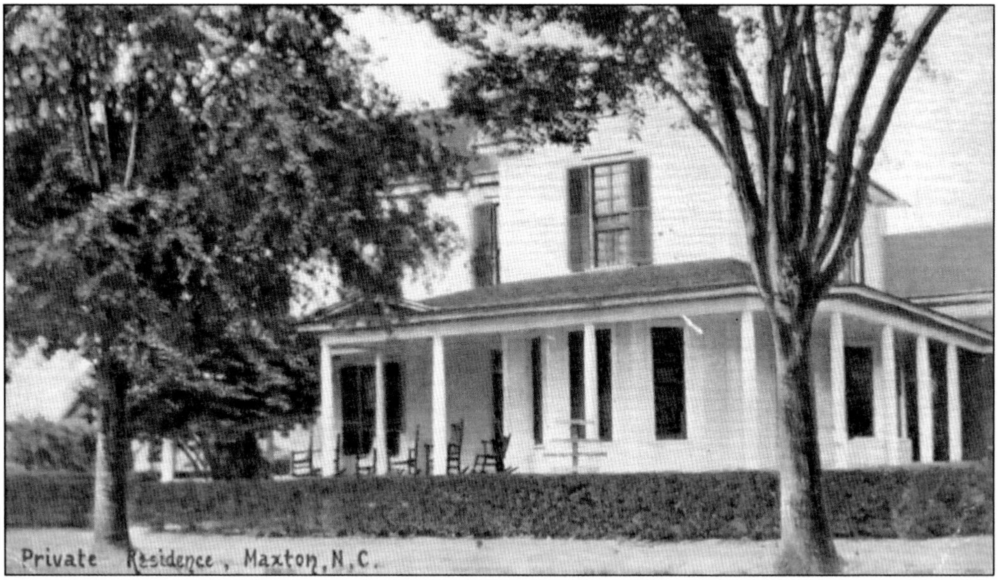

McKINNON RESIDENCE. According to the April 14, 1891, issue of the *Maxton Union*, this home was built for Maj. A. J. "Sandy" McKinnon. The home is a transitional style with elements of both the Queen Anne and neoclassical Revival styles. The McKinnons moved to their new home on Florence Street in 1906. The home was purchased by cotton merchant Rufus Williams; later it was operated as a boarding house by Sallie McLean and her sister, Mrs. Redding.

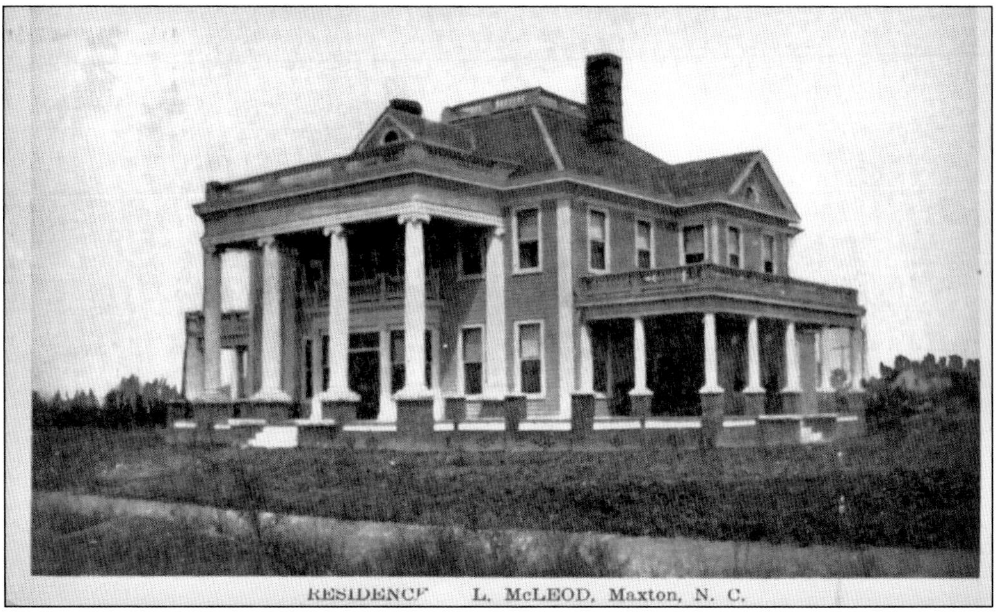

R. L. McLEOD RESIDENCE. This Maxton neoclassical Revival house was built in 1908 for Robert Lee McLeod. He was a large farmer and lumberman; his sawmill processed all of the lumber for the house. The architect suggested that the home face Florence Street and the new residence of A. J. McKinnon. McLeod, however, did not want the back of his home toward the Presbyterian church, so the home was built facing Graham Street. After McLeod's death in 1942, it was home to his daughter, Ruth McLeod Allen, and her family until 2004. McLeod was active in the development of Carolina College for Women in Maxton.

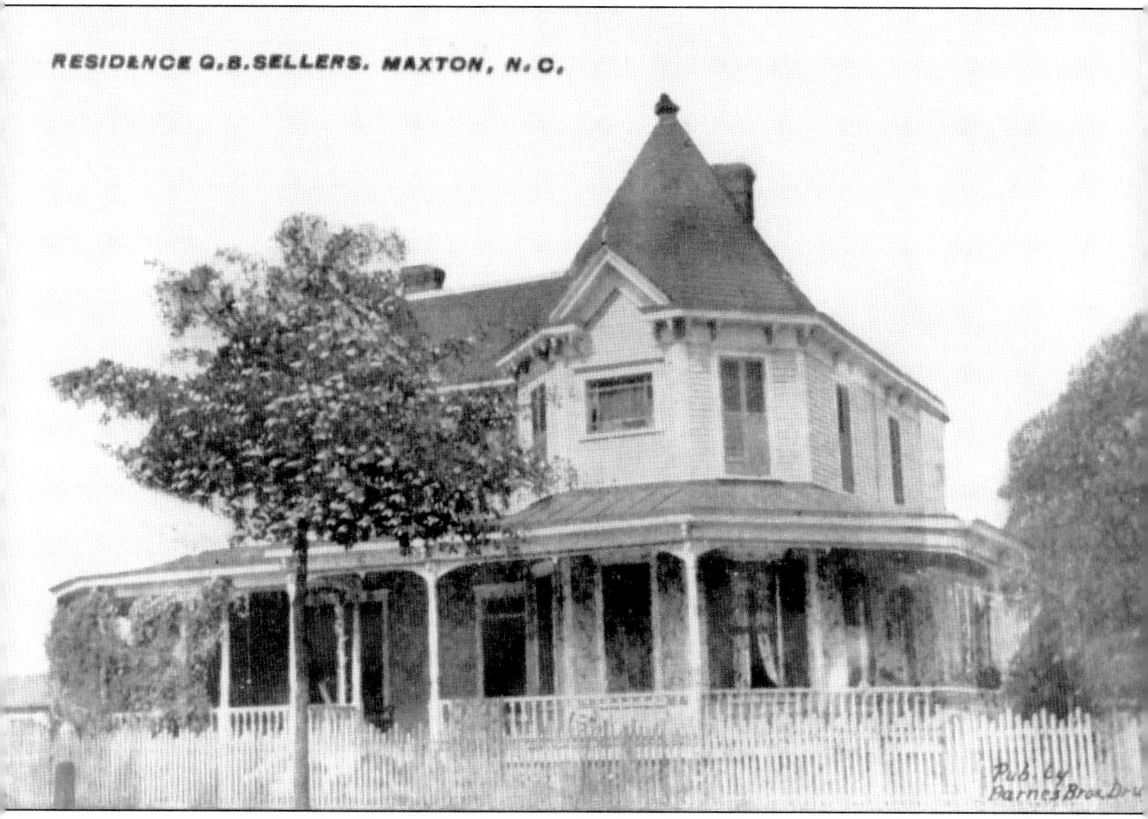

RESIDENCE G. B. SELLERS. Gilbert Bethea Sellers began construction of his Maxton town home soon after his marriage to Flora McKay. The December 10, 1896, *Wilmington Star* reported, "Capt. Sellers has the lumber on his lot on Main Street, ready to begin in the erection of a dwelling as soon as weather will permit." He was major of the 3rd Battalion of the 2nd Regiment of the State Guards and served in the North Carolina House of Representatives. The home is now owned by his granddaughter, Flora Lou Morgan Morton. The Sellers family first settled east of Maxton on the banks of the Lumber River in the 1790s; between 1791 and 1798, Archibald Sellers had thirteen grants from the State of North Carolina, totaling nearly 1,300 acres. (Courtesy North Carolina State Archives.)

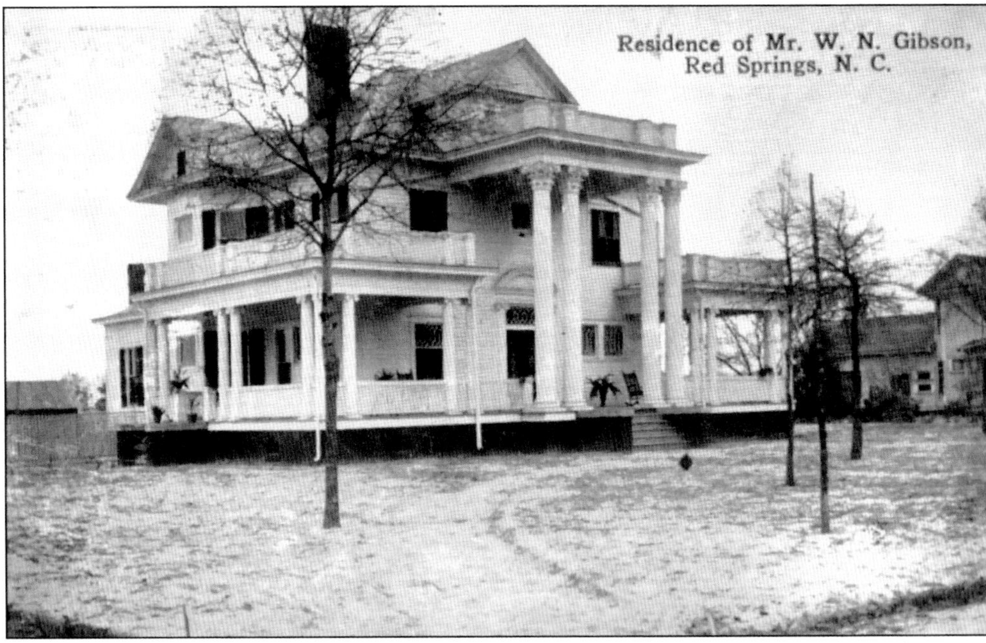

Residence of W. N. Gibson. This impressive home has graced Main Street, Red Springs since 1912. Built for William Gibson in the neoclassical style, the home features a dramatic two-storied pediment Corinthian portico.

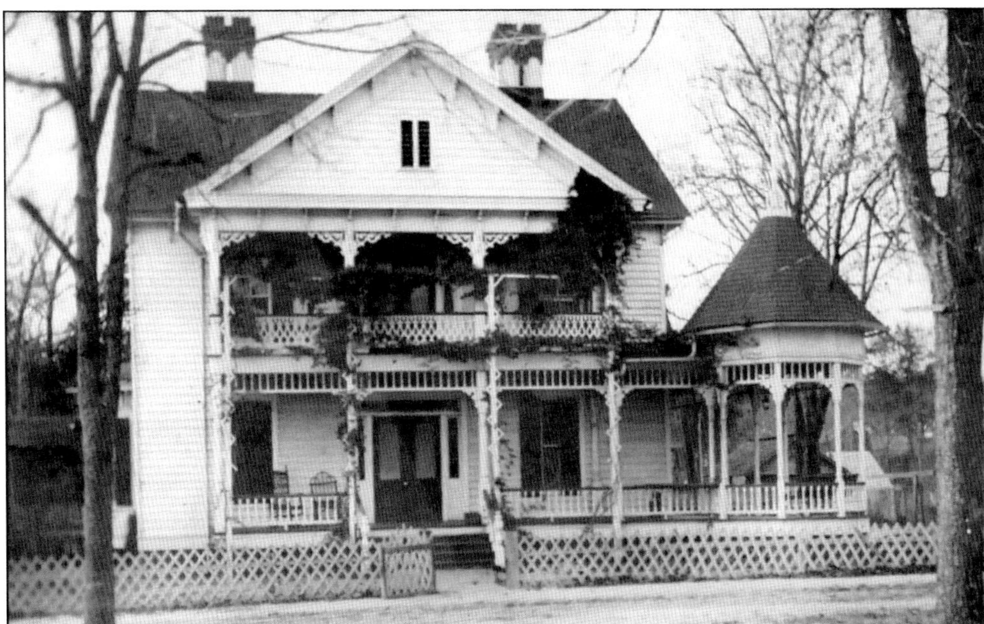

Residence of Locke Shaw. This two-story Victorian home, with an attached gazebo, was built in St. Pauls by merchant and farmer Locke Shaw. Shaw and his brother-in-law, Alexander R. McEachern, worked with Angus Wilton McLean to bring the Virginia and Carolina Southern Railroad to the St. Pauls area in 1907. Shaw and McEachern owned the land surrounding the railroad, which was divided into lots and sold at auction.

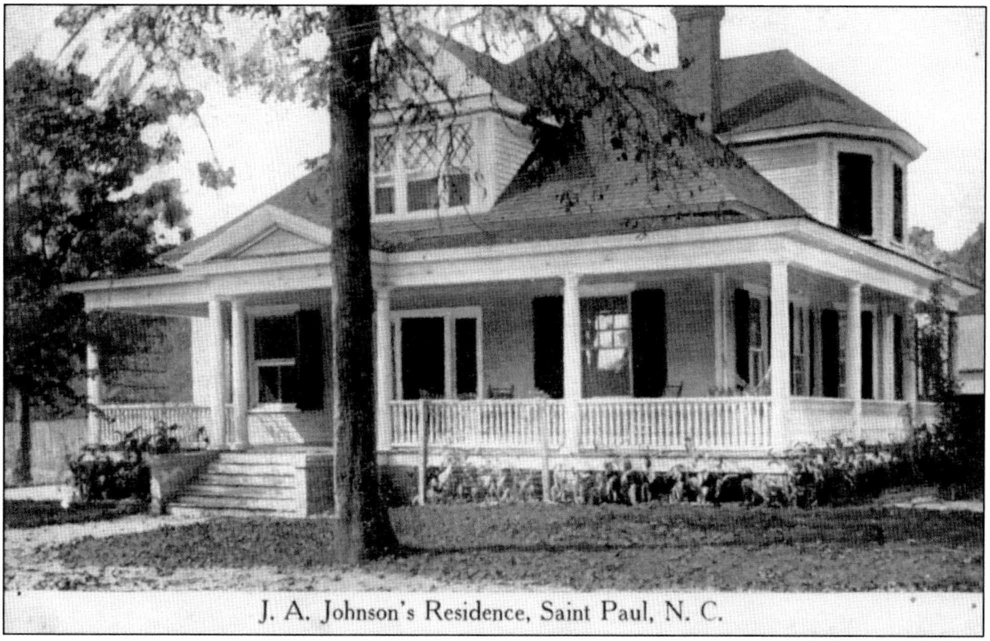

J. A. Johnson's Residence. James A. Johnson built this home on Old Stage Road at the time that it was the main business and residential section of St. Pauls. He and his brother, Walter D. Johnson, operated large farms and business interests that included Johnson Brothers Lumber Company, McEachern-Johnson-McGeachy Company, St. Pauls Cotton Mill, and the Bank of St. Pauls.

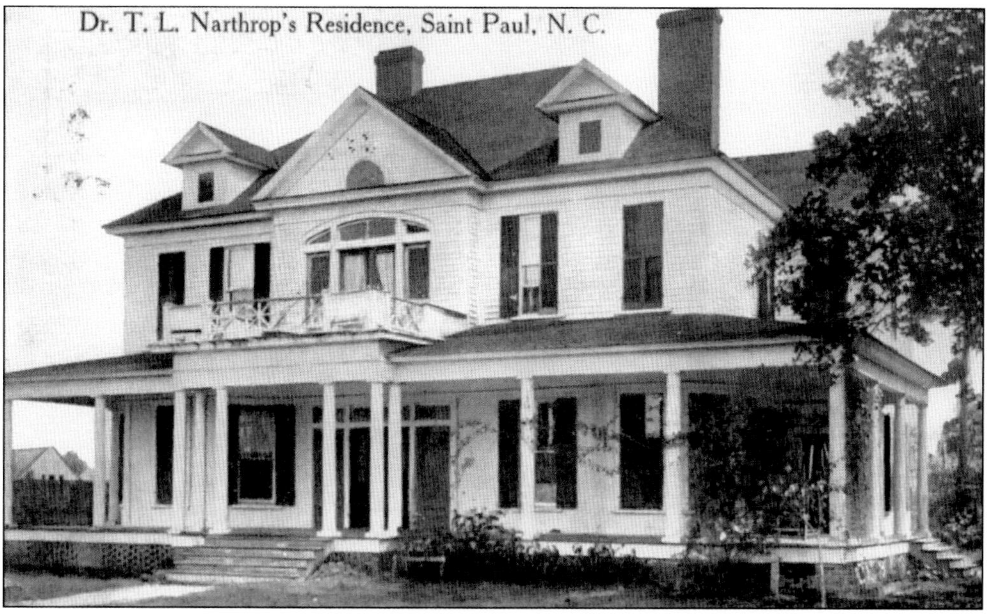

Dr. T. L. Northrop Residence. When Dr. Northrop built this home beside the St. Pauls Presbyterian Church, he included his medical office in it. In addition to providing excellent medical care for the citizens of the northern part of the county, Northrop owned large farming interests. His business interests included serving as a director of the St. Pauls Cotton Mill and the Bank of St. Pauls.

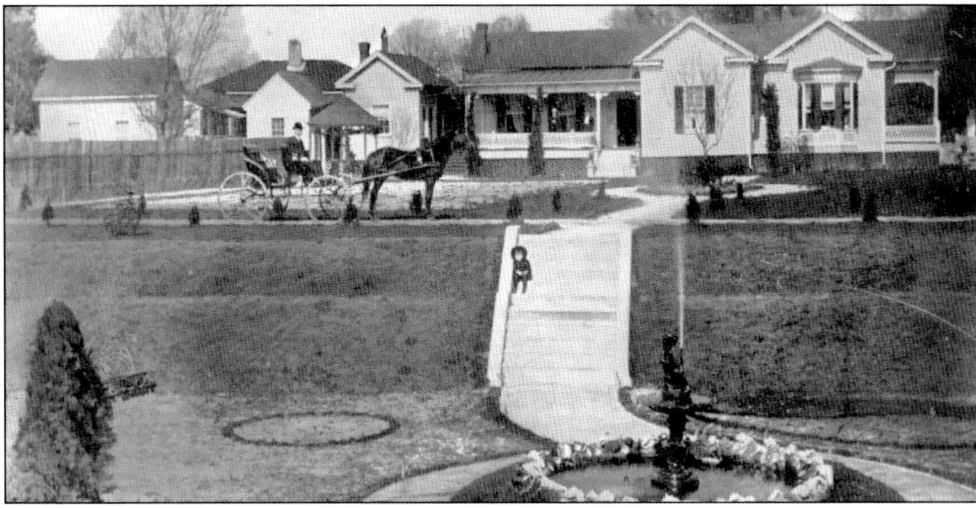

R. D. CALDWELL RESIDENCE. This beautiful home was built by Robert D. Caldwell and featured a sunken garden. Caldwell was first in partnership with William W. Carlyle in the mercantile firm of Caldwell and Carlyle; after Carlyle's death, the firm was renamed R. D. Caldwell and Sons. He was instrumental in the founding of the National Bank of Lumberton, the Lumberton, Dresden, and Jennings Cotton Mills, the Lumberton Building and Loan Association, and the Robeson County Loan and Trust Company. He has also been referred to as the father of the Baker Sanatorium because of the role of support that he provided for his daughter, Annie Ruth, and her husband, Dr. Horace Baker Sr., as they worked to open the hospital in 1921. He was chairman of the board of the deacons of the First Baptist Church for a quarter of a century.

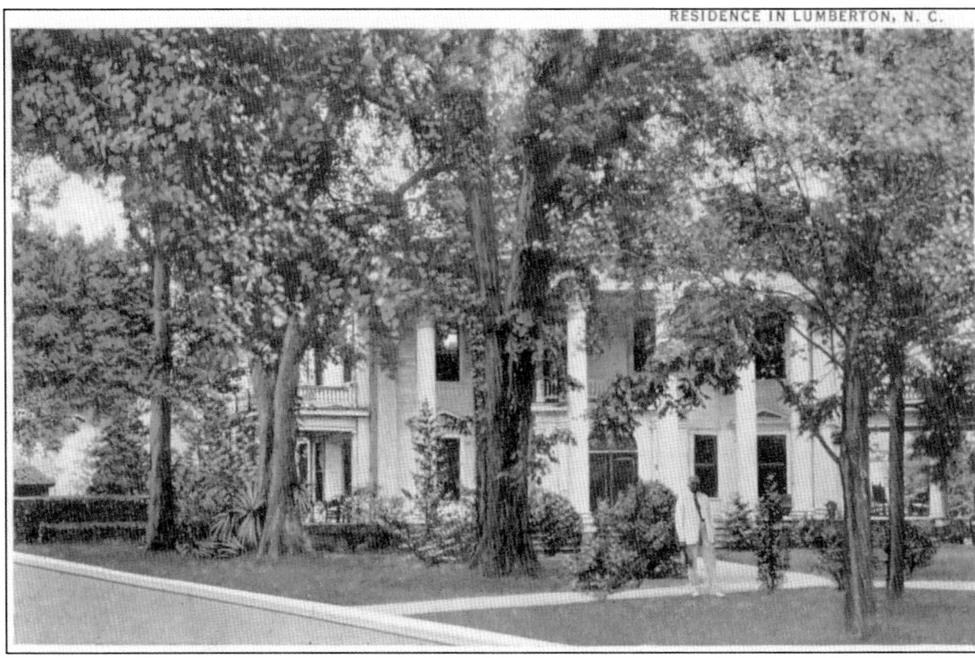

A. E. WHITE RESIDENCE. This wonderful home was located across Chestnut Street from the First Presbyterian Church in downtown Lumberton. Albert Edward White was in partnership with Frank Gough in the mercantile business White and Gough. White, with Angus Wilton McLean and Robert D. Caldwell, organized the Bank of Lumberton.

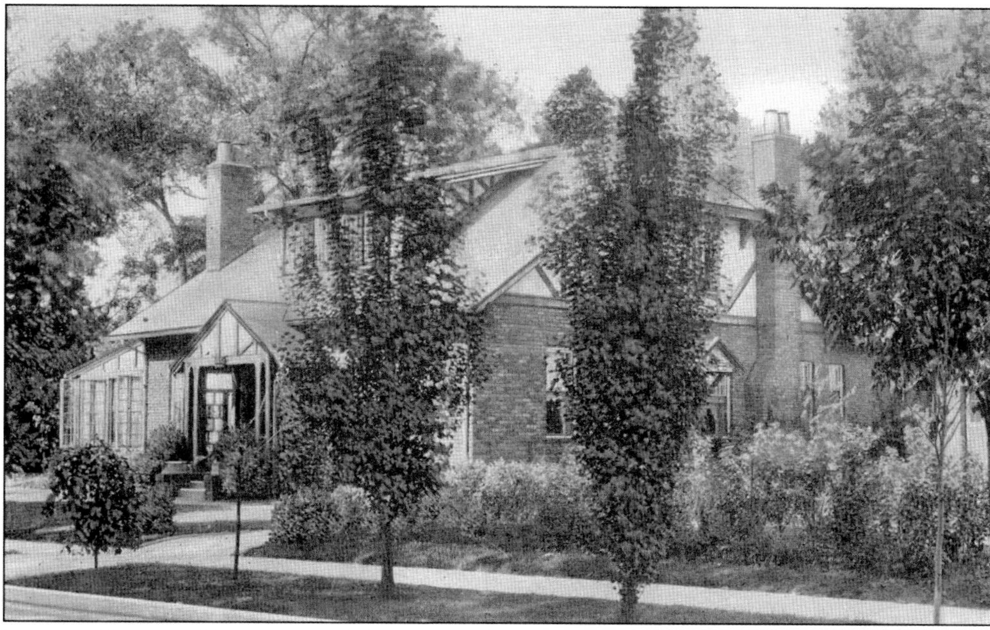

FRANK GRAVES RESIDENCE. The home of Frank Graves was located on Chestnut Street in Lumberton.

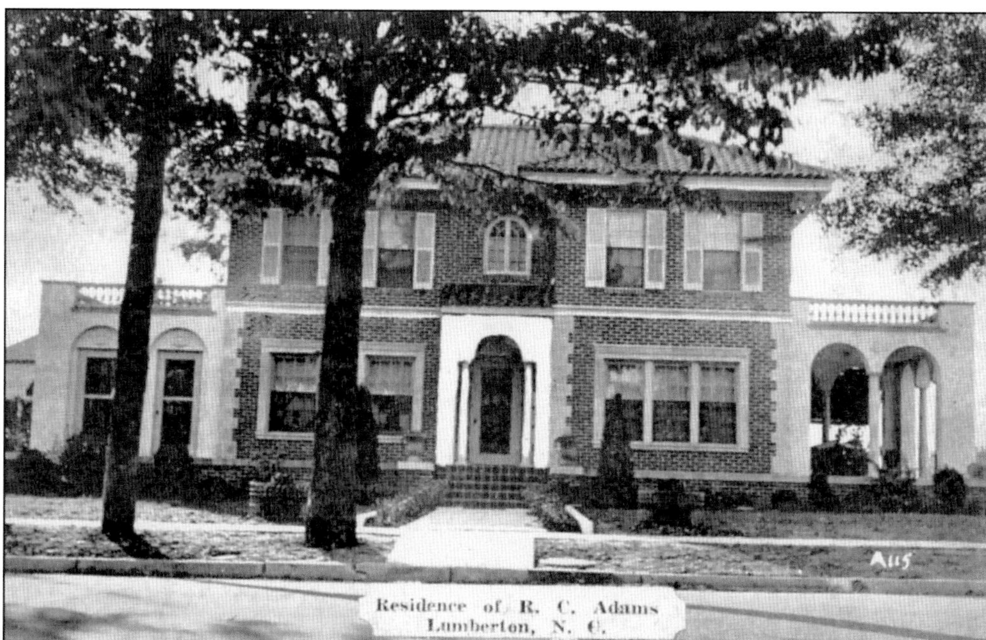

RESIDENCE OF R. C. ADAMS. Lumberton builder, Thomas Matthew Burney, built this home located at 401 Elm Street for Robert C. Adams in 1933. Adams was president of the Lumberton Investment Company and secretary-treasurer of the Robeson manufacturing company and the Ada McLean Mills.

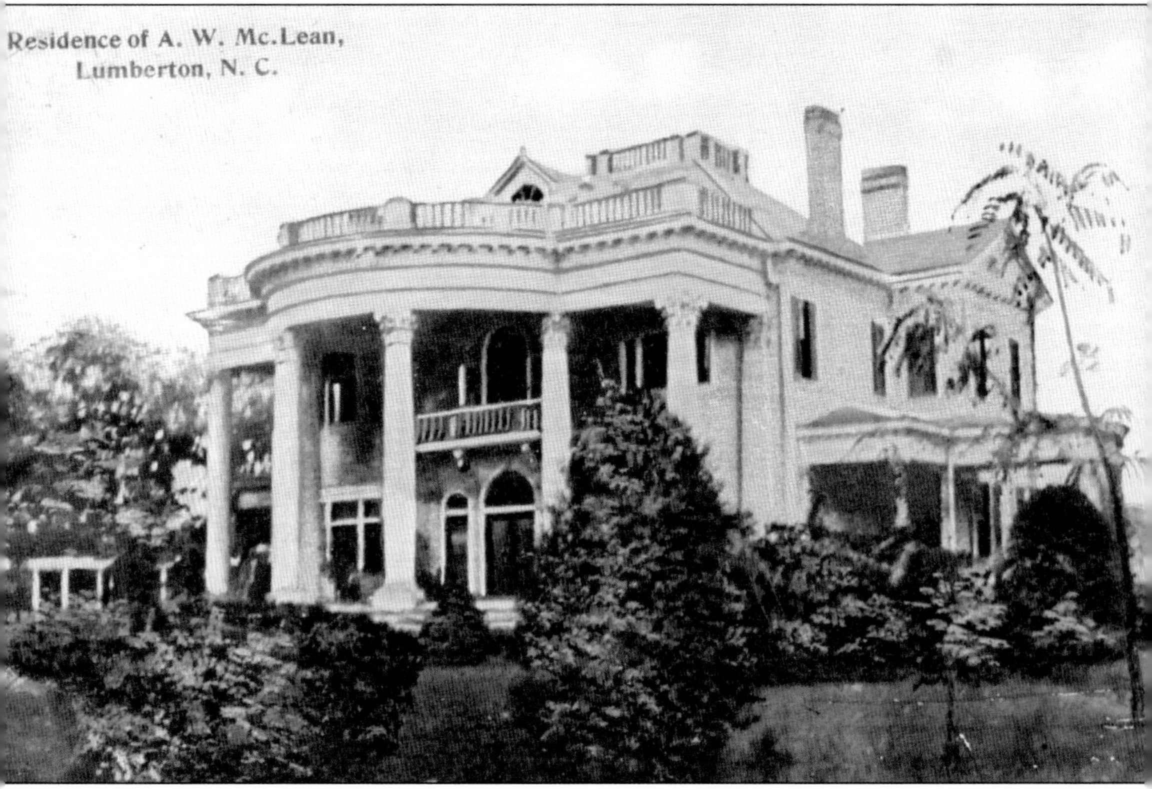

McLean Residence. Angus Wilton McLean and his wife, Margaret Jones French, with their three children lived in this landmark of downtown Lumberton. McLean served as director of the U.S. War Finance Corporation and Assistant Secretary of the Treasury. In 1925, McLean was elected governor of North Carolina. He undertook the task of expanding the powers of the executive branch. With the new power to direct the state finances, he could reduce legislative appropriations, cut salaries, and appoint commissions. He brought all the state agencies under one budget process supervised by the Governor's Office. He also organized many of the county's business such as the National Bank of Lumberton in 1897, which later became Southern National Bank; the Lumberton and Dresden Cotton Mills; and the Virginia & Carolina Southern Railroad. Governor Angus Wilton McLean was claimed by death on June 20, 1935. In 1952, Governor McLean's son, Hector MacLean, was named attorney and assistant to the president of his father's bank. He was named president and chairman of the board in 1955 and headed the bank until 1990. In addition to his banking interest, Hector MacLean served as mayor of Lumberton, North Carolina, from 1949 to 1953 and state senator from 1961 to 1971. He was the president of the board of directors of Medical Foundation of North Carolina from 1971 until 1993; under his guidance, endowment grew from $5 million to $40 million. Like his father, Hector MacLean was very interested in history and served as chairman of many commissions and foundations concerned with history such as the North Carolina Commission on the Bicentennial of the U.S. Constitution, North Carolina Confederate Centennial Commission, North Carolina Bicentennial Foundation, North Carolina Bicentennial Commission, Robeson County Bicentennial Commission, and the Robeson County Bicentennial Foundation. MacLean received many honors including being a 1996 inductee of the North Carolina Business Hall of Fame for his contributions to the banking industry of North Carolina, and in 1997, a portion of Interstate 95 going through Lumberton, North Carolina was named the "Hector MacLean Highway." (Courtesy Paul Valenti and Carla Baxley.)

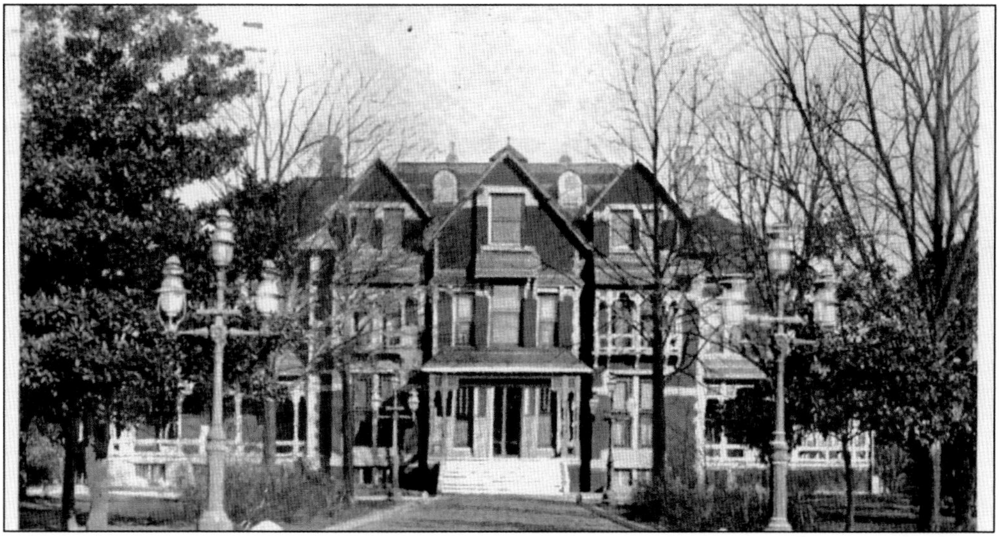

GOVERNOR'S MANSION. After McLean was elected governor in 1924, preparations began for his family to move from their Lumberton mansion to the executive mansion in Raleigh. The McLeans found the official residence in poor physical condition; in fact, it is said that clouds of dust could be seen as one walked from room to room. Carpets and furniture were worn, and the first-floor walls and floors were unsound. Mrs. McLean worked with local decorator Elizabeth Thompson to refurbish the home. Mrs. McLean brought large amounts of furniture, linens, and china to use at the mansion. She also made special purchases of furniture using the McLean private funds to furnish the rooms.

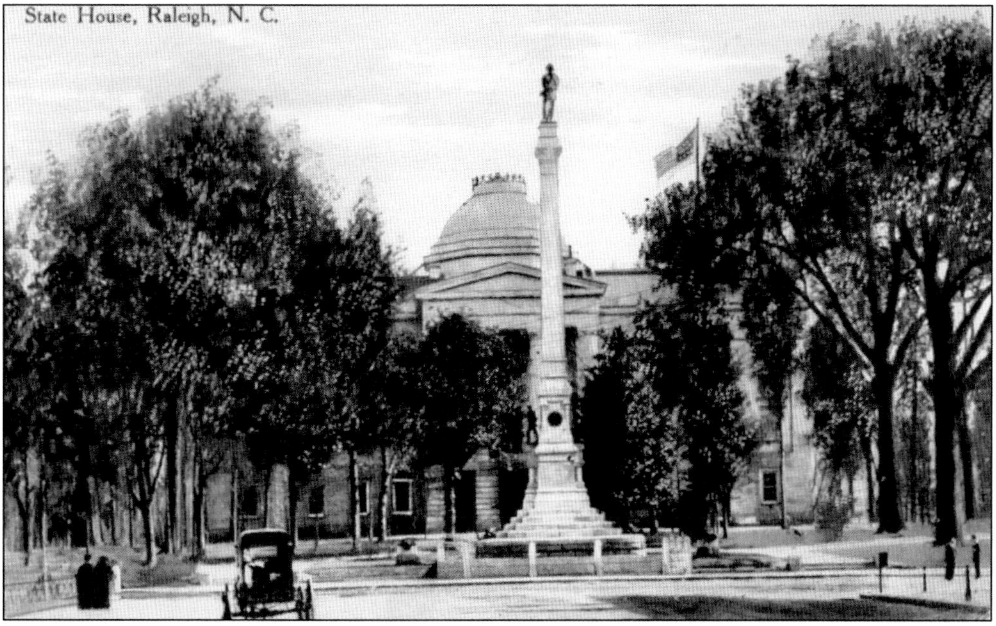

STATE HOUSE. The North Carolina State Capitol, known as the State House, was completed in 1840 and is one of the finest and best-preserved examples of a major civic building in the Greek Revival style of architecture. Governor McLean's office was located in this building. The rotunda of the Capitol houses a reproduction of the Canova's statue of George Washington, as Cincinnatus, that was unveiled by McLean's son, Hector MacLean, in 1970.

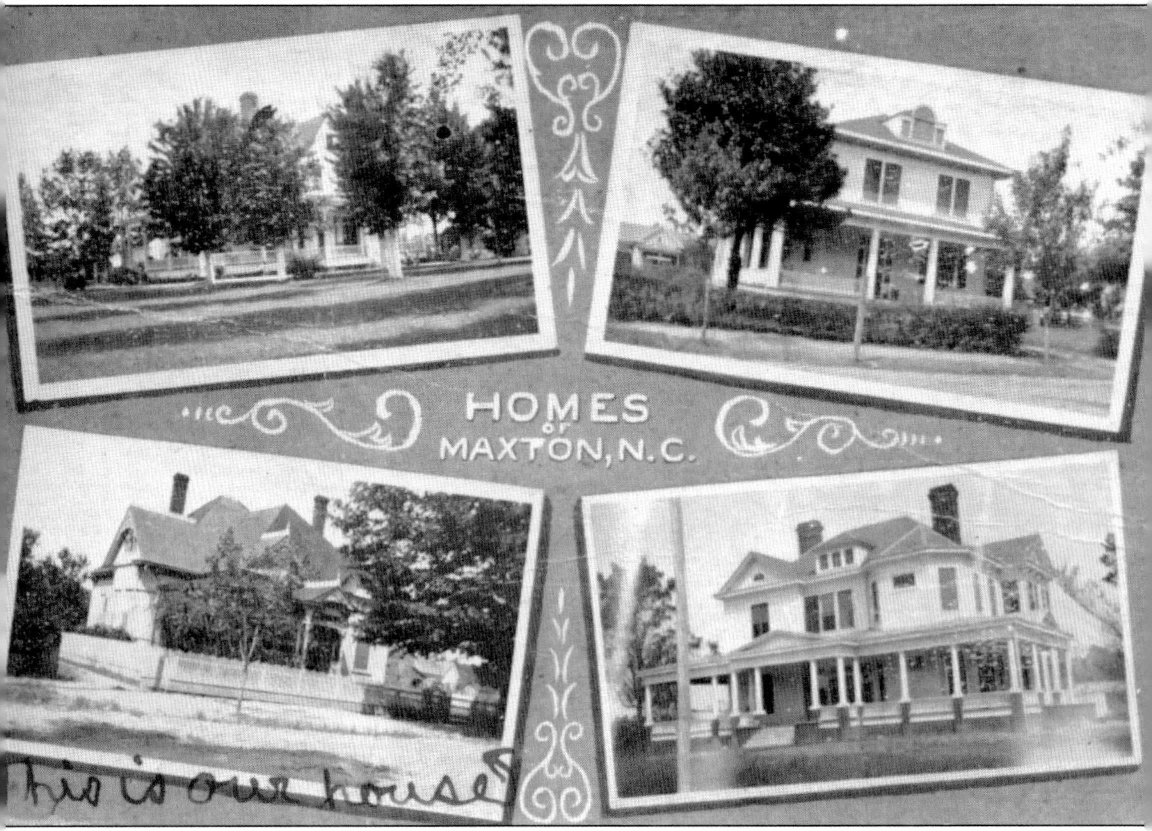

HOMES OF MAXTON. This postcard features four Maxton homes, unfortunately only the Lathrop-Carter House, in the top left-hand corner, and the Rory McNair House, in the bottom right-hand corner, are identifiable since the county has lost many older homes. Built in 1890 by E. S. Lathrop and later occupied by the J. W. Carter family, this Italian Victorian served as the Bird Song Bed and Breakfast for several years in the early 21st century. The Lathrops sold the house to Eva McLaurin as a gift for her niece, Sue Kelly McRae. Although the house was only four blocks from the railroad that ran through the center of town, McRae chose not to live there saying it was too far out in the country. In 1912, Rory McNair built his neoclassical home on the 500-acre Argyle Farm. In addition to cotton on the farm, he produced cantaloupes and watermelons, shipping between 15 and 25 railcars of melons each year.

Six

Education

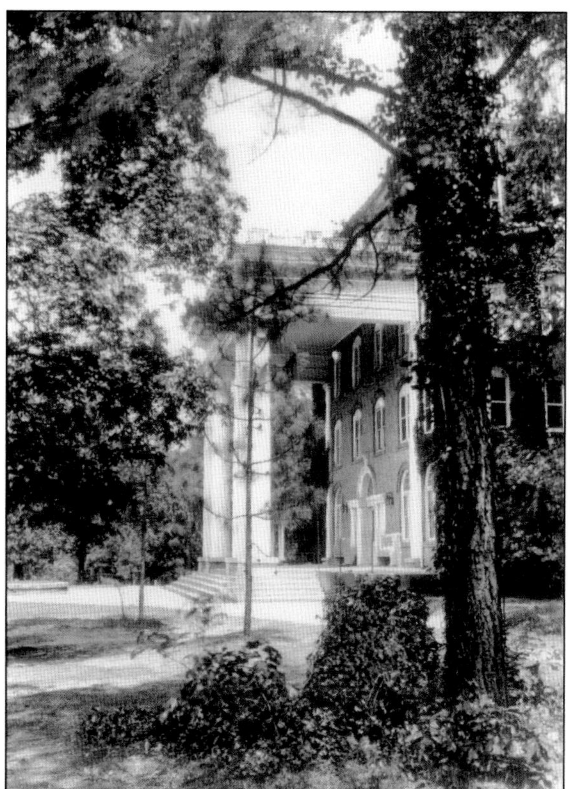

Flora MacDonald College. Not only the most photographed school in the county, Red Springs's Flora MacDonald College more than likely ties with the 1908 Robeson County Courthouse as the most photographed building in the county.

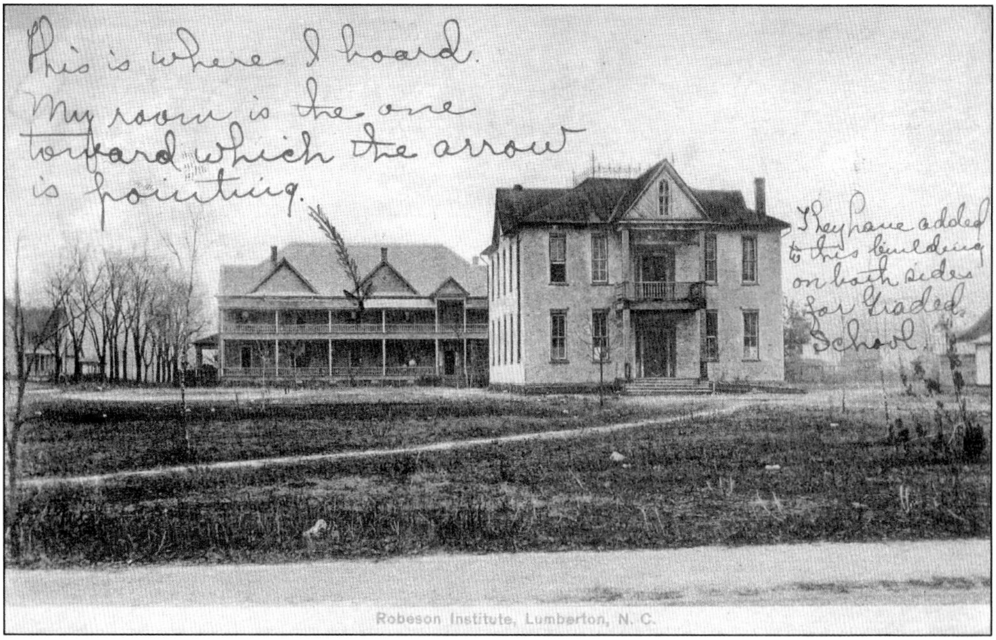

ROBESON INSTITUTE. R. D. Caldwell, Berry Godwin, Frank Gough, A. C. Melke, and E. K. Proctor Jr. founded the Robeson Institute in Lumberton in 1891. Operated until 1907, the school was lead by John Duckett (former superintendent of public instruction of Wake County), and Gen. Thomas F. Toon. The school's motto was "do right."

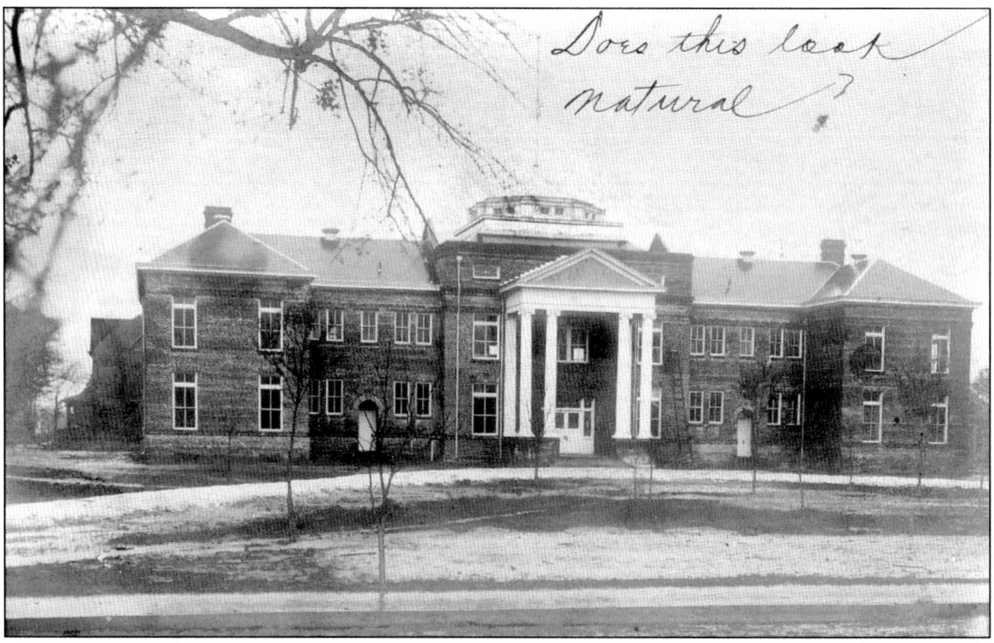

LUMBERTON GRADED SCHOOL. After the Robeson Institute was closed in 1907, the property was deeded to the city of Lumberton to be used as a grade school. Two wings and a dome were added to the building. In the background, the building that was used for boarding students can be seen.

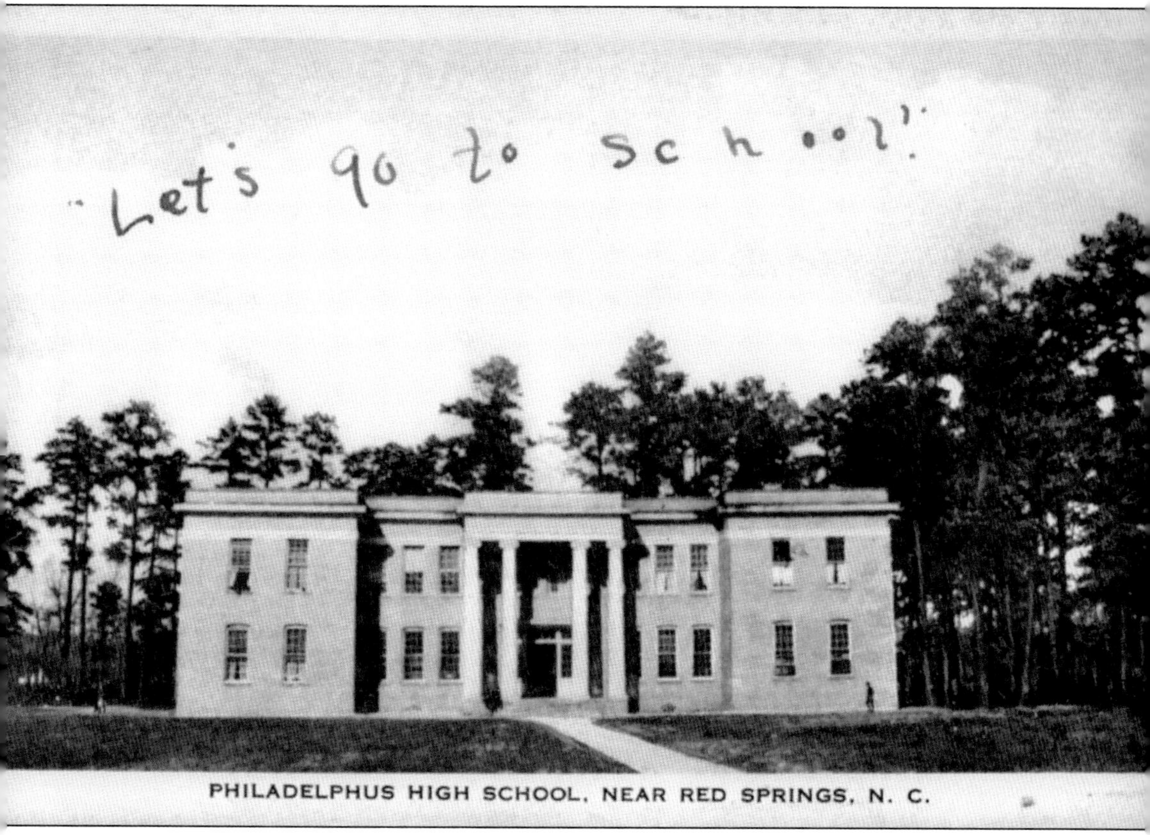

PHILADELPHUS. This large brick school building that was built in 1921 replaced an earlier wooden school that burned. The school was near the Philadelphus Presbyterian Church and about two miles from Buie. The new building had water, electric lights, and steam heat. It featured 16 classrooms, a superintendent's office, a library, and an auditorium. The campus was 25 acres and also contained separate dormitories for girls and boys. The school was for grammar, science, French, Spanish, agriculture classes, home economics, and music. Three types of diplomas were offered: academic, for those whose talents were literary so that they could enter college easier; home economics, for girls to be prepared for business of home making and included the study of food, shelter, and clothing; and agriculture, for boys whose talents were in agriculture or mechanics. The school hosted three literary societies: the Deuropean for high-school girls; the Athenian for high-school boys, and the Euzelian for grammar grades.

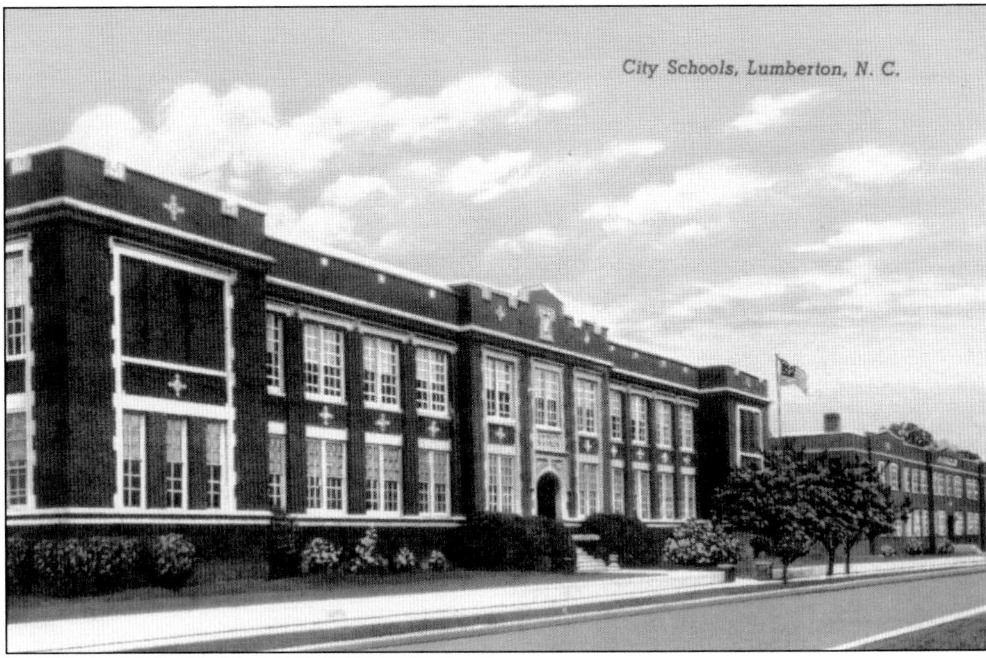

LUMBERTON CITY SCHOOLS. Lumberton, in an effort to upgrade its education system, built a new modern school in front of the old grade school. Also on the property were a modern gymnasium and cafeteria.

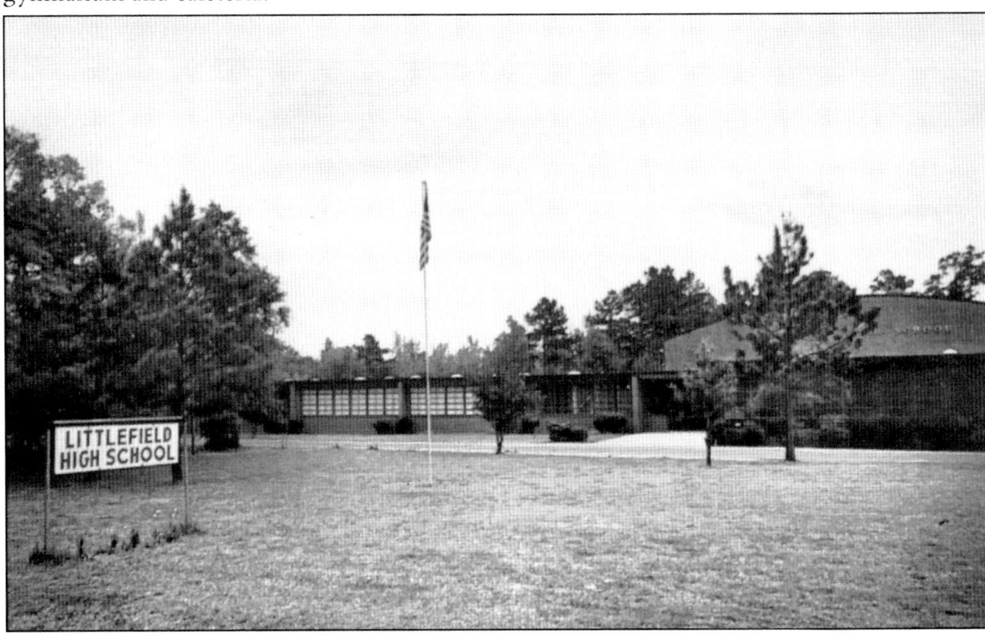

LITTLEFIELD SCHOOL. Smith's, Allenton, and Barker Ten-Mile Schools consolidated into a new high school in the fall of 1955. The new school, located on 17.7 acres six miles east of Lumberton on North Carolina 41 and named after B. E. Littlefield (then superintendent of Robeson County Schools), served the 273 original students of these high schools. In 1972, an addition was made to the building. The last high school graduation from the school was in spring 1991. With consolidation of the county school system, Littlefield was turned into a middle school.

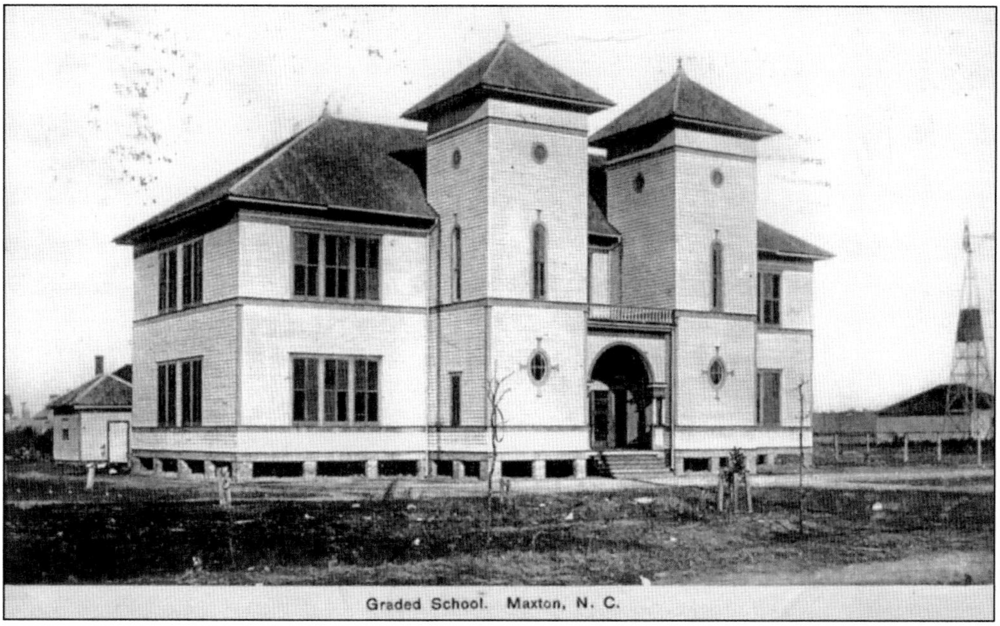

MAXTON GRADE SCHOOL. This building was located on the corner of Graham and Florence Streets at the corner site of the Gilbert Patterson Law Office that houses the maxton Historical Society Museum. The school published their first catalog for the 1902-1903 school year. It reported 10 pupils with Joseph E. Avent as the superintendent and Sallie A. McLean, Elizabeth B. McLean, Maggie K. Patterson, and Annie L. McRae as teachers.

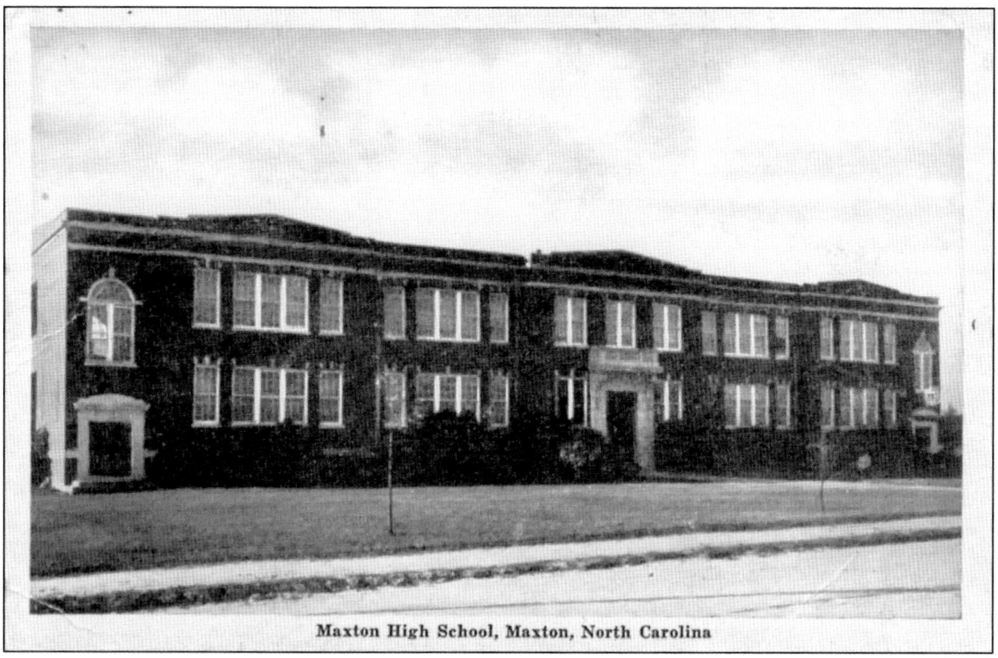

MAXTON HIGH SCHOOL. This Georgian Revival high school was built in 1924; it was designed by Leslie N. Boney of Wilmington, North Carolina. The building featured terra-cotta trim in contrast to the deep-red bricks. The local high school was merged with the Prospect High School in 1979, and this building was later torn down.

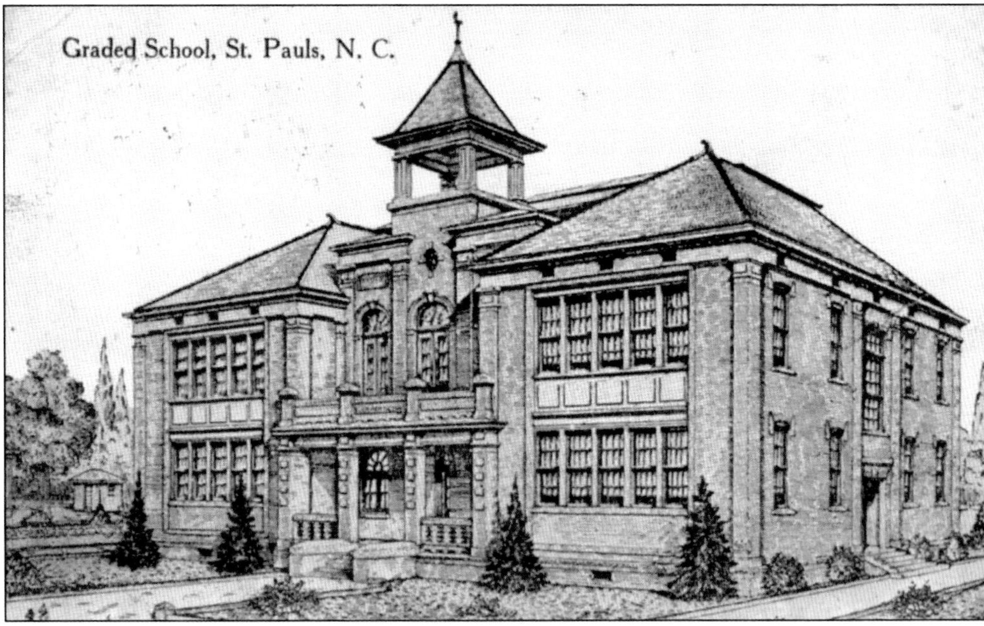

GRADED SCHOOL. This nine-room brick school was built in 1913 on Northrop Street in St. Pauls. It served all grades until 1923, when a new building was built on Shaw Street near Highway 301. The new building was used for high school and upper primary, while the old building was used by the lower primary grades. The building was later used by the local National Guard.

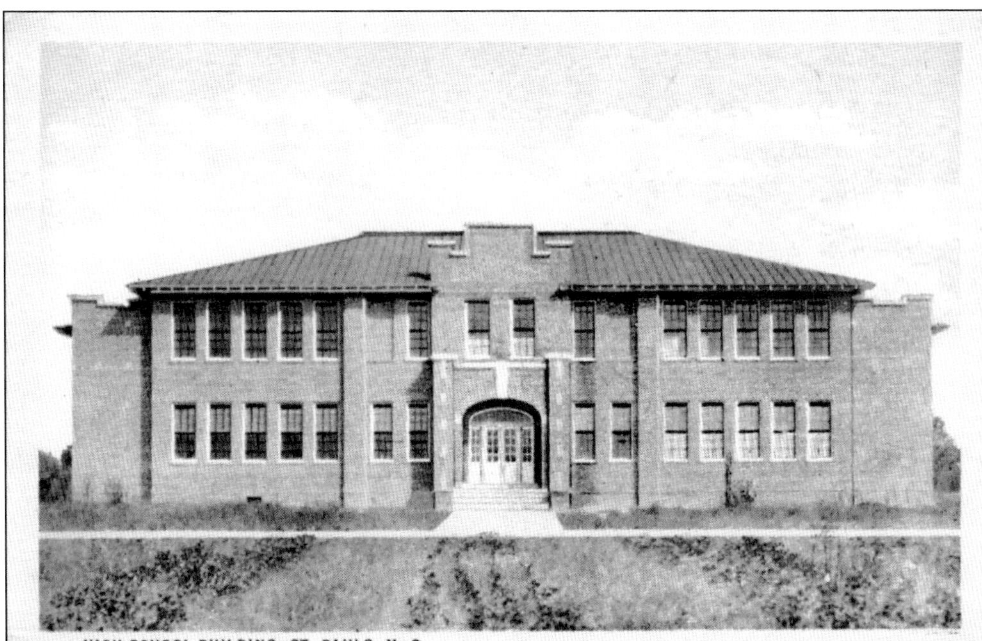

HIGH SCHOOL BUILDING. One of the first buildings on the new campus on the corner of Shaw Street and Highway 301, this building features classrooms on both floors and a large auditorium on the lower level.

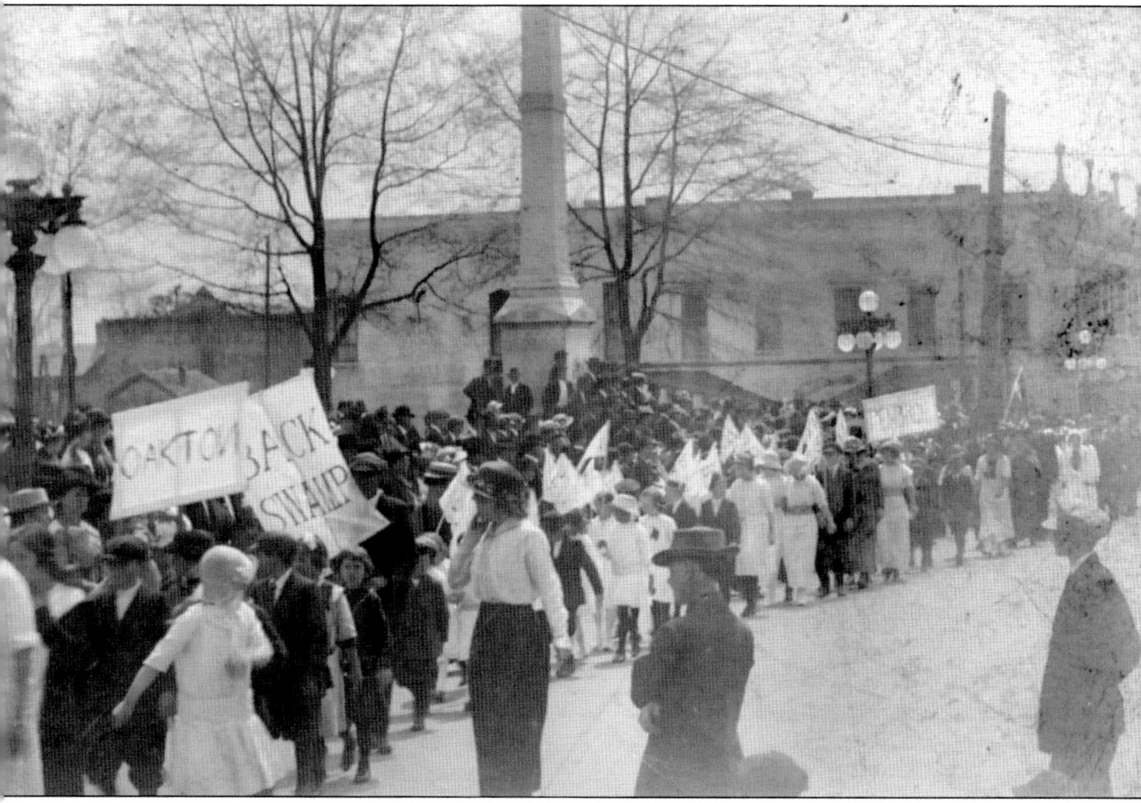

COMMENCEMENT DAY PARADE. The commencement day parades for Robeson County were held in downtown Lumberton. They would march north on Elm Street past the courthouse. This scene shows class groups from Oakton, Back Swamp, and Pembroke.

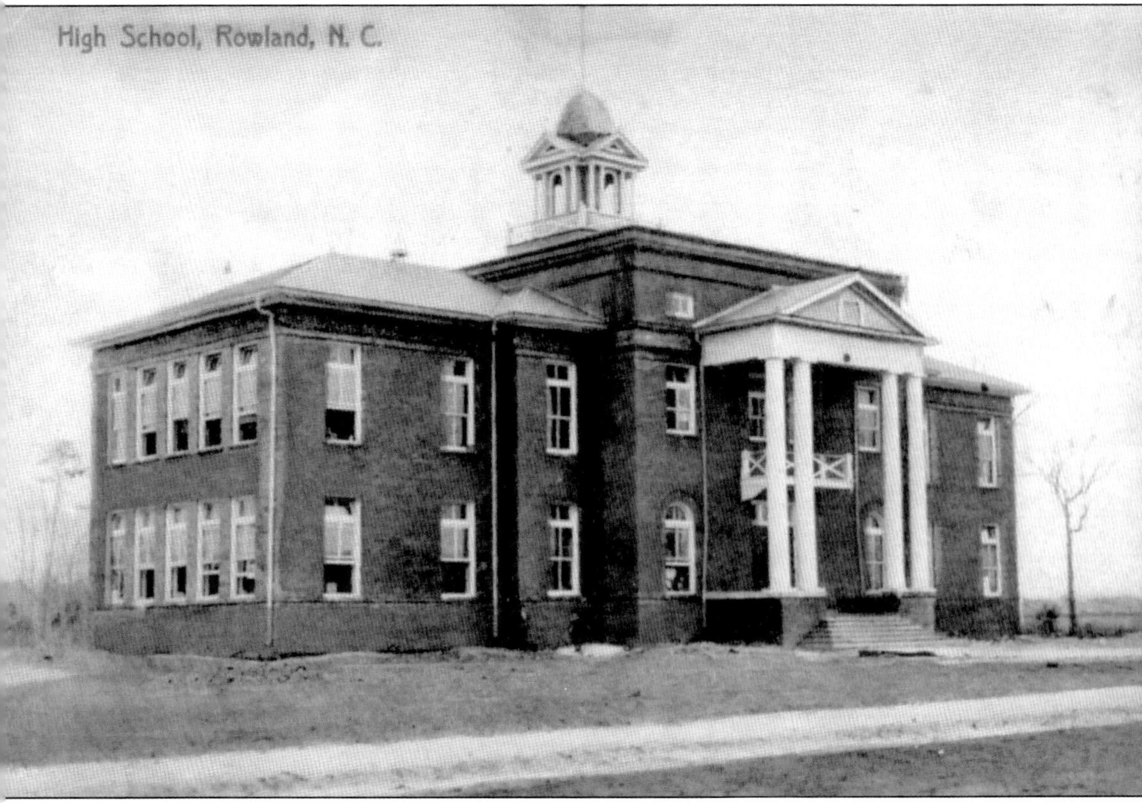

ROWLAND SCHOOL. The high school was located in the town of Rowland on the border of North and South Carolina and cost $14,000 at the time of construction. In 1905, the school was under the direction of Principal William C. Herbert, and the school committee was made up of Graham McKinnon, P. H. Barnes, and John A. McCormic.

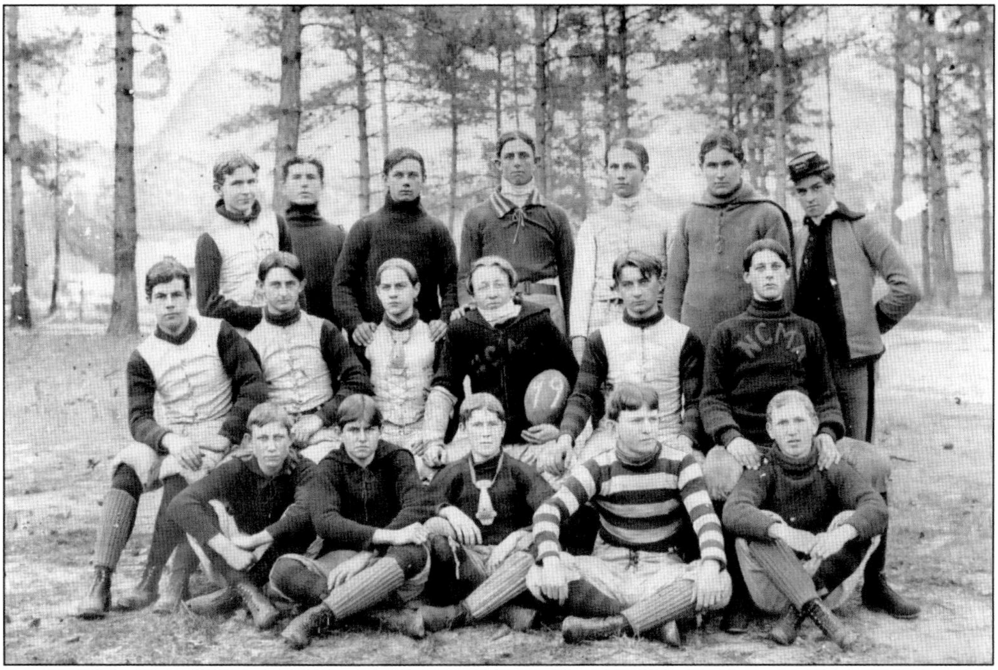

Football Team. The football team of the North Carolina Military Academy looks like they are ready to not only play during the 1899 season, but to win. (Courtesy North Carolina State Archives.)

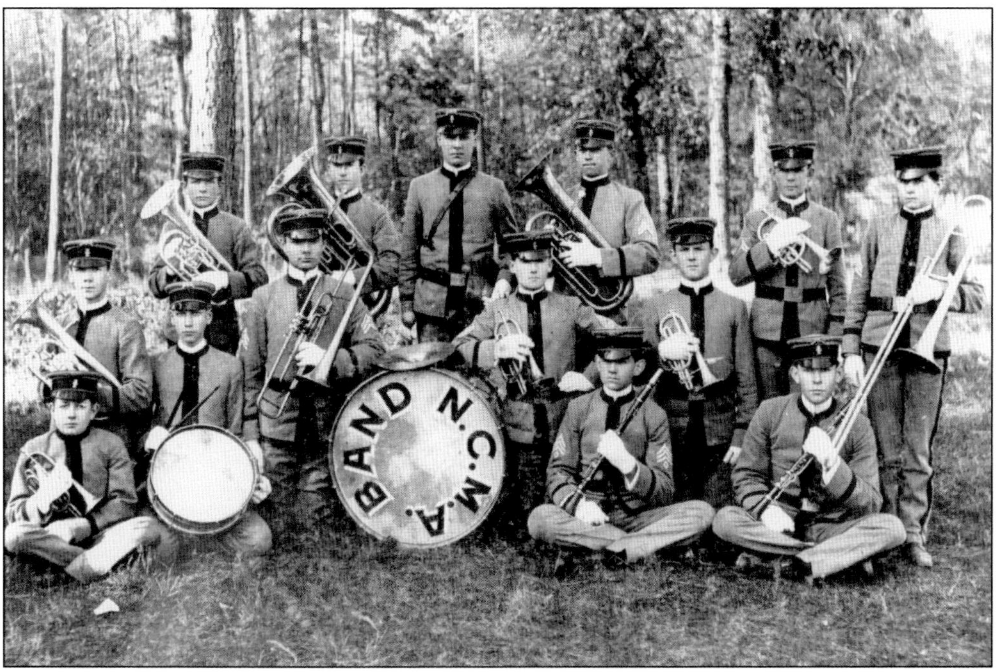

Band. Prof. Marcellus Wooten moved the North Carolina Military Academy from Fayetteville to Red Springs in 1899. This photograph of the band was taken about the time of the move. The academy flourished until 1908. Students that attended the academy included Dr. H. H. Hodgin, Chesley McCaskill, and Tom DeVane. (Courtesy North Carolina State Archives.)

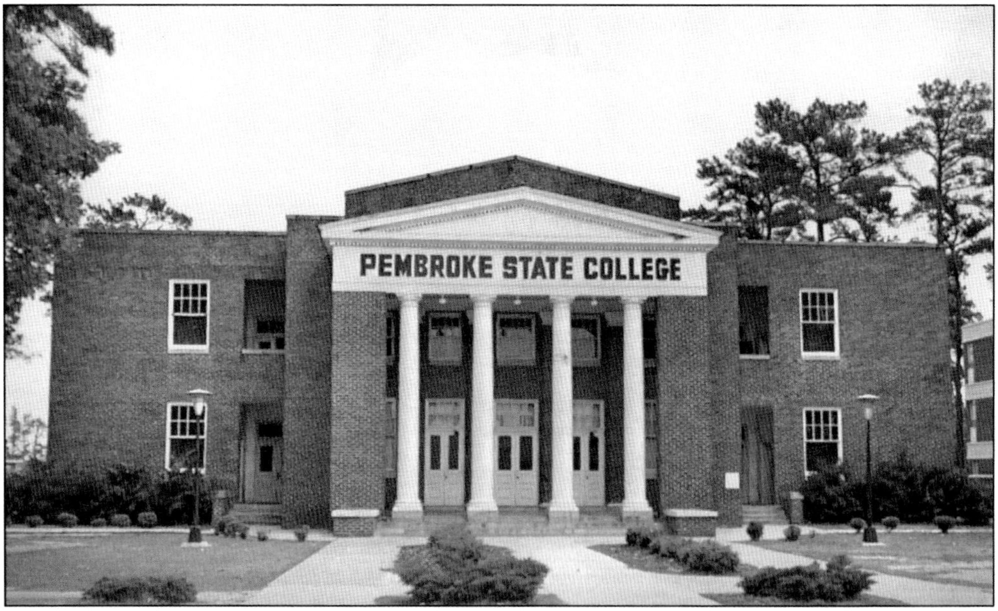

OLD MAIN. On March 7, 1887, the General Assembly of North Carolina enacted legislation, sponsored by Rep. Hamilton McMillan of Robeson County, creating the Croatan Normal School. The normal school was founded to train Native American public school teachers. After many name changes, the school officially became The University of North Carolina at Pembroke on July 1, 1996.

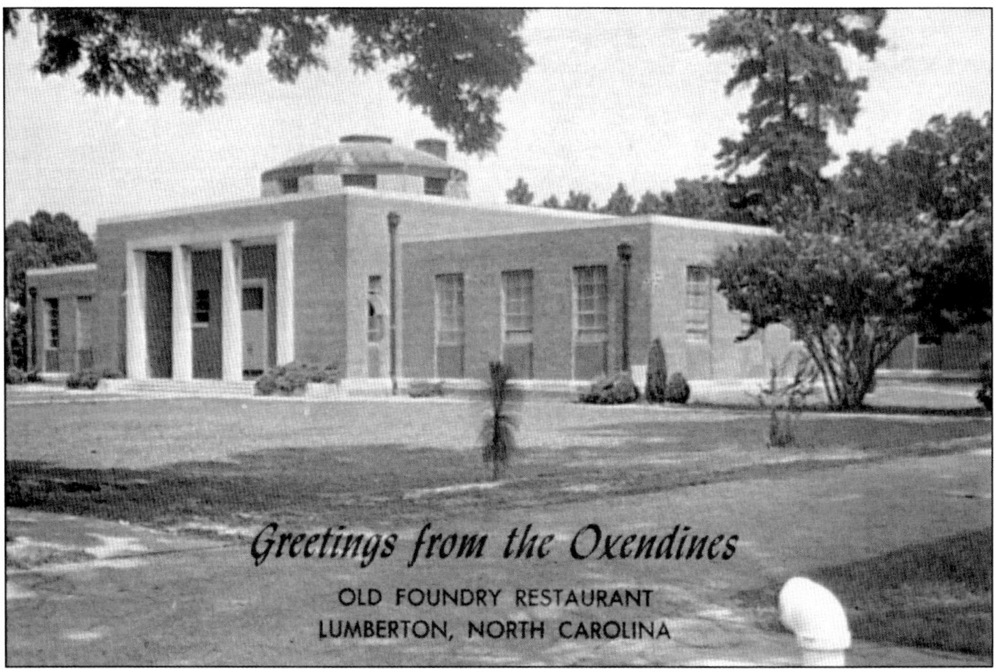

SAMPSON HALL. Named in honor of Oscar R. Sampson, an educator and former chairman of the board of trustees, this building housed the college's administration and the library. The building was torn down, and the current library is named the Sampson-Livermore Library in honor of Sampson and Prof. Mary Livermore.

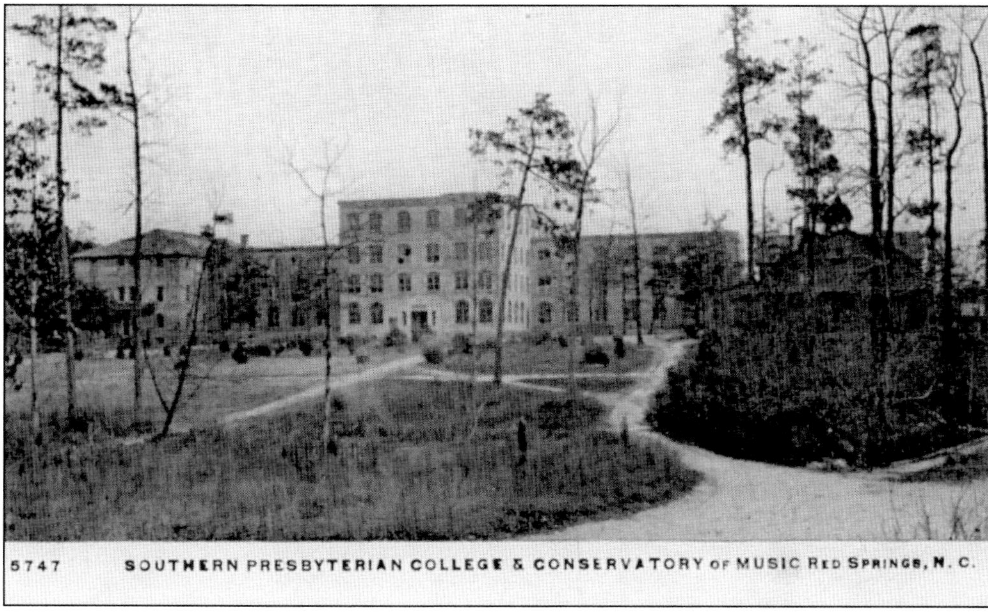

NEW AND OLD. A movement in North Carolina for the higher education of women led to the founding of Red Springs Seminary in 1896. The Fayetteville Presbytery decided to establish a seminary for girls somewhere in the area. Red Springs came forward with the promise of $2,500, four acres of land, and 40 students if the school was located there. The offer was immediately accepted. The name was changed in 1903 to Southern Presbyterian College and Conservatory of Music and in 1916, to Flora MacDoanld College. This postcard shows the modern multi-story brick building. Also to the front-right, the original wooden building can be seen.

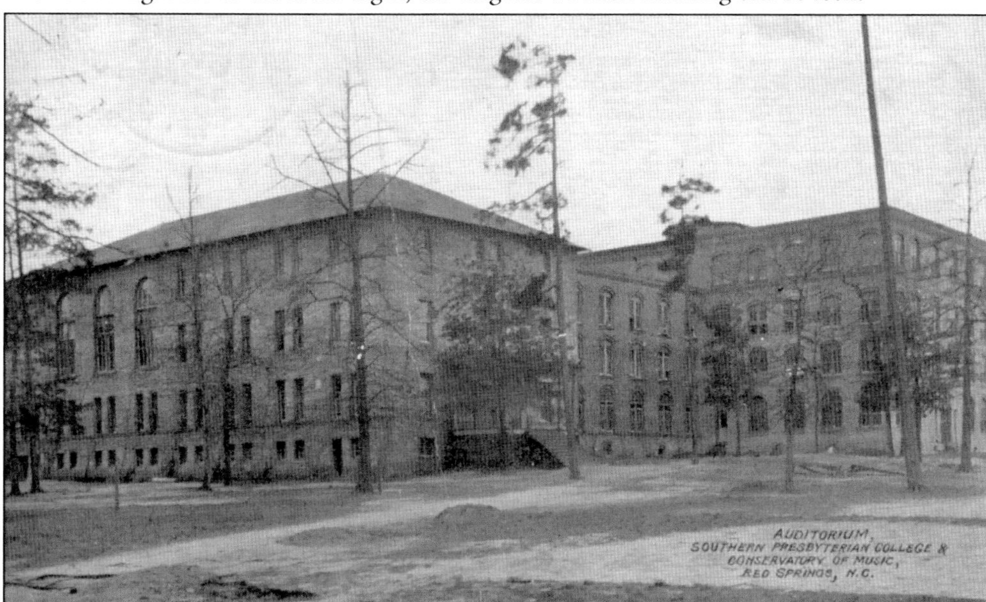

AUDITORIUM. In some ways, the auditorium was the center of life for the Southern Presbyterian College and Conservatory of Music. The auditorium features a massive pipe organ. An orchestra of students, faculty, and community members provides many concerts for the public. (Courtesy Paul Valenti and Carla Baxley.)

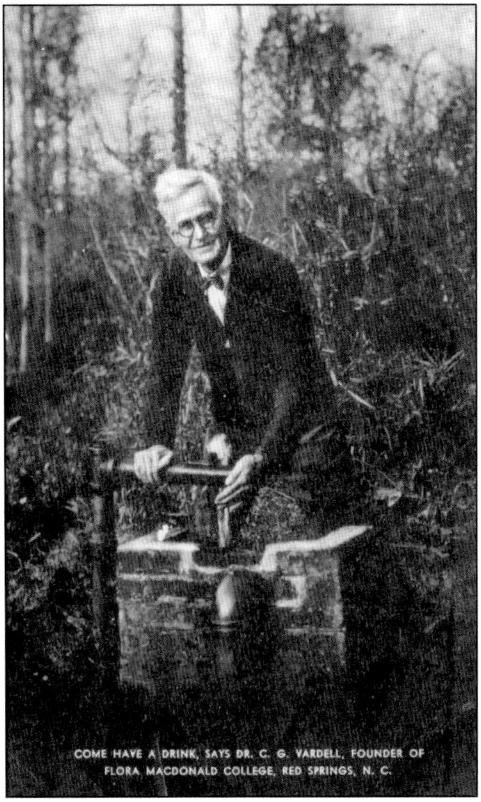

DR. VARDELL. Dr. Charles G. Vardell, president of Flora MacDonald, originally started the college gardens. Under his guidance and that of his capable assistant, Dexter Garner, the gardens became nationally known. Considerable damage was done by a 1984 tornado, and restoration has brought them back to a point where one can still walk the meandering paths. Many of the original plants gathered by Vardell still survive.

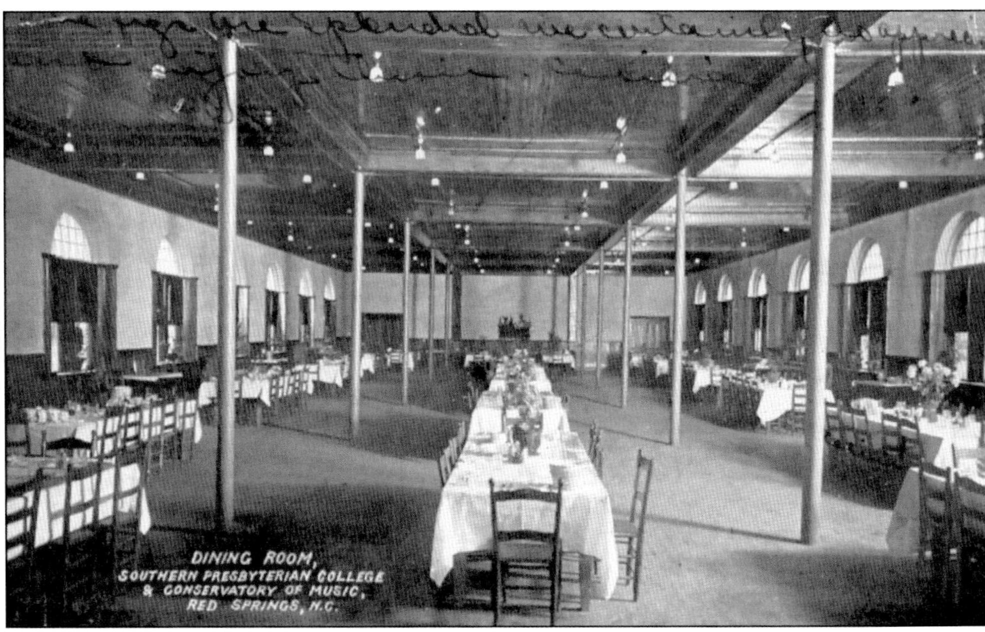

DINING ROOM. This postcard features the large dining room of the college that is often used for dances.

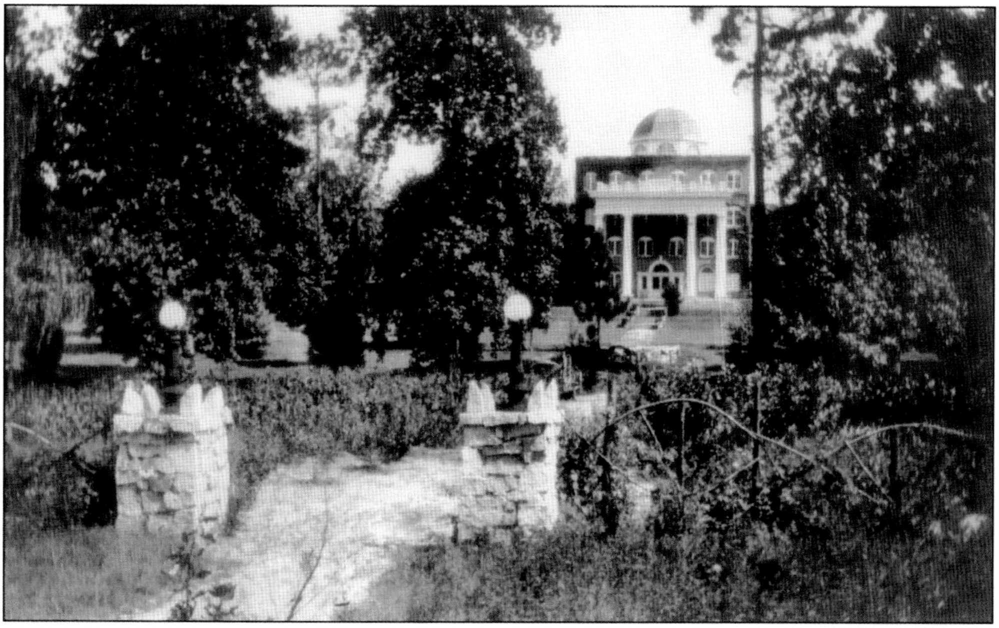

UNUSUAL FENCE. This view of the college was taken sometime after the dome was added in 1919. Notice the unusual woven twig fence that ran across the front of the property.

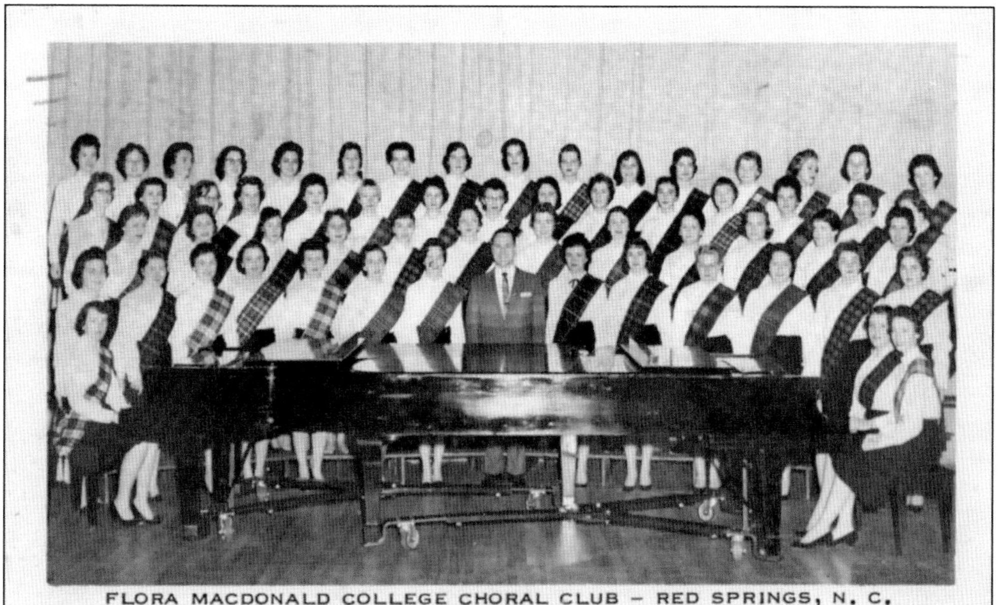

CHOIR. Just as in the days when the school was known as Southern Presbyterian College and Conservatory of Music, the choir of Flora MacDonald provided wonderful entertainment for the public as well as touring to other areas.

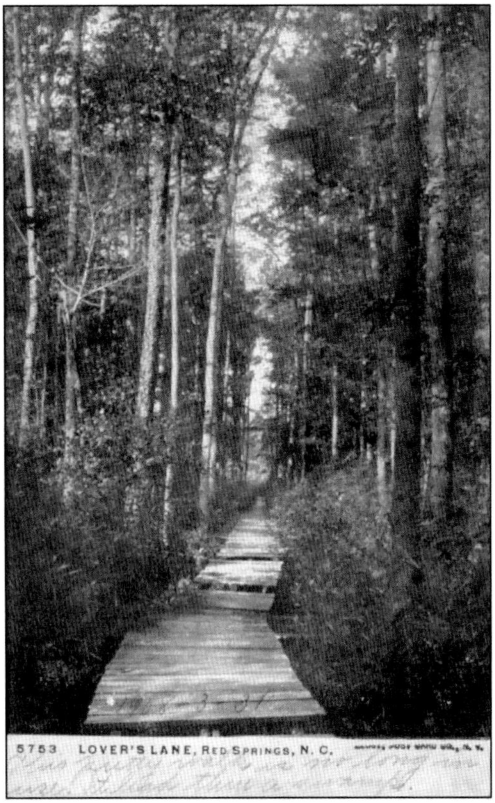

LOVER'S LANE. This Lover's Lane through the gardens of the college has seen better days. The sender of the postcard notes on the back the condition of the lane.

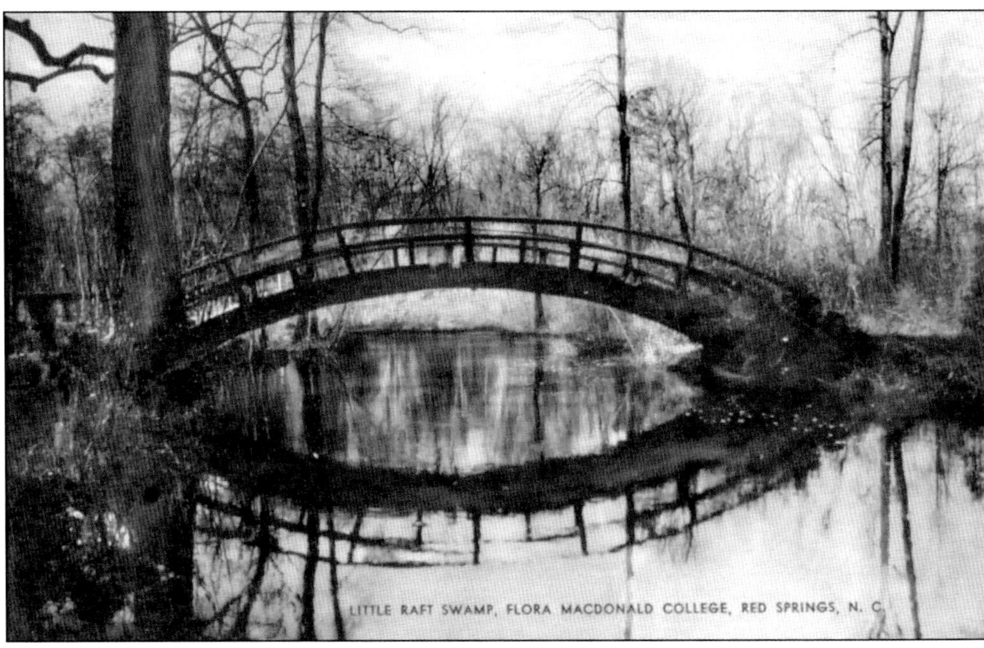

BRIDGE. This beautiful bridge was located in the gardens of the college and crosses over the Little Raft Swamp, which runs through the gardens.

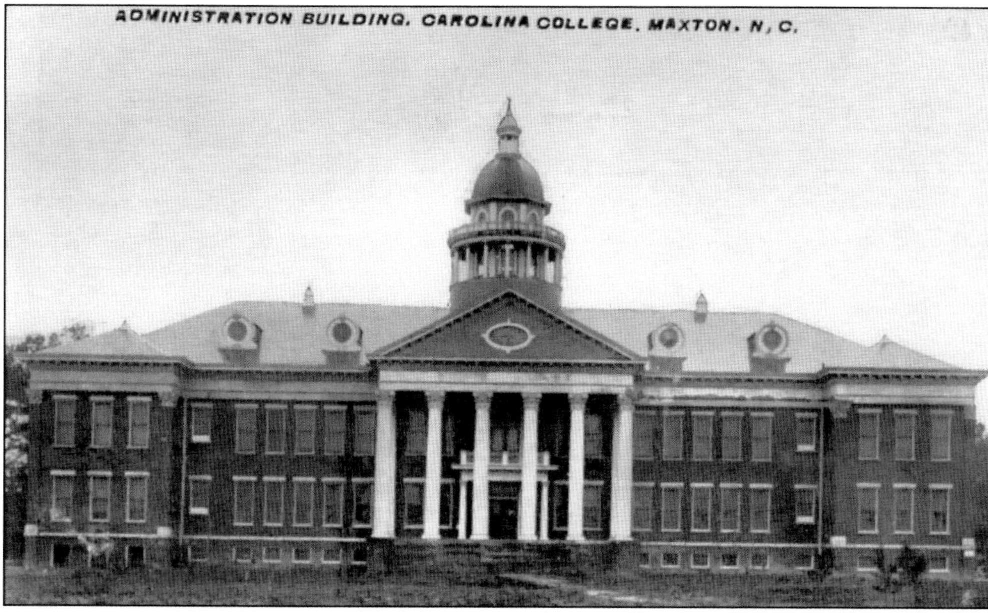

CAROLINA COLLEGE. The cornerstone for Carolina Methodist College for Women was laid in 1908, but construction was not finished until 1912. The school's opening enrollment was 65 girls. By 1926, Duke University had received its large legacy from Buck Duke; one condition of Duke's legacy was that the university accept women. As a result, the North Carolina Methodist Conference voted in 1926 to close Carolina College.

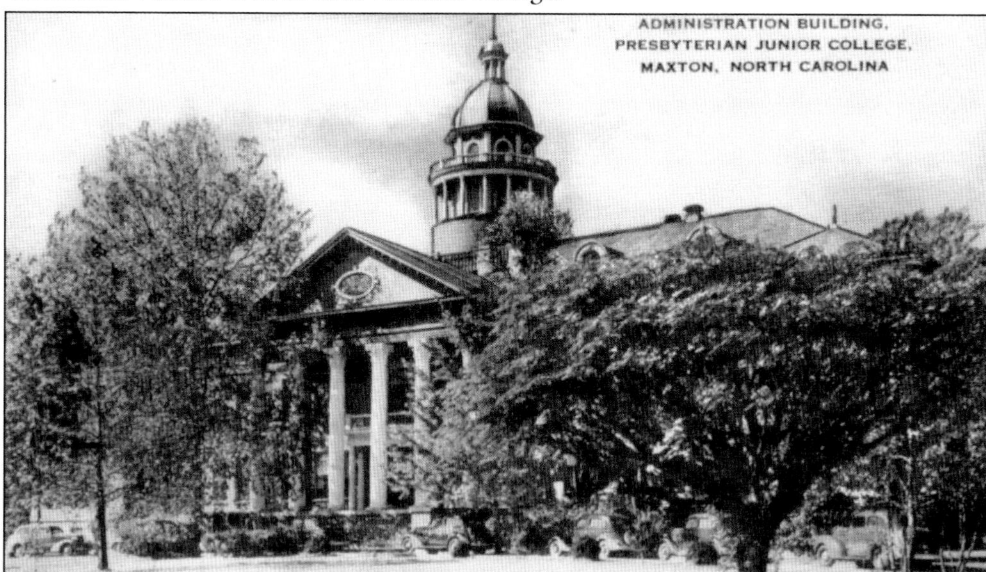

PRESBYTERIAN JUNIOR COLLEGE. In 1927, an interested group made a presentation to the Fayetteville Presbytery asking them to establish a junior college for boys. The presbytery decided to acquire the former Carolina College property for $35,000, which was the outstanding debt for the facility. The new college opened for its first session on September 11, 1929. In 1961, it merged with Flora McDonald College to form St. Andrews Presbyterian College and moved to Laurinburg. The old campus was used for the next ten years for the Carolina Military Academy until the main building burned in 1973.

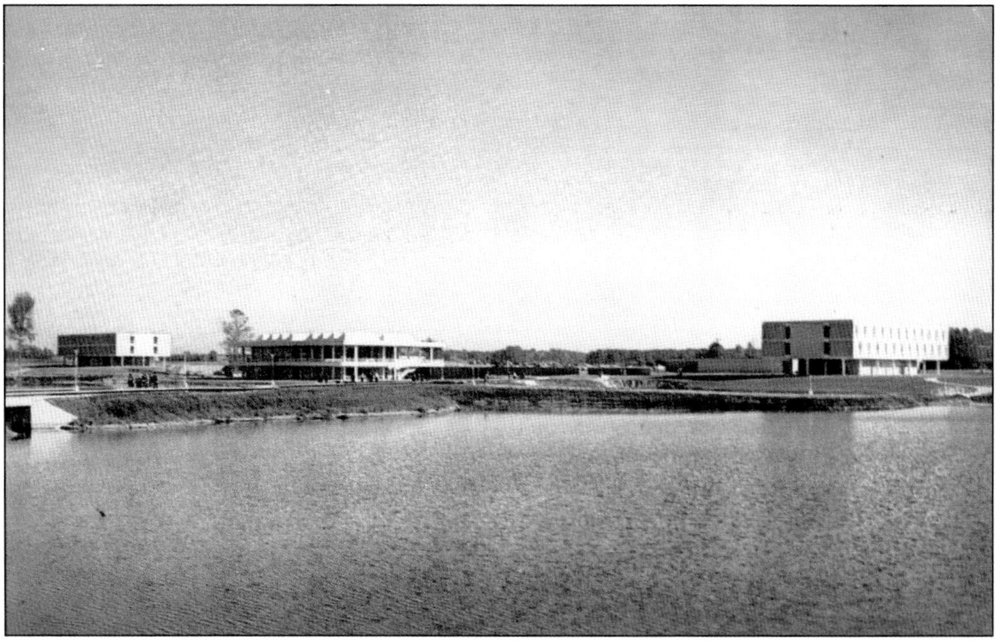

DORMITORIES. Seen across one of the beautiful lakes are three of the modern buildings that were built after the merger of Flora MacDonald College and Presbyterian Junior College in 1961, which created St. Andrews Presbyterian College. Pictured from left to right are Mecklenburg and Wilmington Dormitories and the Belk Student Center.

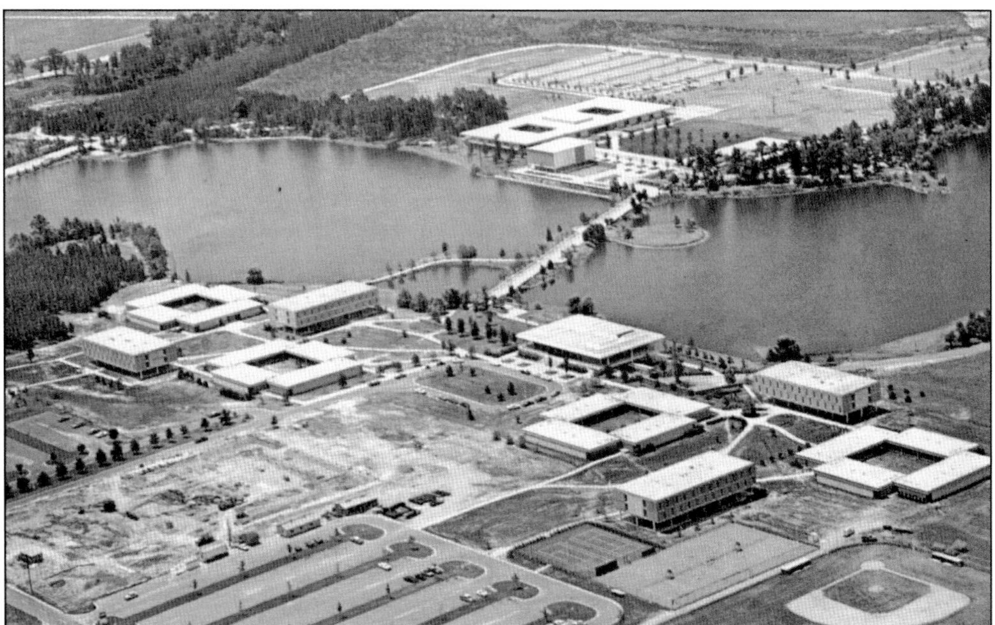

NEW CAMPUS. This aerial postcard shows the large campus of St. Andrews Presbyterian Church in Laurinburg which was built on both shores of a beautiful lake.

Seven

MILITARY

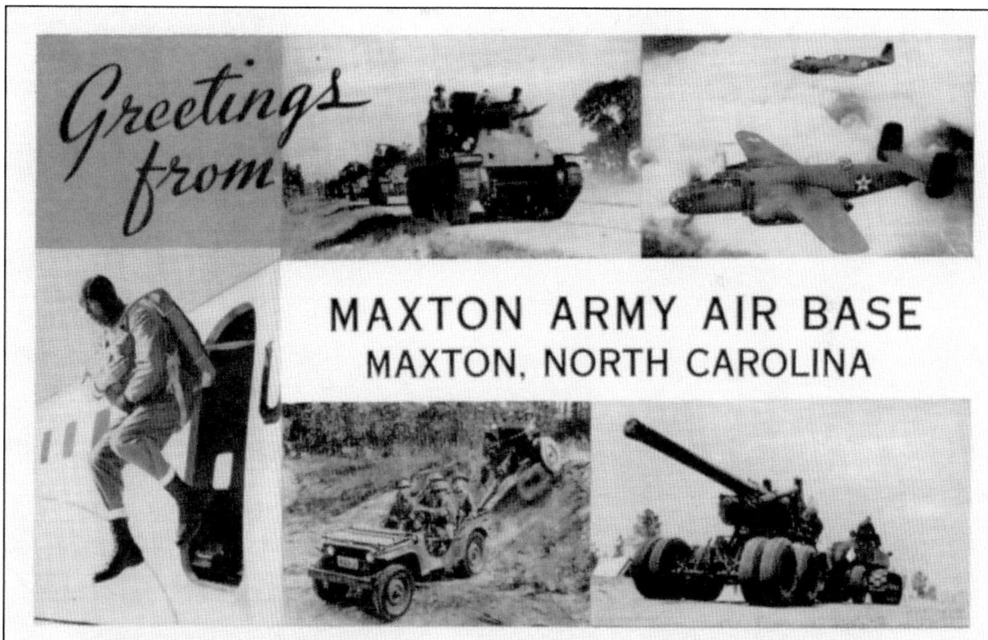

LAURINBURG-MAXTON ARMY AIR BASE. On December 23, 1941, at a Maxton town meeting, it was announced that the federal government wanted to locate an air training school in the vicinity of Maxton. The Town, along with the City of Laurinburg, Scotland County, and Robeson County, purchased 583 acres to lease to the government to be used as a military reservation. Construction was authorized on April 20, 1942; much of the labor was provided through the WPA. The cost was over $10 million and netted 20 miles of paved roads within the compound.

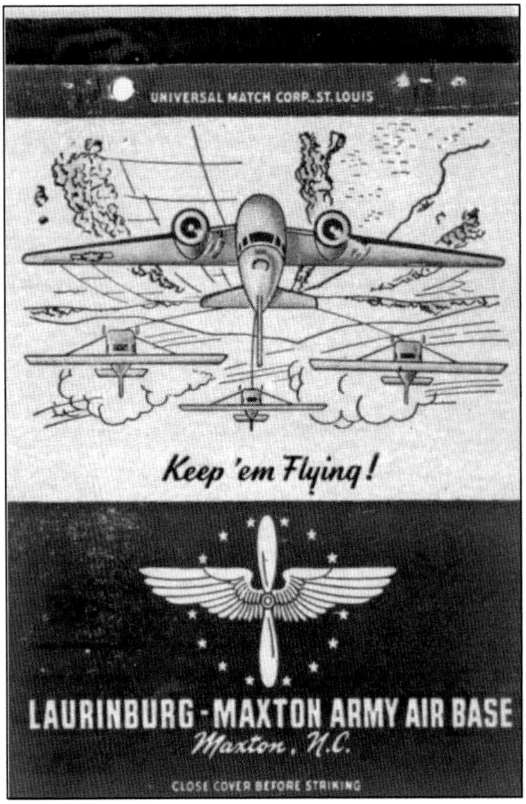

MATCHBOOK COVER POSTCARD. This unusual postcard was an answer to the shortages that happen during war. Beginning its life as a matchbook, it was designed so that it could be sent as a postcard once the matches were used.

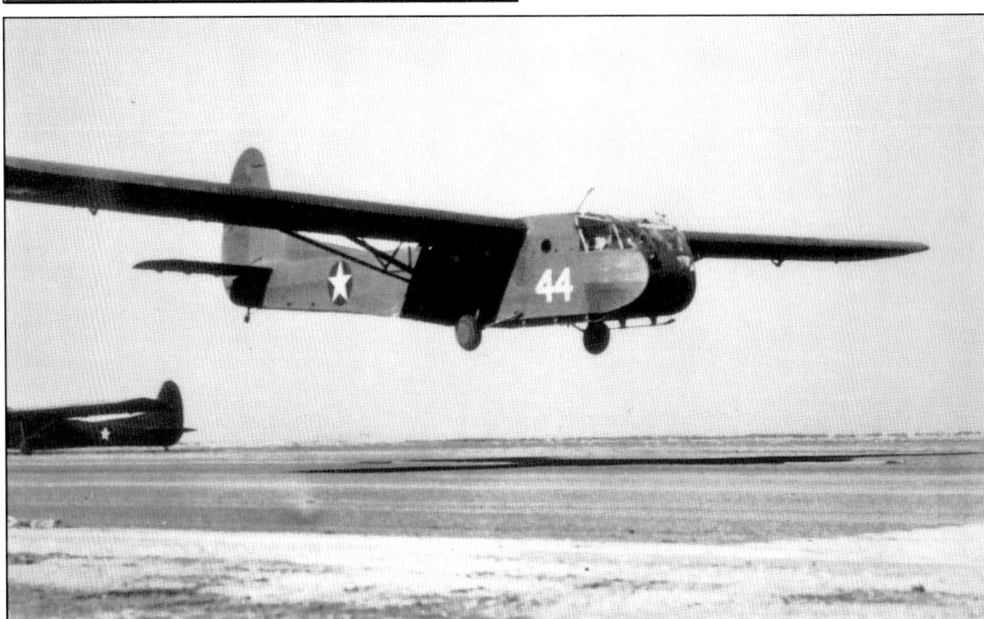

GLIDER LANDING. The Laurinburg-Maxton Airbase was the largest glider training base in the world and trained the glider pilots that were used during the D-Day Invasion. The Waco CG-4A was designed to carry 13 men or 4 men and a jeep. The base was closed after the end of World War II, and the property is now an airport that is operated by Maxton and Laurinburg.

PARATROOPERS. Construction began on what was originally known as Hoffman Airborne Camp on November 8, 1942. The camp was meant to be used by Fort Bragg and the Laurinburg-Maxton Airbase to help train troops; here they were to receive basic training in addition to perfecting their parachuting and gilder skills. In 1943, the camp was named in memory of Pvt. John Thomas Mackall; he served in the 2nd Battalion, 503rd Parachute Infantry Regiment.

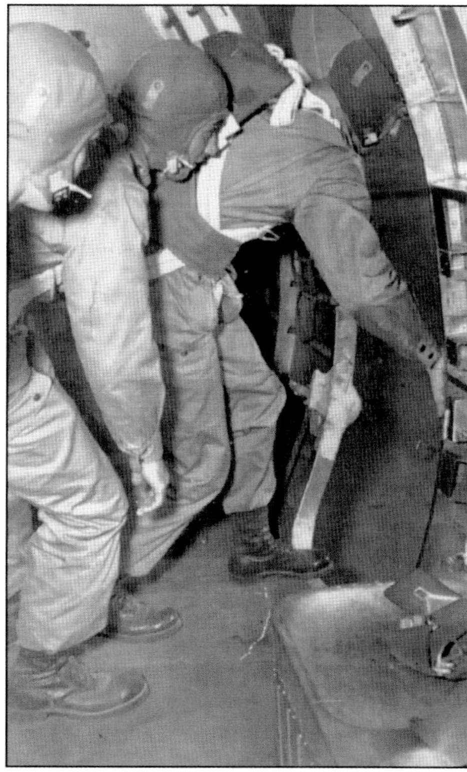

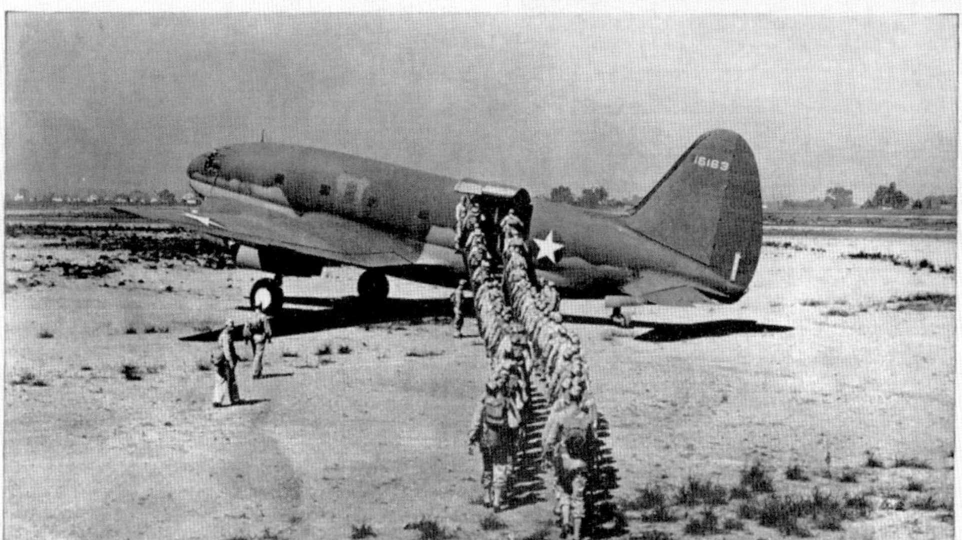

No. 1622 Paratroops Boarding Transport Plane—CAMP MACKALL, N. C. *Photo by U. S. Army Signal Corps*

PARATROOPERS BOARDING TRANSPORT PLANE. The troops stationed at Camp Mackall jumped into the fields of the base as well as flew in and unloaded gliders. Such training always includes risks; on February 16, 1944, eight paratroopers drowned in Kenny Cameron Lake at Camp Mackall when their pilots miscalculated the drop zone.

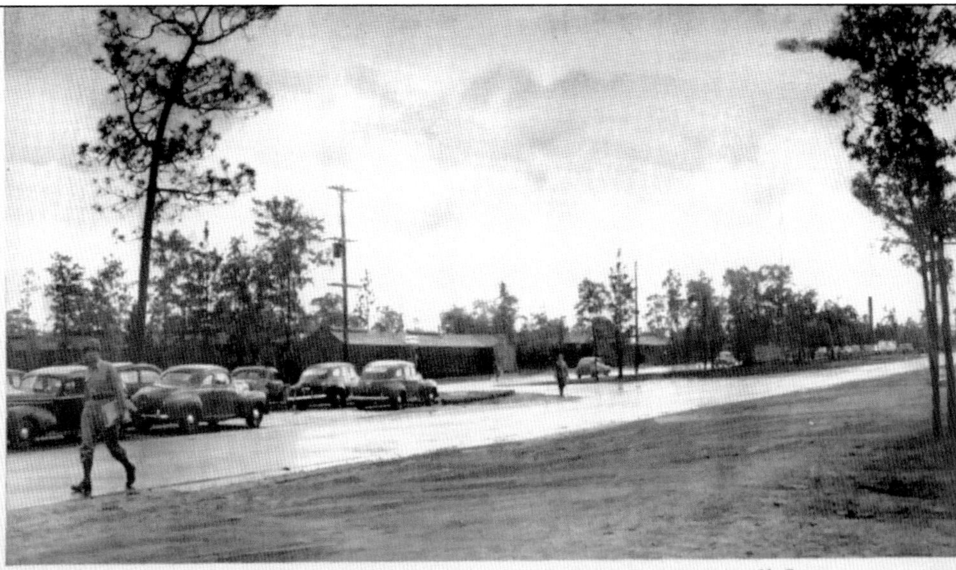

No. 1625 STREET SCENE AND ONE OF THE DIVISION HEADQUARTERS—CAMP MACKALL, N. C.

STREET SCENE AND ONE HEADQUARTERS BUILDING. A portion of the over 56,000 acres that became Camp Mackall was a hunting preserve set up by the Baltimore Barber Steamship Company. They created Mossgeil Lake and built a log cabin on the shore. This would later serve as the commander's home during World War II. The DuPont Corporation purchased the property in 1930, adding a lodge that became the Camp Mackall's Officers' Club.

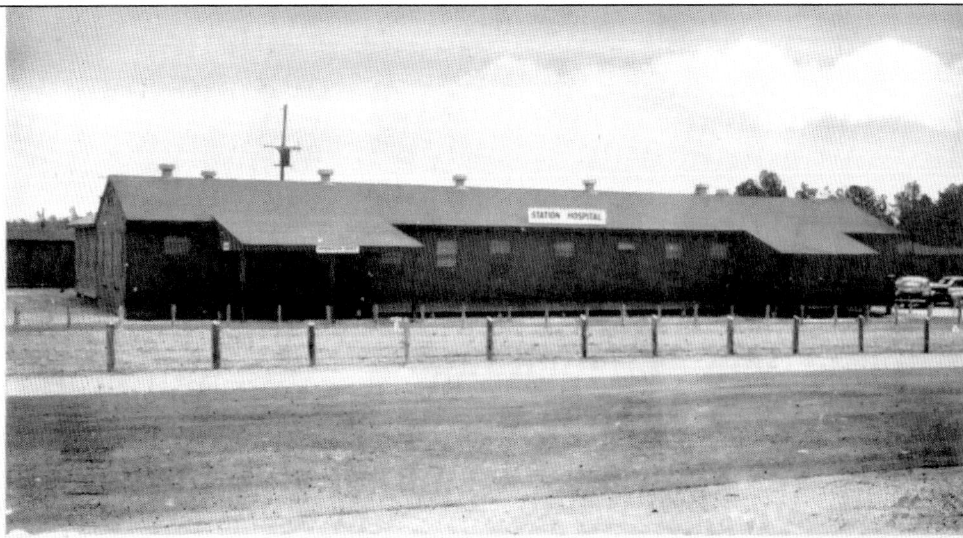

No. 1623 STATION HOSPITAL—CAMP MACKALL, N. C.

STATION HOSPITAL. The 56,002.91 acres that made up the camp were obtained from the Department of Interior and purchased from local landowners. The Army erected 1,750 buildings, mostly of the theater of operations type. These one-story buildings were rough plank siding covered with tar paper and heavier-grade tar paper as roofing material. Construction included seven service clubs, two guest houses, three libraries, 16 post exchanges, 12 chapels, a hospital, 65 miles of roads, and three 5,000-foot runways in a triangle. Those buildings included headquarters for the U.S. Army Airborne Command, the garrison command, and the division headquarters. There were also numerous service buildings.

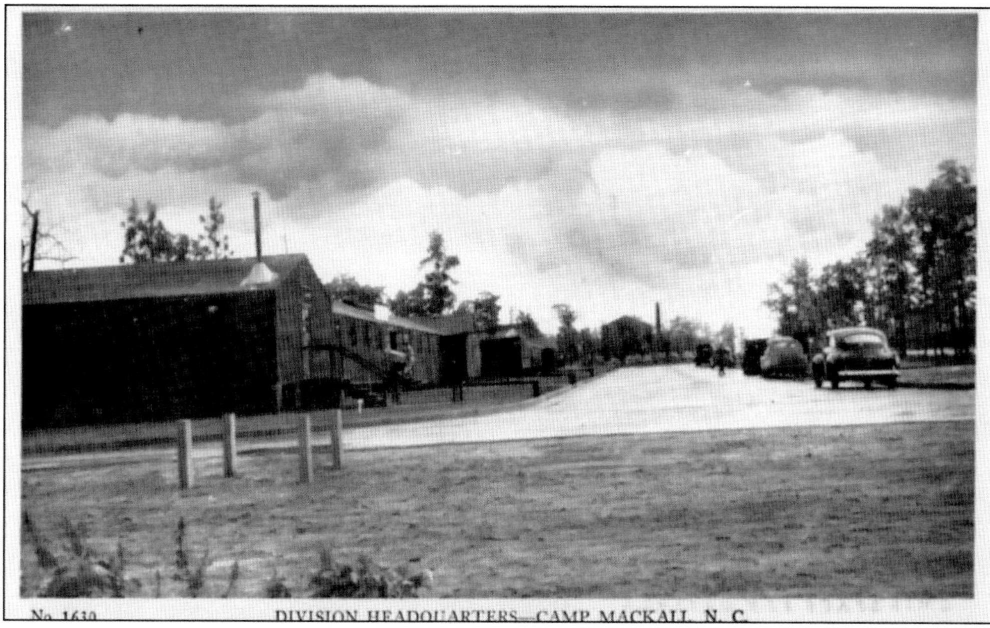

Division Headquarters. Three Airborne Divisions were formed at Camp Mackall in 1943. The 11th Airborne Division, known as The Angels, was formed February 25. They used gliders at Aparri, the only time gliders were used in the Pacific Theater. The 17th Airborne Division was formed April 25; they participated in the Battle of the Bulge. They used 1,305 gliders with only 172 being salvageable. The 13th Airborne Division was formed August 13.

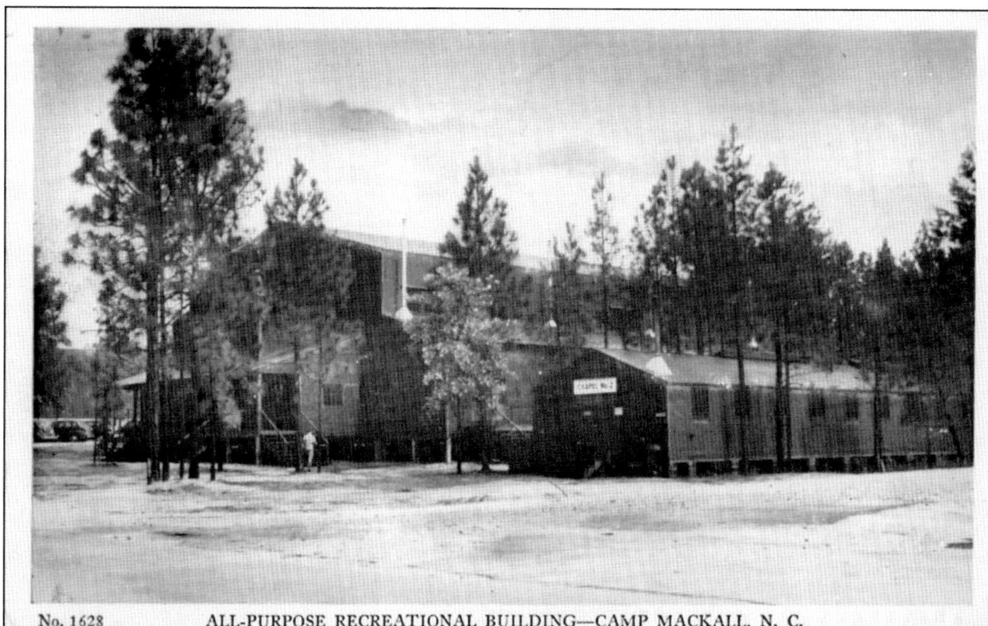

Recreation Building and Chapel. The camp was also home to a prisoner-of-war camp for German prisoners. The POWs and their guards lived in Winter Rise, actually a framed tent structure. The camp had a capacity of 500 but usually housed 250 to 350. POWs worked at the camp, as well as being hired out to local farmers.

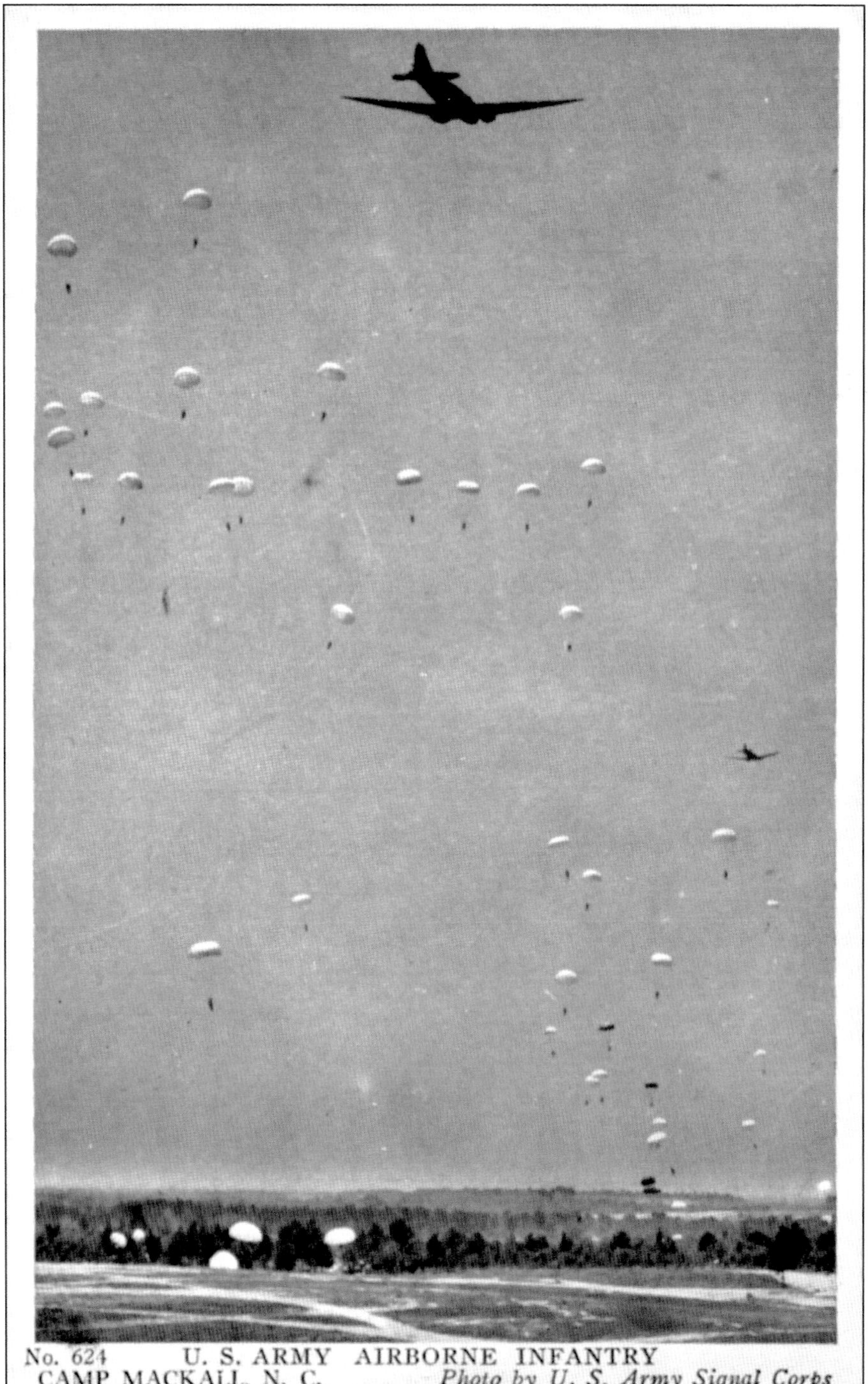

U.S. ARMY INFANTRY. The camp crossed many county lines being located in Hoke, Richmond, Moore, and Scotland Counties. Portions of the camp were disposed of from 1945 to 1949. In 1952, the recently-established U.S. Army Special Forces began training at the camp. The site is used to train anti-terrorism teams and houses the 19-day course in Survival, Evasion, Resistance, and Escape (SERE) that was established around 1967.

Eight

Religion

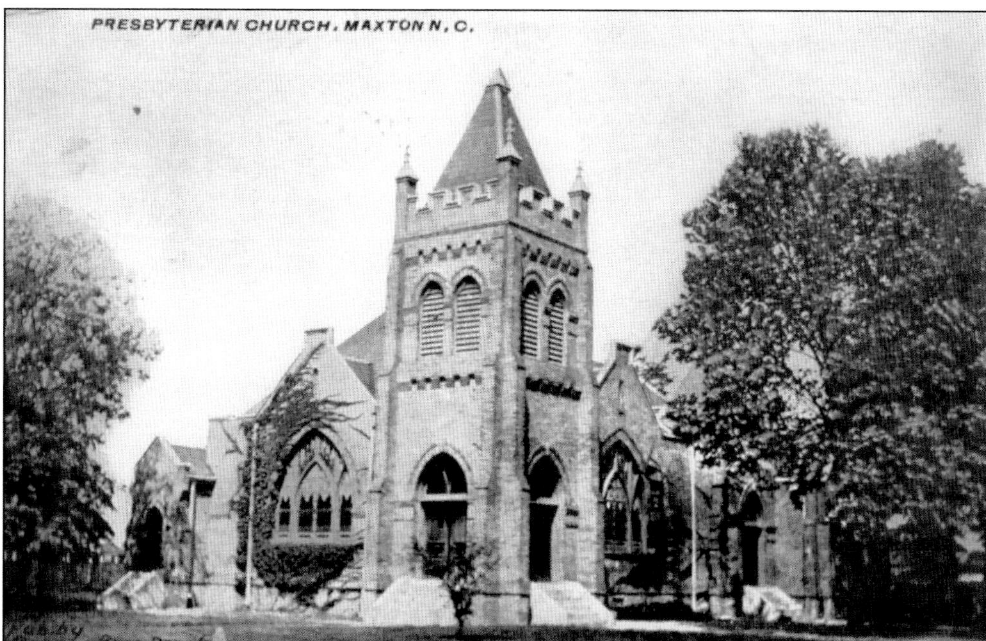

Presbyterian Church. The First Presbyterian Church of Maxton was one of the first churches organized in what was then called Shoe Heel. It was a member of the Presbyterian Church, U.S., until its reunion in 1983 with the Presbyterian Church (UPUSA) to form the Presbyterian Church (USA).

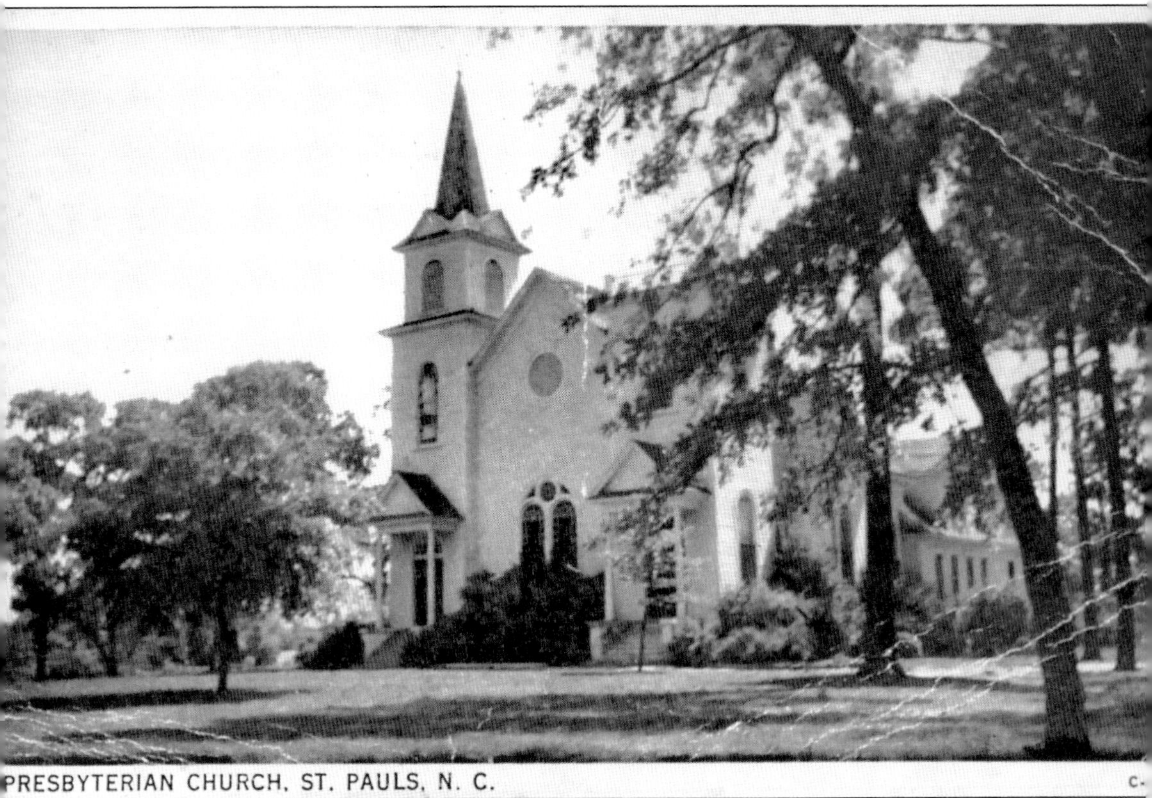

ST. PAULS PRESBYTERIAN. The St. Pauls Presbyterian Church was founded in 1799 north of the present day St. Pauls near the farm that became known as the William Davis Farm. This site is at the intersection of Highway 301 and Interstate 95 across from the BP Gas Station. The Rev. Daniel Brown preached the first sermon and was the supply pastor for about one year. In 1848, the church moved to its current location on Old Stage Road, building on property given by Deacon Neill Crawford. The dedication for the second building was held in 1850. The third church building, shown on this postcard, was built at a cost of $4,000, and the dedication was held on September 20, 1908. The church building was razed and a new brick church built in its place in 1969.

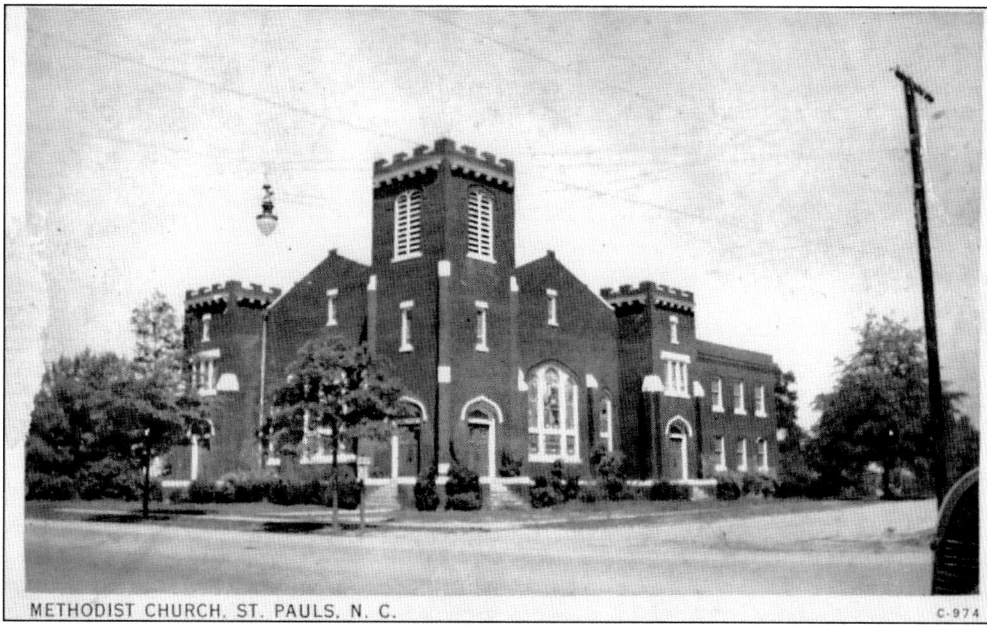

ST. PAULS UNITED METHODIST CHURCH. In 1908, a small group of Methodists in St. Pauls began to hold prayer services using the St. Pauls Presbyterian Church. The group grew and soon began using a two-story frame on West Broad Street. The current building, pictured here, was built in 1919.

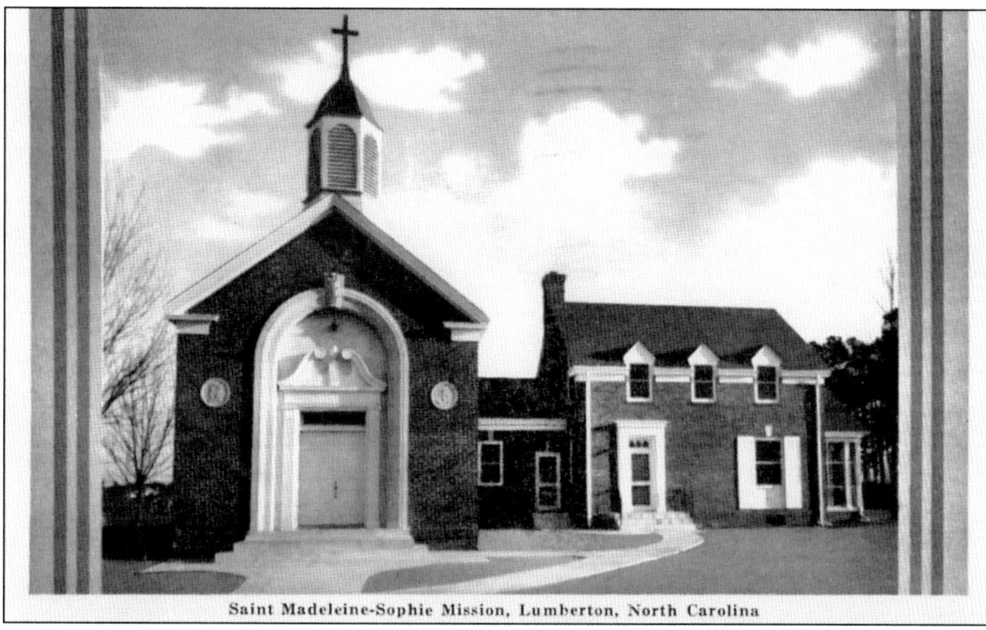

SAINT MADELEINE-SOPHIE MISSION. The Saint Madeleine-Sophie Mission was located in Lumberton. This postcard was sent by Mrs. Walter Polston of North Lumberton to Maybelle Arnold in Harbor View, Ohio, in 1945. It was a hobby of many people to engage in postcard exchanges. People would advertise in newspapers and magazines that they would like to begin an exchange. Polston asks Arnold what type of postcards she likes best and tells her that her favorite are waterfalls and churches.

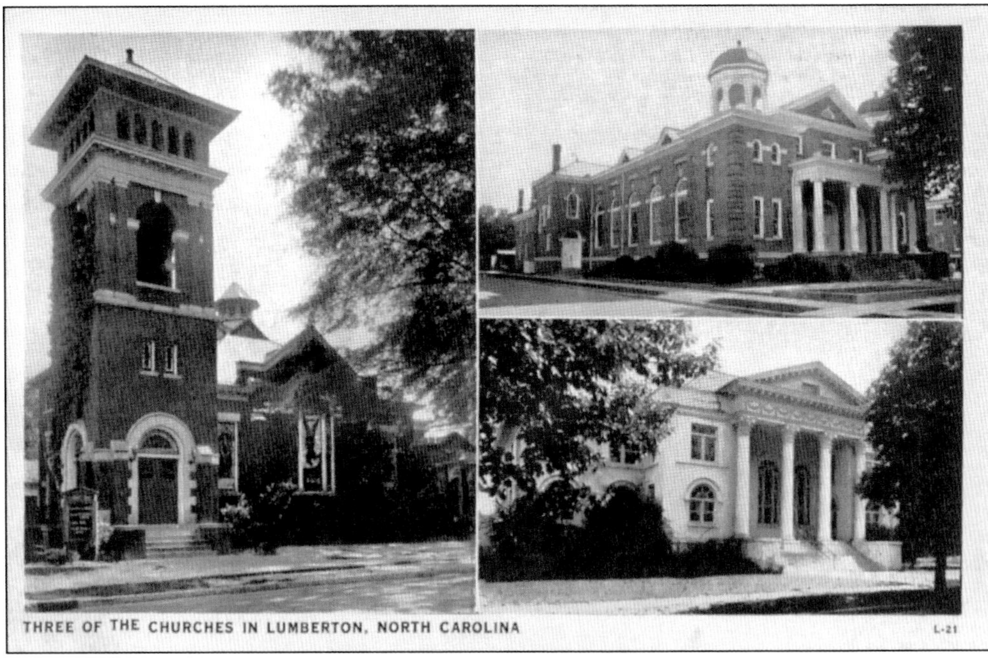

THREE CHURCHES. These three downtown Lumberton churches, clockwise from the top right, are First Baptist, First Presbyterian, and Chestnut Street Methodist. Chestnut Street Methodist was founded between 1787 and 1803; the building pictured was built from 1911 to 1913.

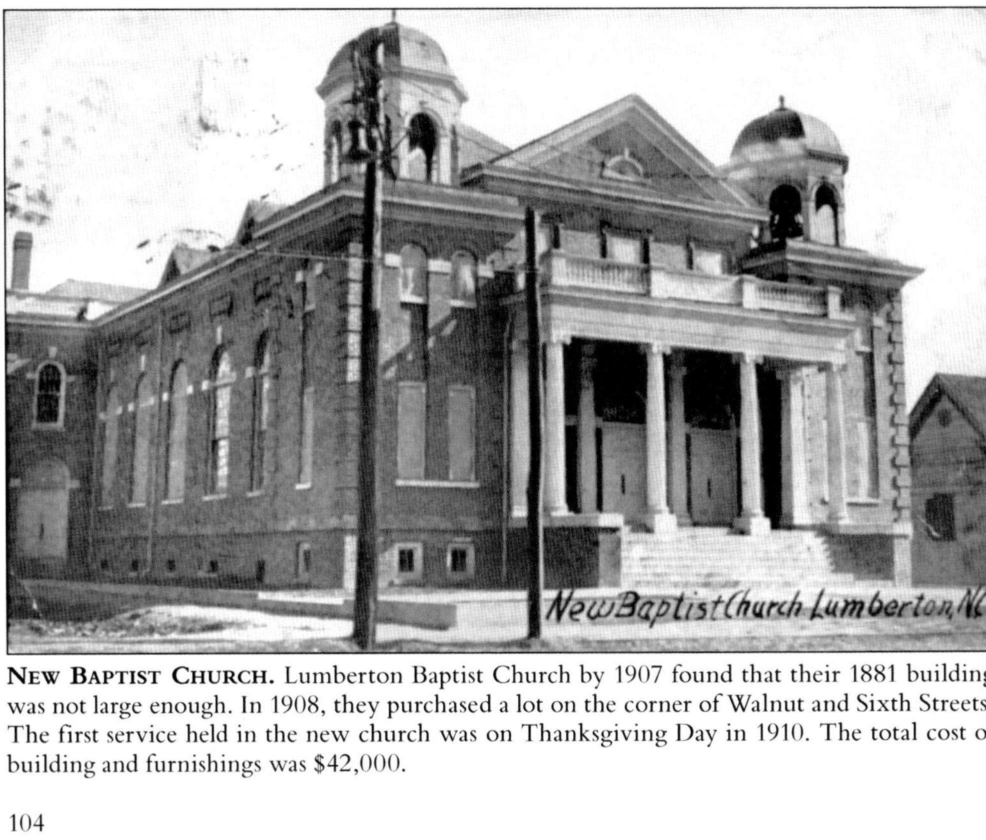

NEW BAPTIST CHURCH. Lumberton Baptist Church by 1907 found that their 1881 building was not large enough. In 1908, they purchased a lot on the corner of Walnut and Sixth Streets. The first service held in the new church was on Thanksgiving Day in 1910. The total cost of building and furnishings was $42,000.

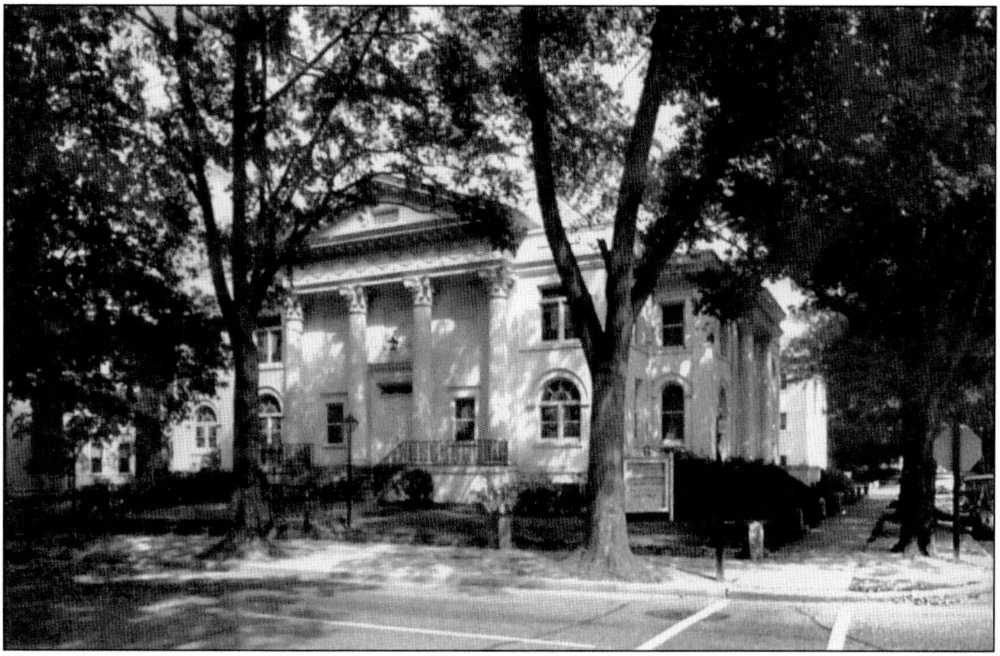

FIRST PRESBYTERIAN CHURCH. The Presbyterians began meeting in 1854 at the Robeson County Courthouse. The church building pictured here was built in 1917 on a lot given by Emily McLeod.

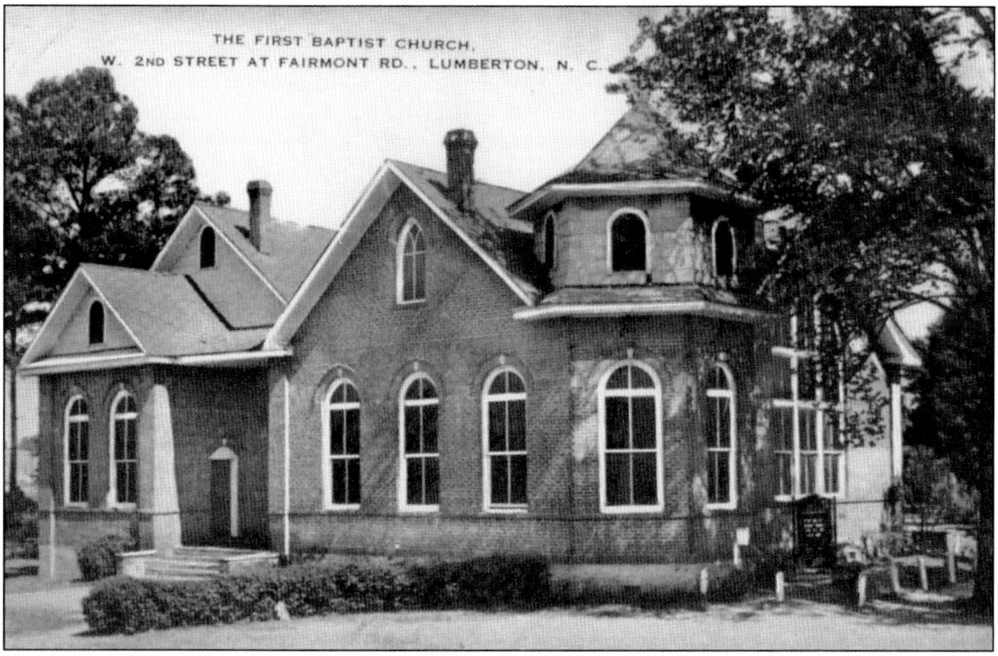

BAPTIST CHURCH. In 1922, the congregations of St. John's and Providence Baptist Churches voted to merge. The purchased property is on West Second Street, at the corner of Fairmont Road in Lumberton. The cornerstone for this building was laid in 1926. This African American church as served the community well throughout the years; Dr. E. B. Turner has been pastor for over 45 years.

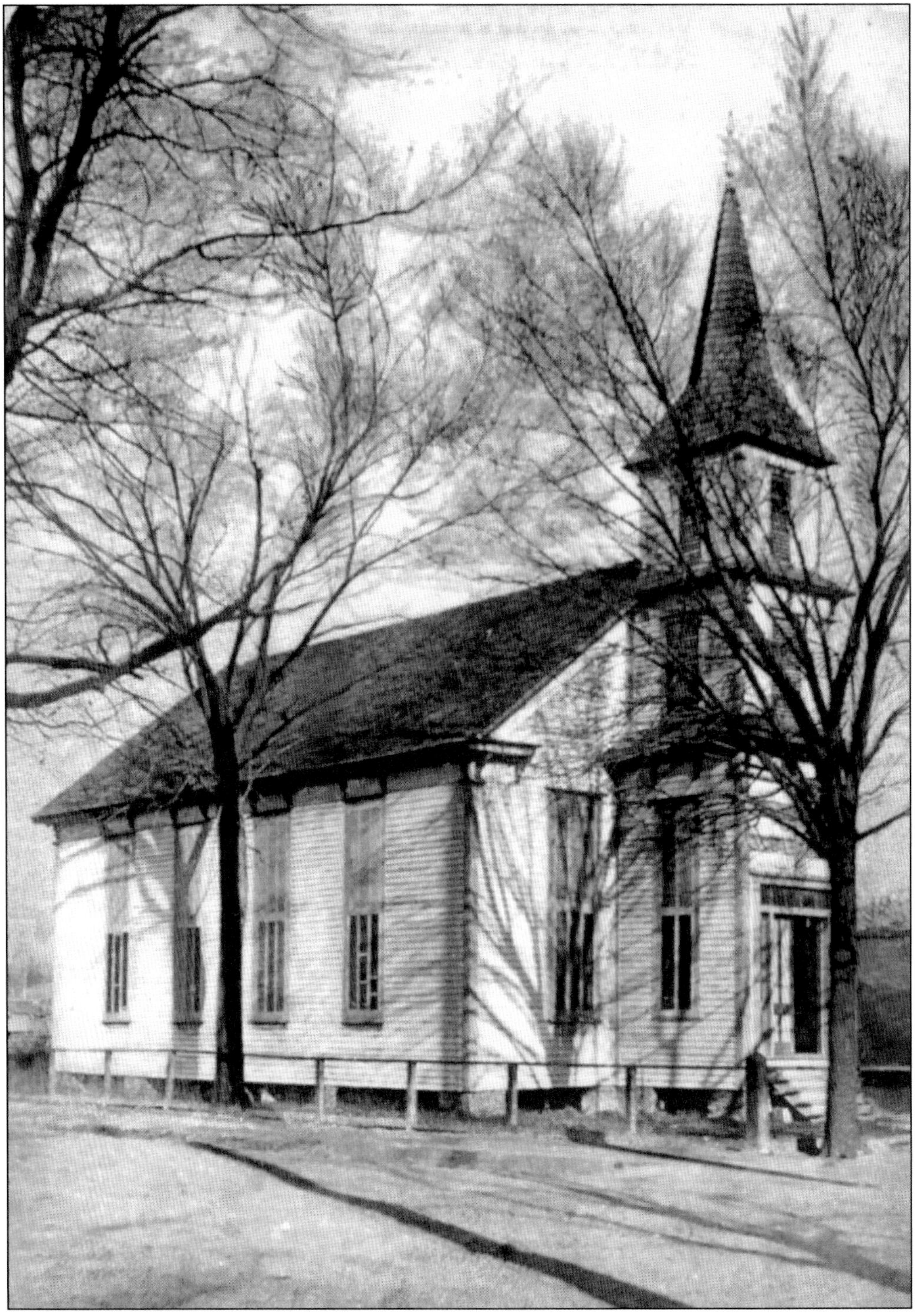

METHODIST CHURCH. This frame church was built in 1885, and it served the Methodists of Maxton until a larger church was built on the opposite end of the block in 1906. The name was originally Ashpole Mission then Shoe Heel Mission. About the time the new building was finished, the name changed to St. Paul's Methodist.

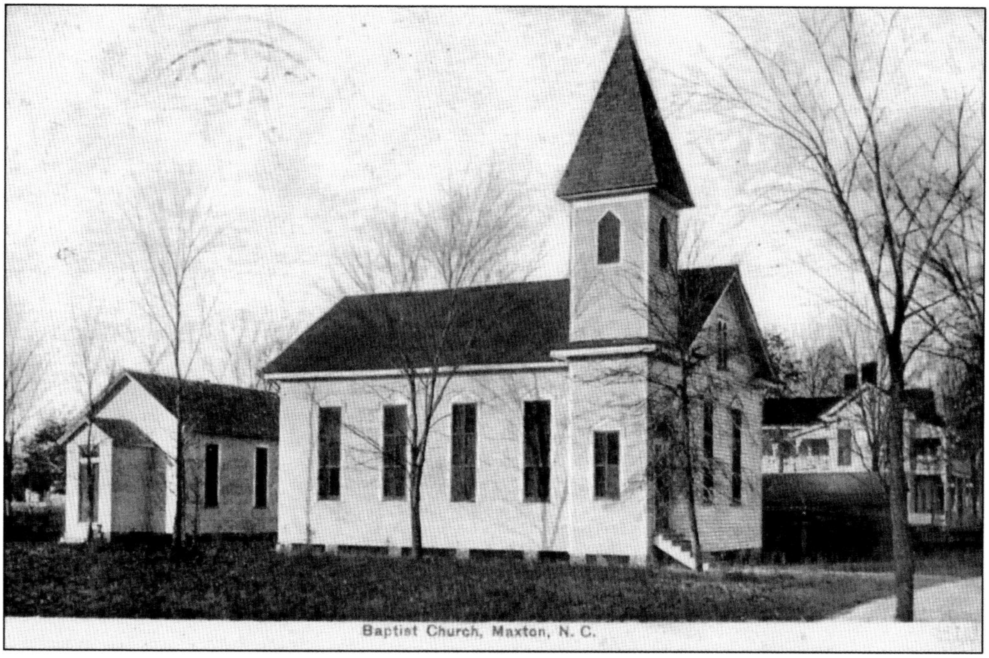

BAPTIST CHURCH. The Baptists in Maxton organized in June 1891, and the building pictured was built in December 1891. It was replaced years later by a modern brick building.

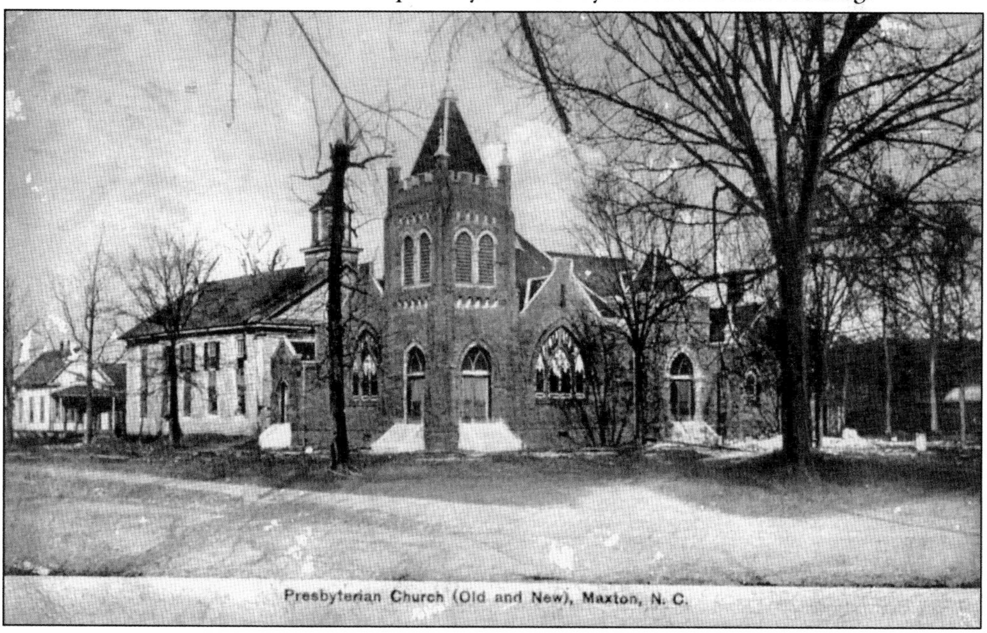

PRESBYTERIAN CHURCH. A group of 29 men and women met in a store building in Maxton, then Shoe Heel, on October 23, 1878, for the purpose of petitioning the Presbytery to establish a Presbyterian church. In April 1879, the Rev. Roger Martin was called as the first pastor, serving both this church and the Centre Presbyterian Church. Also in 1879, Mr. Gilbert Patterson presented the church with a lot for the purpose of erecting a new church building, which was begun in 1879 and completed in 1880. This first building was of frame construction and can be seen behind the 1906 brick building.

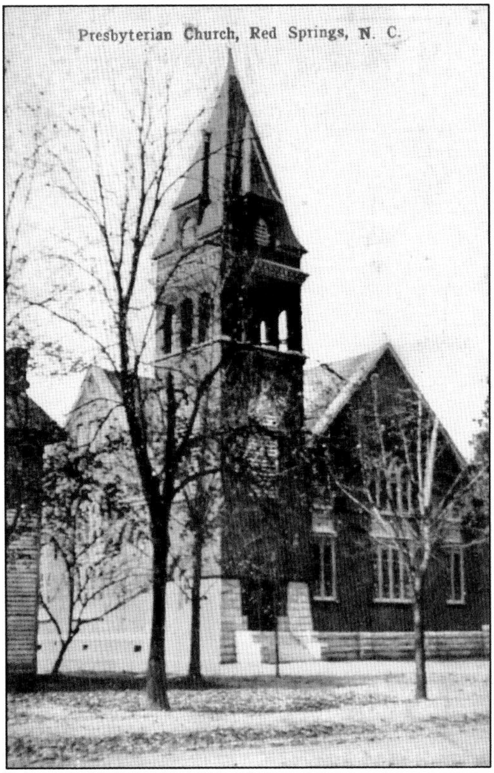

Presbyterian Church. The Red Springs Presbyterian Church was built on land granted by King George III to "Sailor" Hector McNeill and given to the church by one of McNeill's grandsons. The Rev. A. W. Shaw moderated the first meeting on June 5 and 6, 1889, and there were 16 original members.

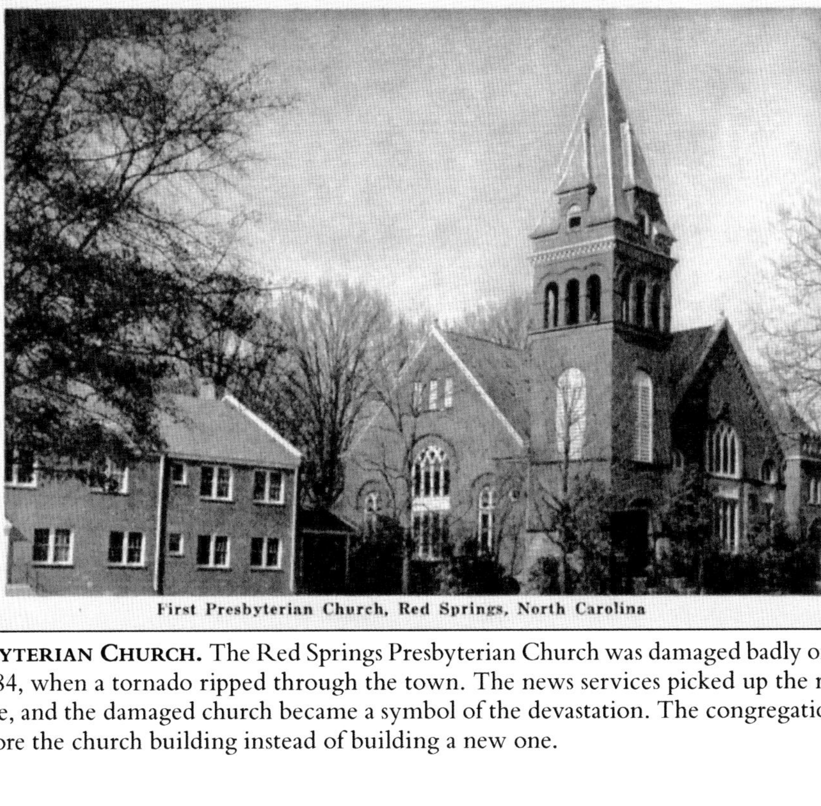

First Presbyterian Church, Red Springs, North Carolina

Presbyterian Church. The Red Springs Presbyterian Church was damaged badly on March 28, 1984, when a tornado ripped through the town. The news services picked up the report of damage, and the damaged church became a symbol of the devastation. The congregation voted to restore the church building instead of building a new one.

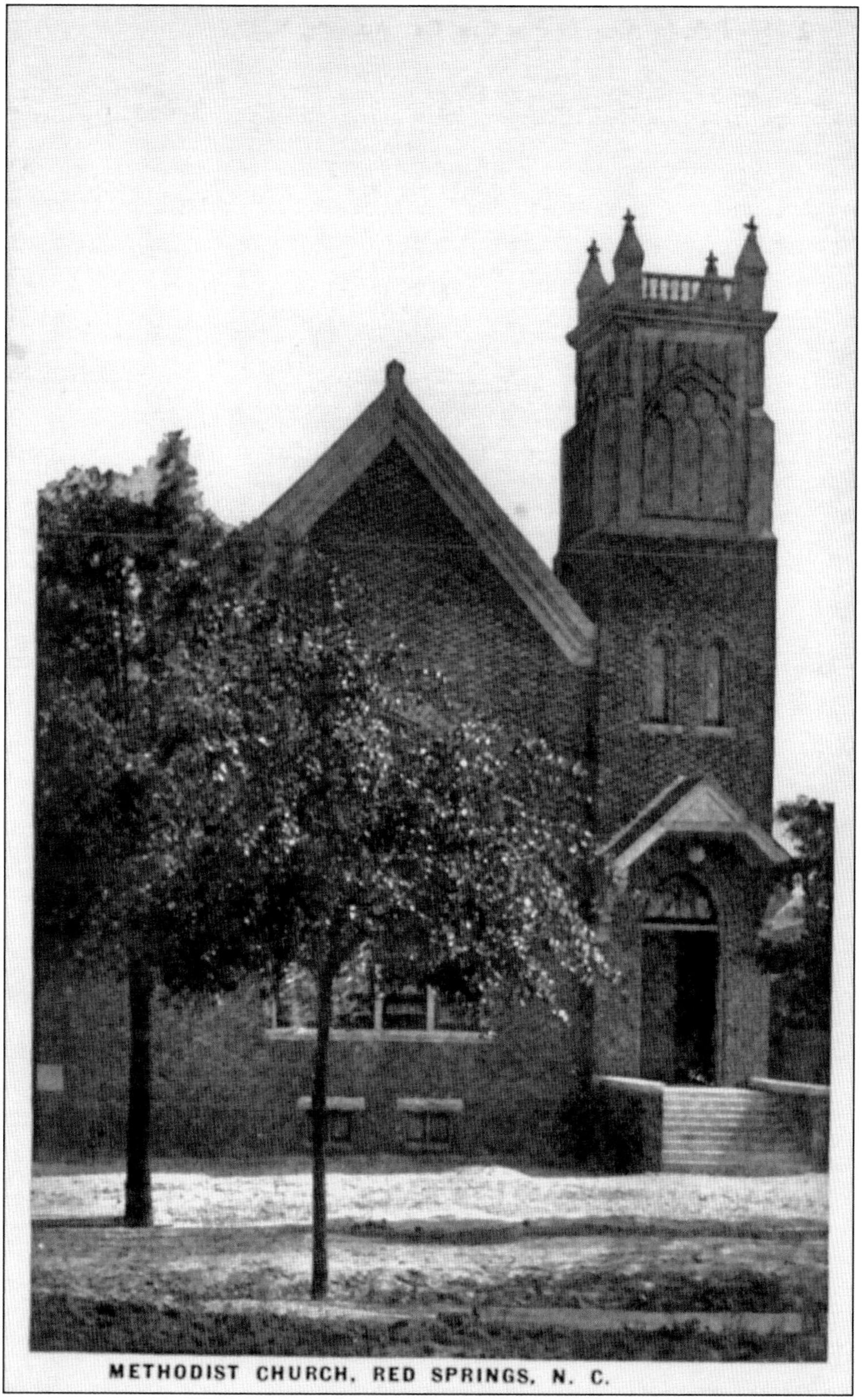

METHODIST CHURCH. The first record of a Methodist service in Red Springs is on February 4, 1877, when Rev. Washington Chaffin, a circuit rider, preached to a group of interested Christians in the McNeills' parlor on the hill. The present Trinity United Methodist Church was organized in July 1889. The building shown here was completed in 1911.

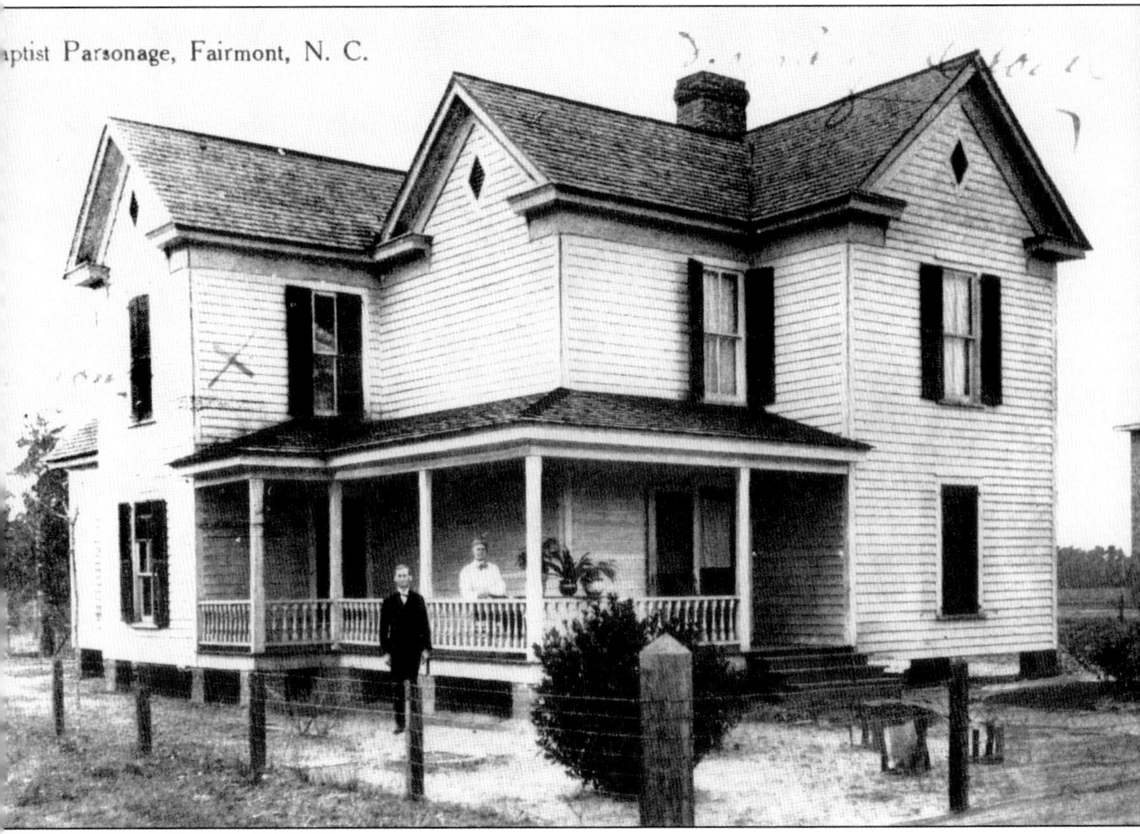

BAPTIST PARSONAGE. This postcard of the Baptist Parsonage in Fairmont was sent by a boarder who stayed there in 1912. He marked the room he stayed in with an X. The Baptist church in Fairmont can trace its roots back to when Isham Pittman settled in the area in 1770. He was licensed to preach by the Saddletree Baptist Church in 1972 and started Pittman's Church. The church was later known as Ashpole Church and finally Fairmont Baptist. (Courtesy North Carolina State Archives.)

Nine

Social Life and Popular Diversions

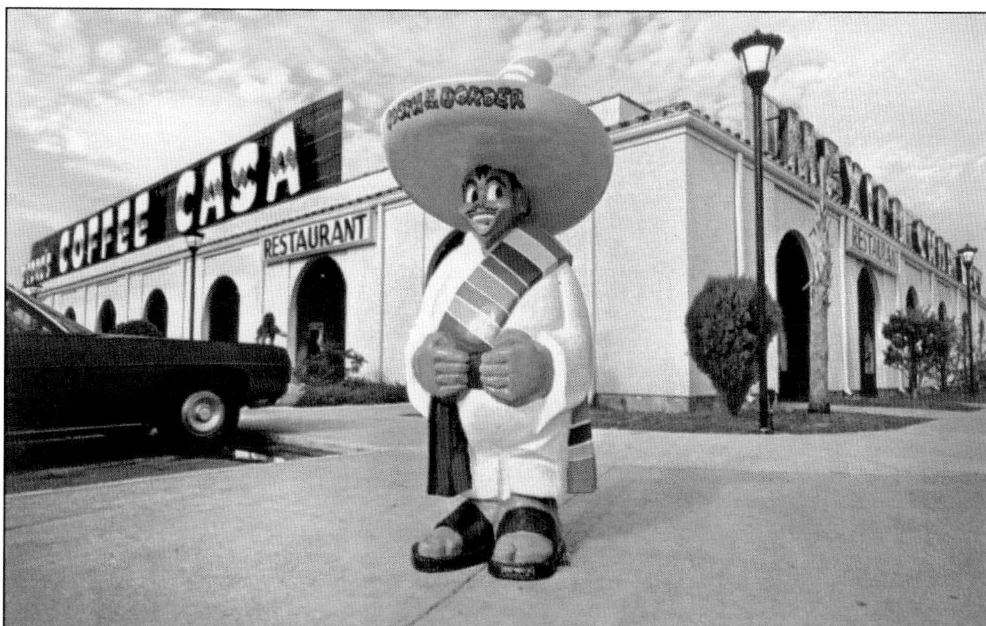

Pedro in front of Coffee Casa. South of the Border's mascot, Pedro, is a common site all over the complex. According to the company's history, Pedro was born when two young Mexican men returned from Mexico to South Carolina with business owner Alan Schafer. The bellboys were called Pedro by everyone, and hence the mascot's name was born.

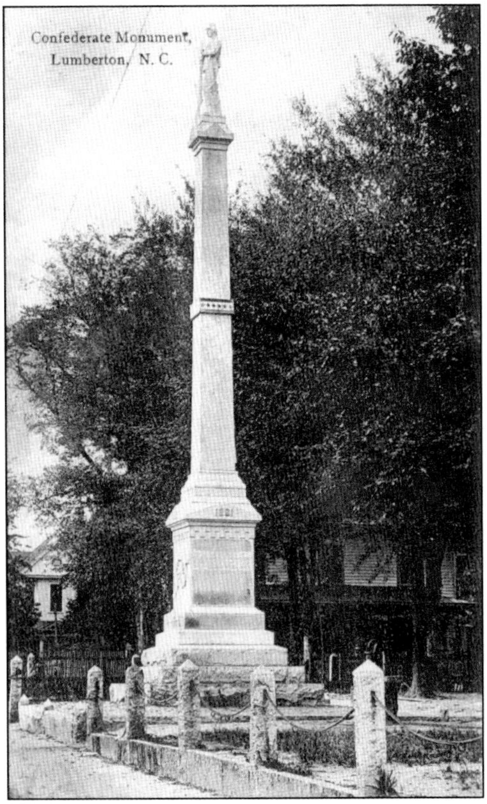

Confederate Monument. The Robeson County Confederate Monument was unveiled on May 10, 1907, before a crowd of 7,000 people including 500 Confederate veterans. The first to donate to the fund-raising project was Lumberton attorney and future North Carolina governor Angus Wilton McLean. The monument has survived two courthouses and a major overhaul to the exterior of the current courthouse. Through time and changes, the Confederate soldier has stood high above Elm Street as a silent reminder of the loss the county suffered during the War Between the States.

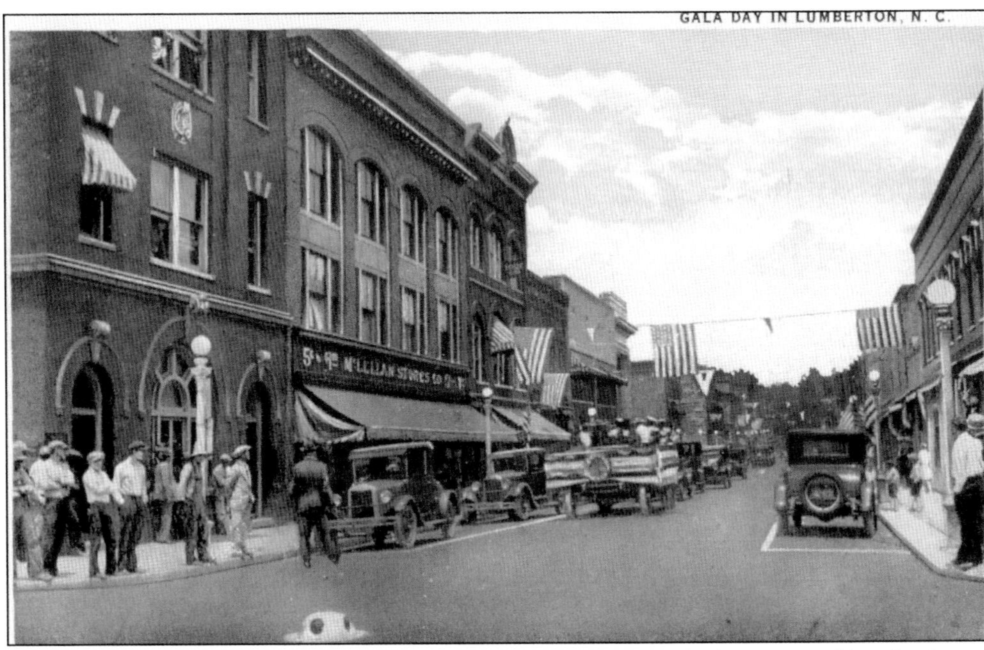

Gala Day. While it is not recorded what particular event this gala day postcard is referring to, Lumberton has always been known for wonderful parades.

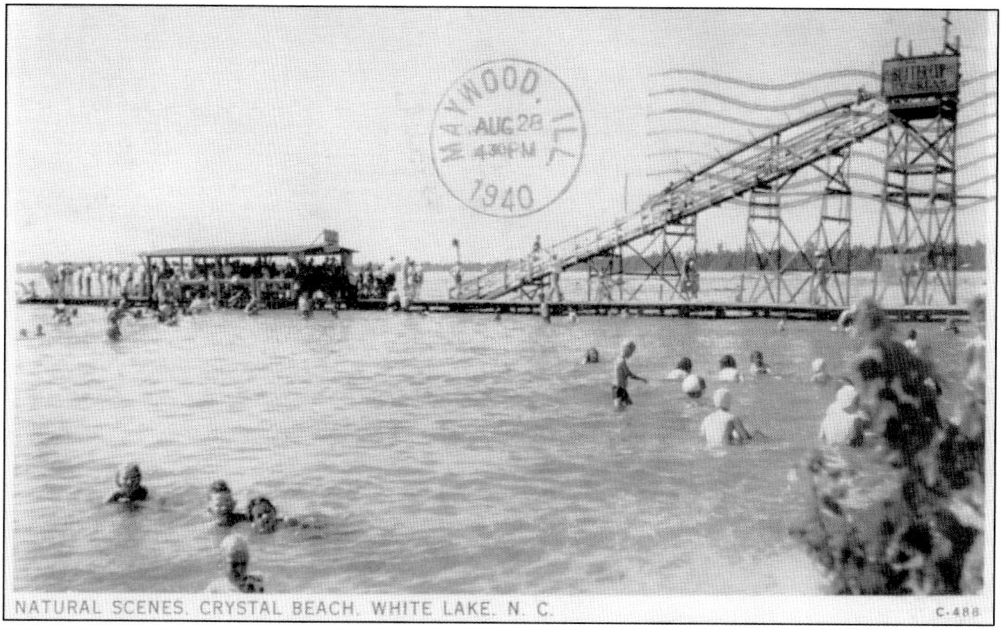

WHITE LAKE. A frequent recreation spot for the people of Robeson County has always been White Lake; the 1,200-acre lake is located in Bladen County. The first commercial operation opened at the lake in 1901, and the town was incorporated in 1951. The lake is home to approximately 500 year-round residents and during the summer, is host to nearly 200,000 tourists. (Courtesy Paul Valenti and Carla Baxley.)

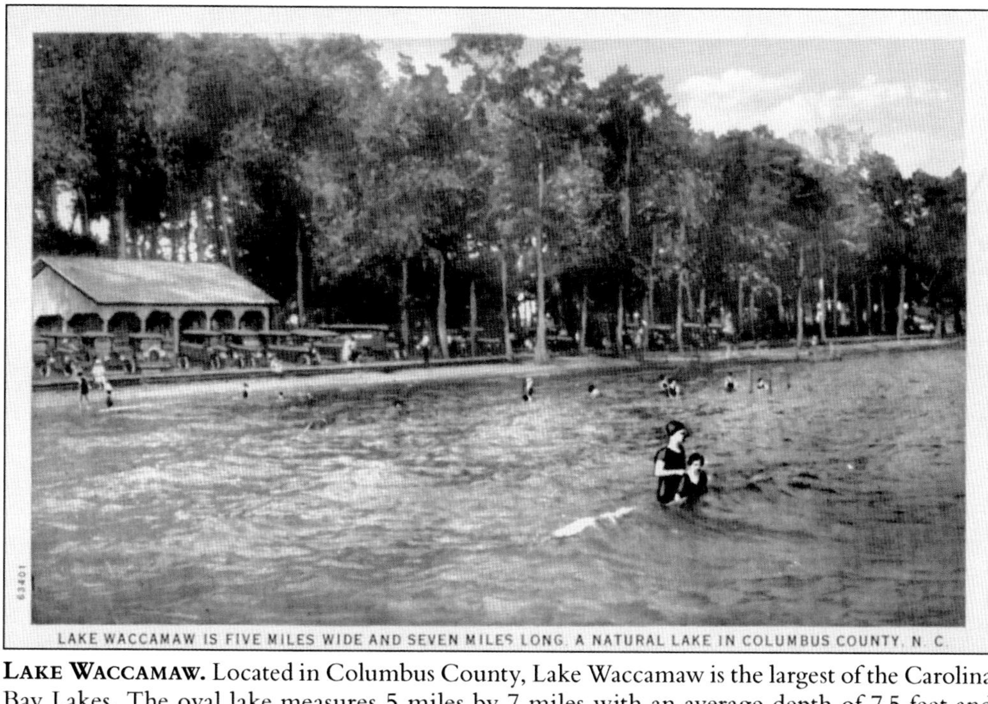

LAKE WACCAMAW. Located in Columbus County, Lake Waccamaw is the largest of the Carolina Bay Lakes. The oval lake measures 5 miles by 7 miles with an average depth of 7.5 feet and covers a total of 8,936 acres. The lake has served generations of Robesonians as a vacation spot, whether for just for a day or an extended stay.

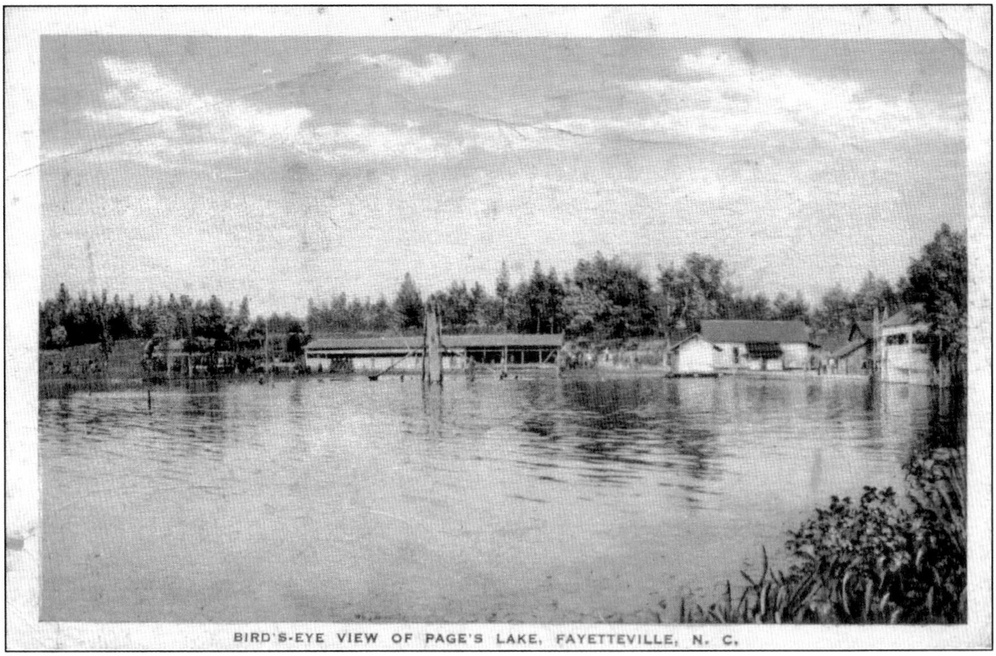

BIRD'S EYE VIEW. Page's Lake, located just over the Robeson County border in Bladen County, was owned and operated by Ulysses S. Page. Page was known to most as U. S. Page or Bladen Bombshell, a nickname that was first given to him during his time in the General Assembly. Page was born in the White Pond section of Robeson County to Ellis Elmore and Elizabeth Britt Page and was married to Lemoyne Rouse.

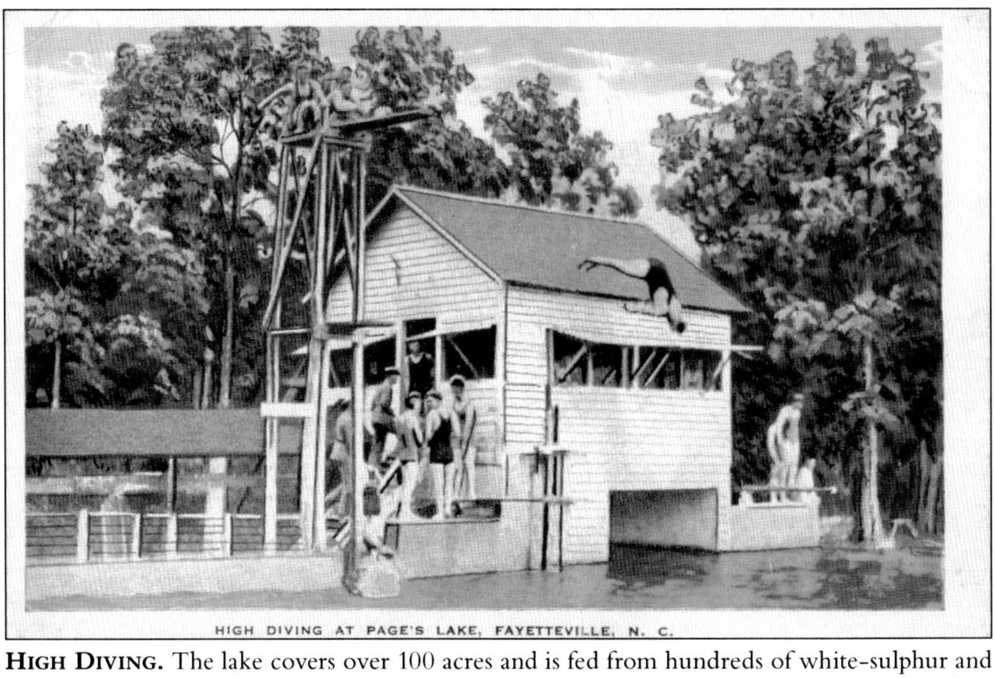

HIGH DIVING. The lake covers over 100 acres and is fed from hundreds of white-sulphur and iron springs. Advertising from the time markets the lake resort as "a clean, safe place for clean people." The lake was known as a site for fishing and boating.

HIGH DIVING. In addition to providing a popular high-diving area, the lake also had a number of furnished cottages for extended stays. Page operated a small general store on the property that also served locals since the site was 16 miles south of Fayetteville and 7 miles east of St. Pauls.

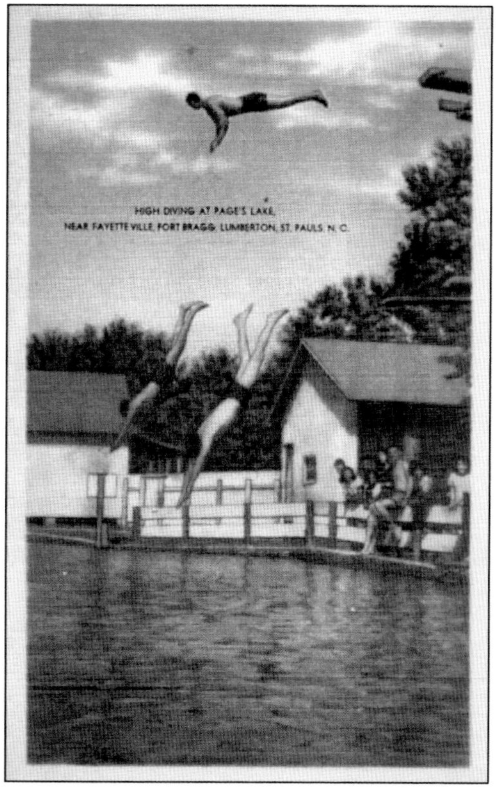

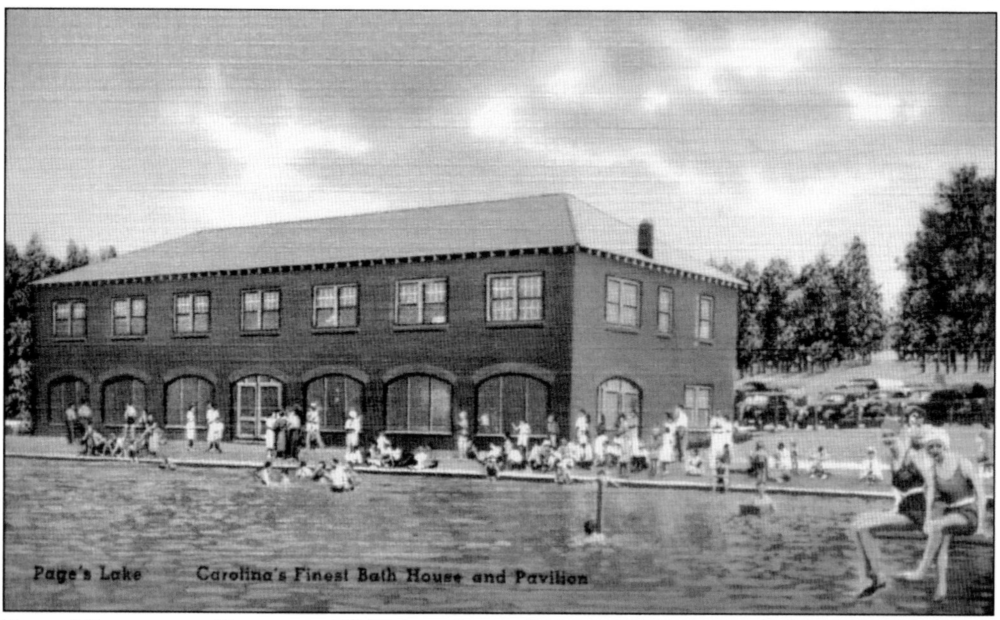

BATH HOUSE AND PAVILION. This view shows the beautiful lawn that led to the sandy beach of the lake. The site proved ideal for banquets, picnics, and all kinds of outings. Page operated the lake from 1922 until 1951, when he was brutally murdered in his lake-side store. Archie Blue Tyner of St. Pauls leased the lake from Mrs. Page for a short time following Page's death, but he soon decided to focus his efforts on his farming interests.

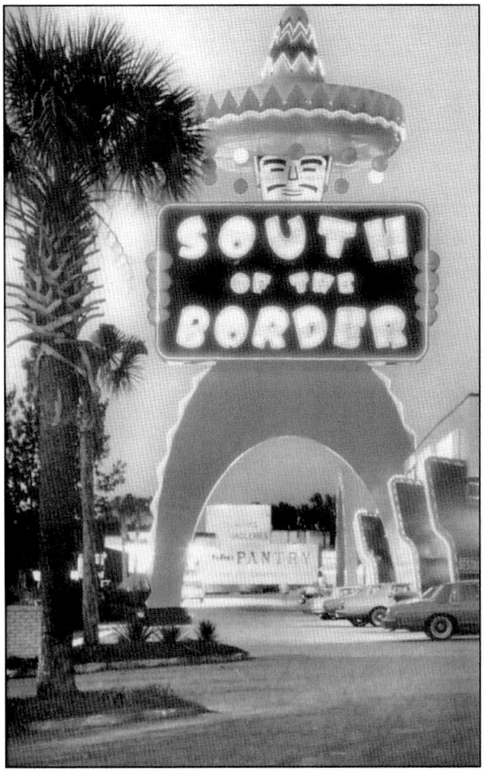

NEON PEDRO. This 110-foot electrical sign of Pedro is the largest and tallest sign of its kind east of Las Vegas and welcomes visitors to South of the Border. This attraction had its start when, in 1949, Alan Schafer opened a small hot-pick beer stand just over the Robeson County border. A year later, the small grill called the South of the Border Drive-In was added when South Carolina governor Strom Thurmond sought to stop the complaints of North Carolina's anti-alcohol forces. Schafer continued to add to his enterprise, and the site grew to 350 acres.

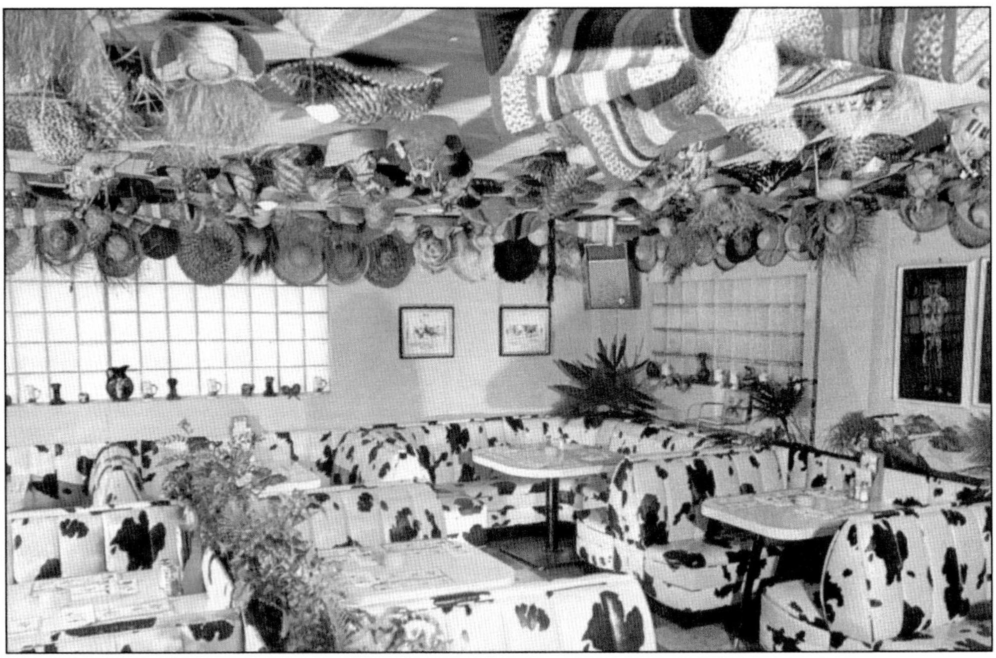

SOMBRERO ROOM. Postcards list this as the world-famous sombrero room featuring Mexican-Confederate cuisine and Confederate cookin' Yankee style. South of the Border was one of the first rest stops between Washington, D.C., and Miami to welcome African Americans during the days of segregation.

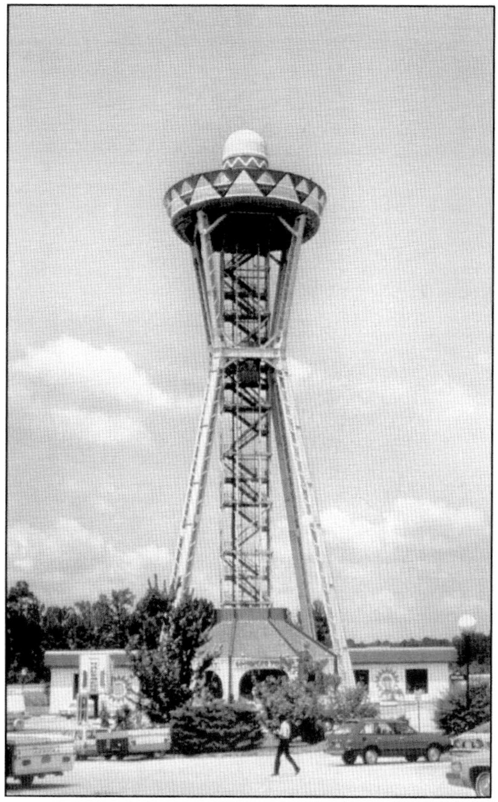

SOMBRERO TOWER. The 200-foot Sombrero Tower features a glass elevator and a 236-foot observation deck that allows visitors to see for miles.

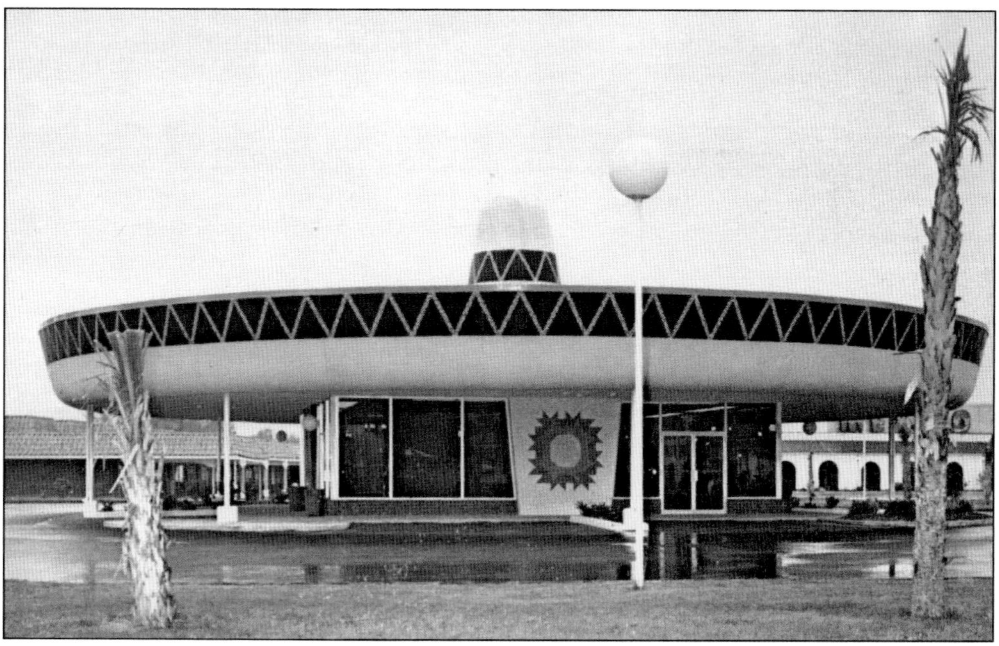

SOMBRERO. This unique attraction is actually part of the motel complex. The sombrero's wide brim provides weather-protected parking for 16 cars.

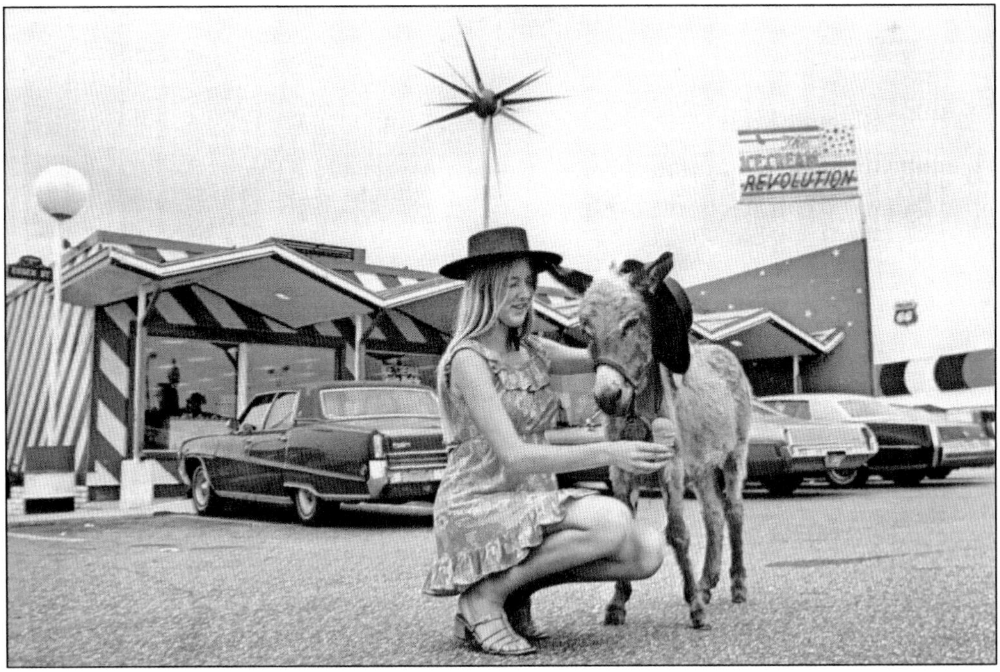

BURRO. This fellow enjoys a chocolate ice cream cone in front of Pedro's Ice Cream Revolution. The ice cream parlor is decorated in the patriotic colors of red, white, and blue.

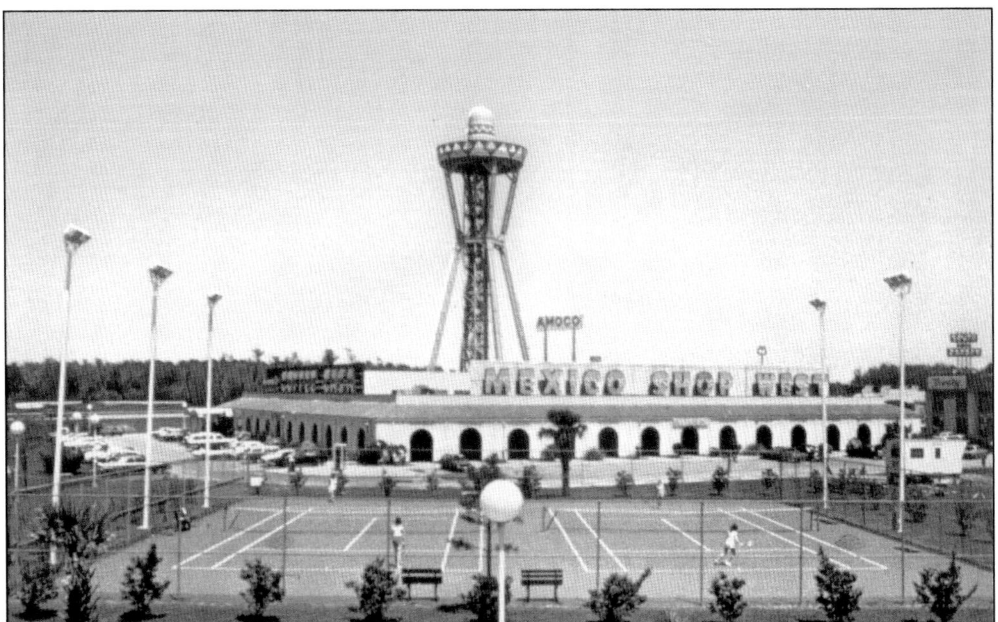

SHOPPING CENTER. This view shows the Coffee Casa and the Mexico Shop West, with the Sombrero Tower in the background. The postcard states that the tower originally cost $1 million to build.

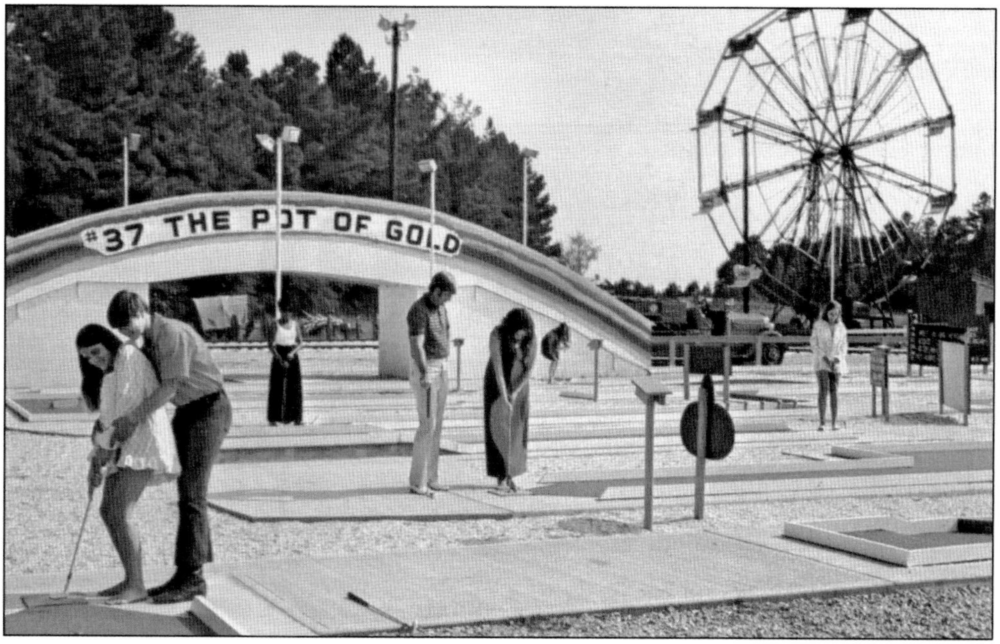

GOLF. Miniature golf, or carpet golf as it was sometimes called, was a big craze in the 1970s. The Amigoland Fun Park was Pedro's 37-hole championship course; hole 37 was 110 yards.

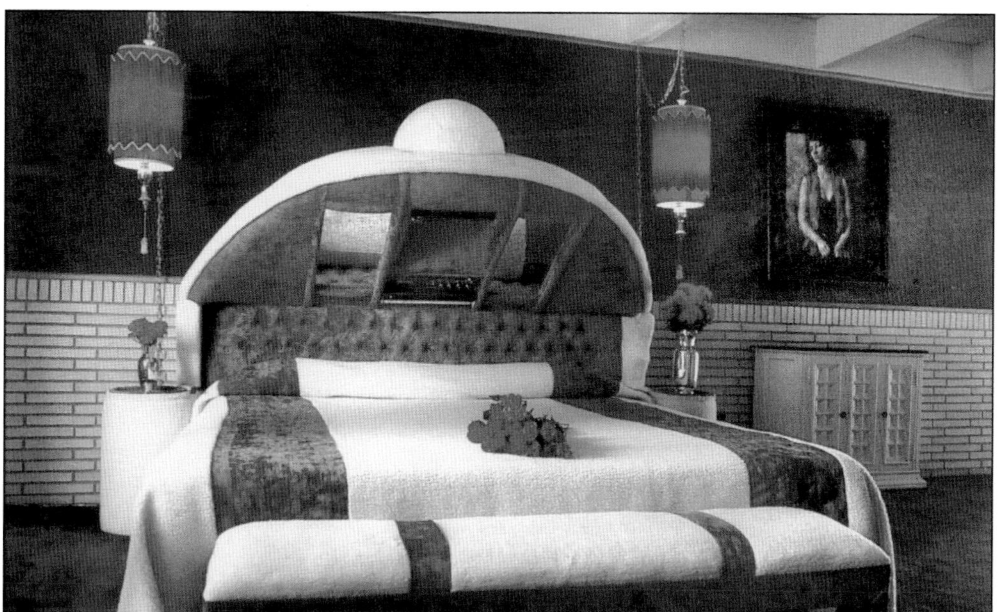

HONEYMOON HEAVEN. This was one of Pedro's 20 honeymoon suites and included the famous everything bed. The sombrero-shaped bed included a television, radio, cassette player, and mirrors. The room has the typical look of the 1970s, including unusual lighting and lots of velvet.

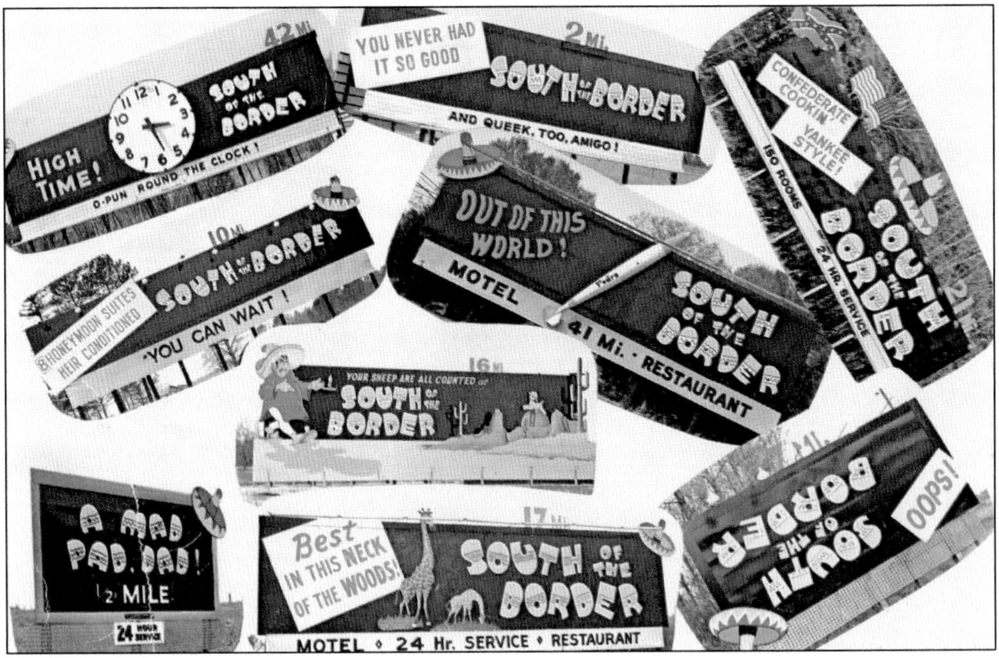

INTERSTATE BILLBOARDS. Billboards advertising South of the Border appear up and down Interstate 95. At one time, all the billboards were the creation of the attractions owner, Alan Schafer. It has been said that he had South Carolina's greatest 20th-century marketing mind and used it to build one of the East Coast's largest tourist attractions. Some of the signs read "Camp weeth Pedro," "Fireworks Capital of the U.S.," and "You never SAUSAGE a place! You're always a WEINER at Pedro's!"

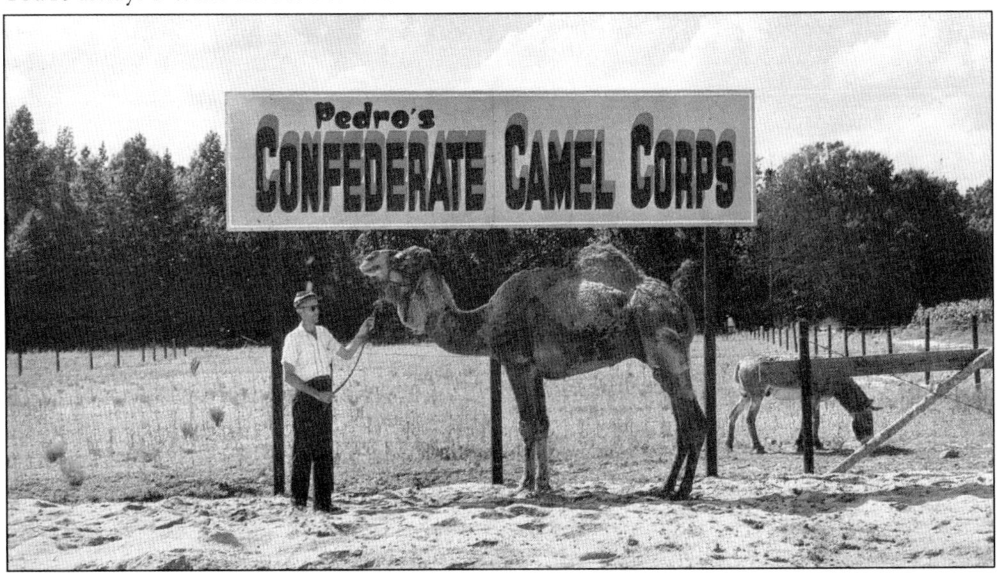

CONFEDERATE CAMEL CORPS. In the late 1950s and early 1960s, as the centennial of the War Between the States drew near, many businesses choose Confederate names and symbols as part of their advertising schemes. South of the Border was no different. In fact, they used the term Confederate and the image of the Confederate Flag on everything from postcards to billboards to areas of the complex. Shown here is Pedro's Confederate Camel Corps at Confederateland, U.S.A.

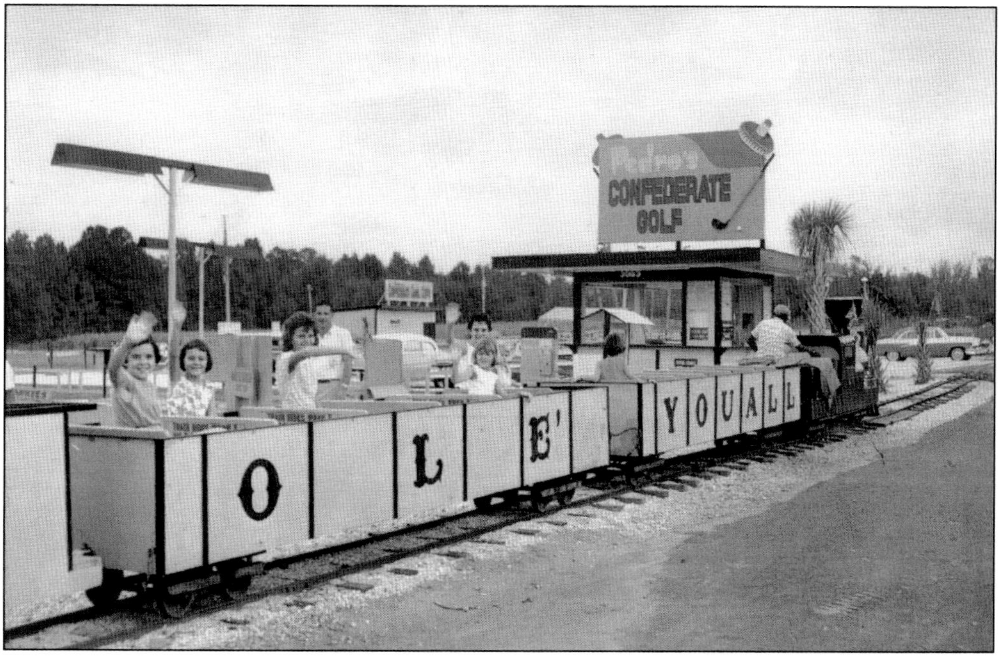

RAILROAD STOP. This postcard shows the Carolina, Confederateland, and Upper Mexico Railroad stopping at Confederateland's Confederate Golf Course.

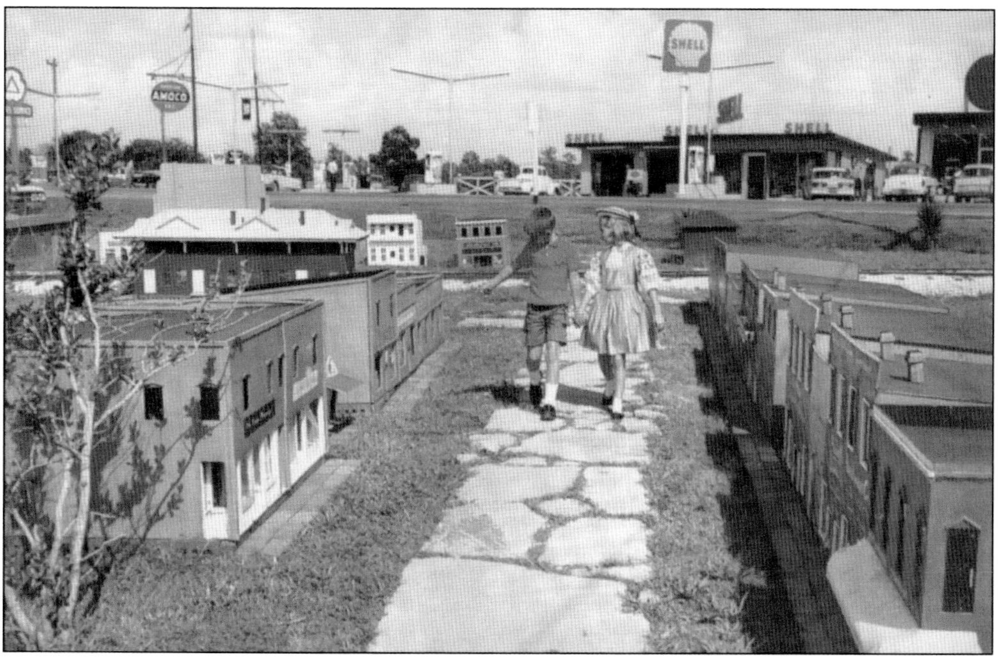

TOURING THE TOWN. A boy and girl, hand-in-hand, tour Confederateland, U.S.A., which is a scale-model replica of local towns as they appeared fifty years earlier.

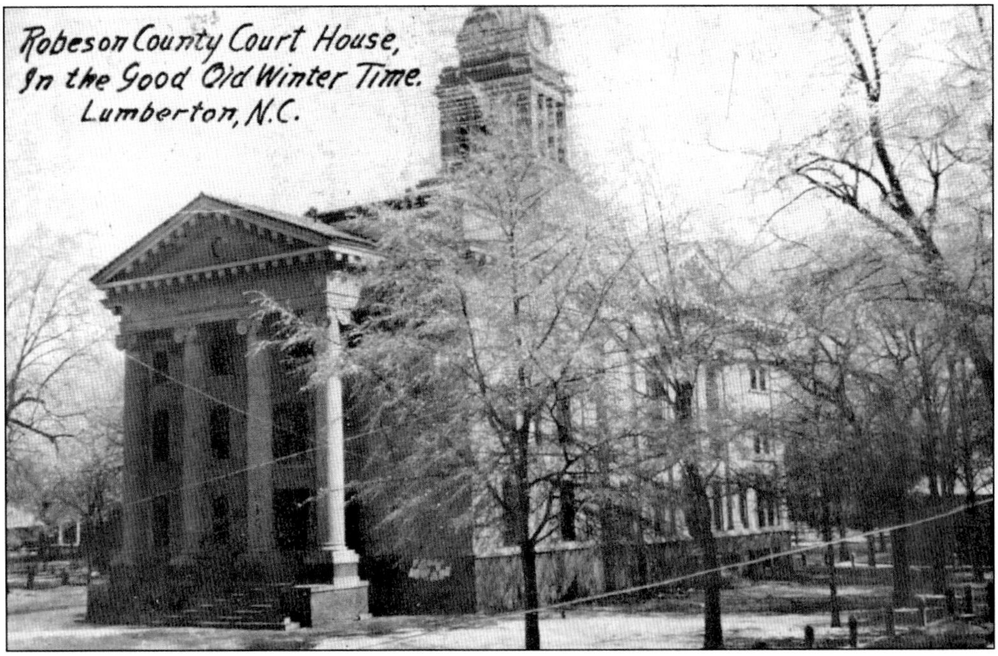

COURTHOUSE IN GOOD OLD WINTER TIME. No look at social life or popular diversions could be complete without what every school child craves during the school year: winter weather. This unusual postcard shows the 1908 courthouse in a frosted state, the result of a winter storm.

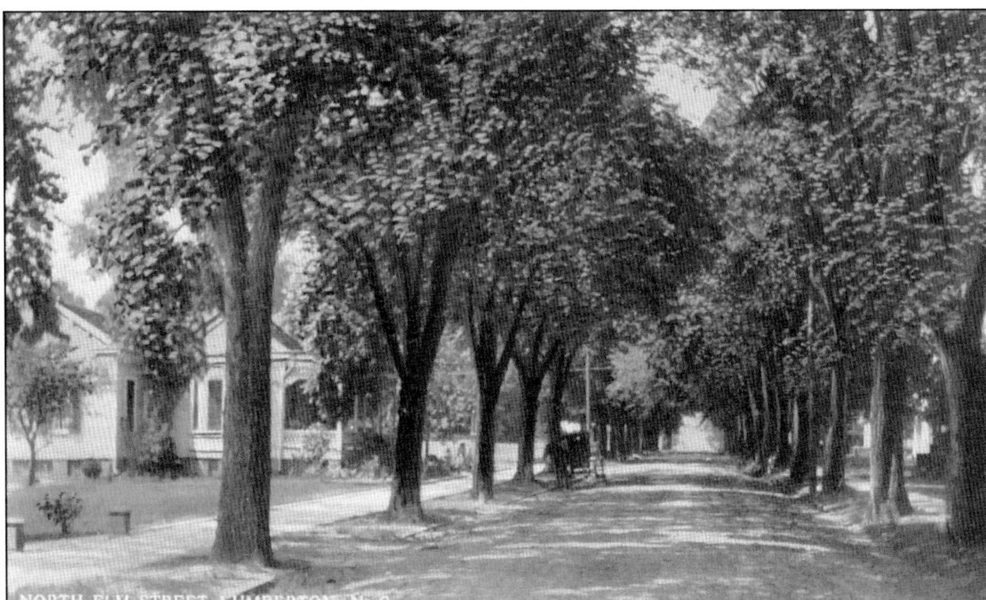

ELM STREET. Sometimes a diversion could be something as simple as a walk down a shady tree-lined street like this view of Lumberton's Elm Street.

Ten

Robeson Lost—Hoke County

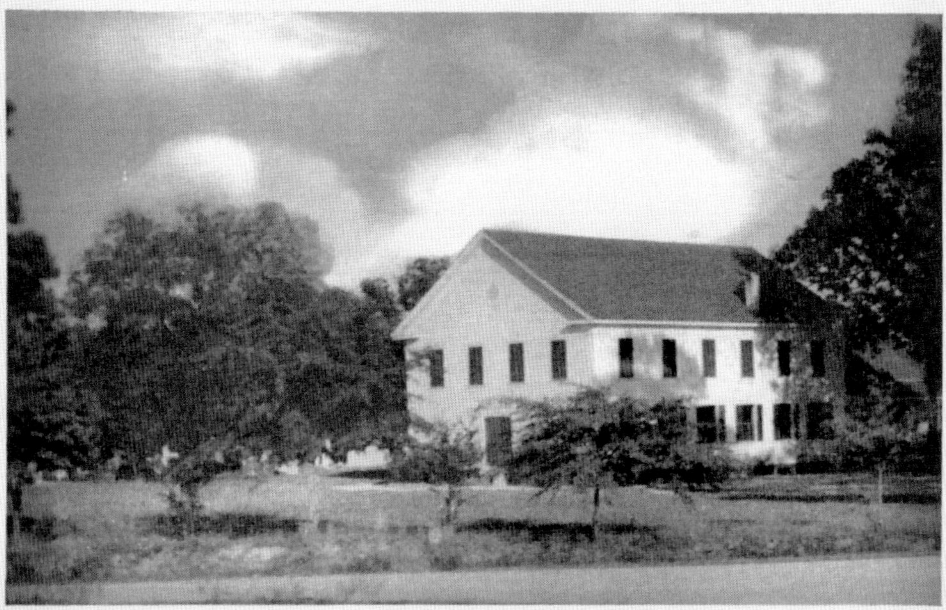

Antioch Presbyterian Church, Red Springs, North Carolina

Antioch Presbyterian Church. When the northern part of Robeson County was lost in 1911 to form part of the Hoke County (the 99th North Carolina county), the historical Antioch Presbyterian Church between Red Springs and Raeford was in that portion. The organizers of this church first met at McPhaul's Mill until their building code could be constructed. Rev. Hector McLean served as Antioch's first pastor.

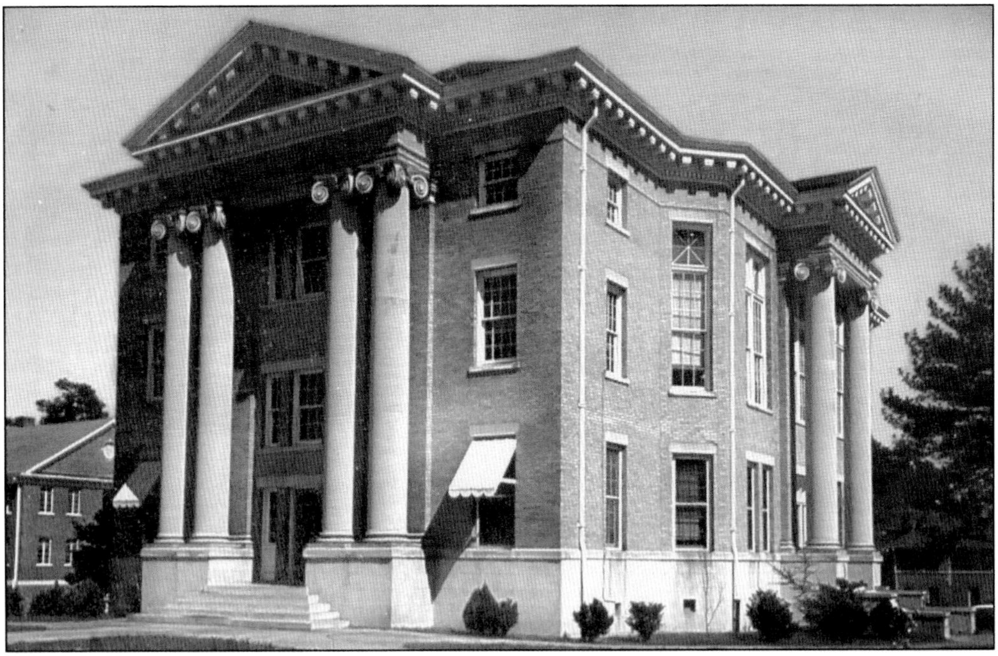

COURTHOUSE. Hoke County was formed in 1911 from Cumberland and Robeson counties. It was named in honor of Robert F. Hoke, a major-general in the Confederate States Army. The Hoke County Courthouse, which serves as the seat of the government, is listed on the National Register of Historical Places.

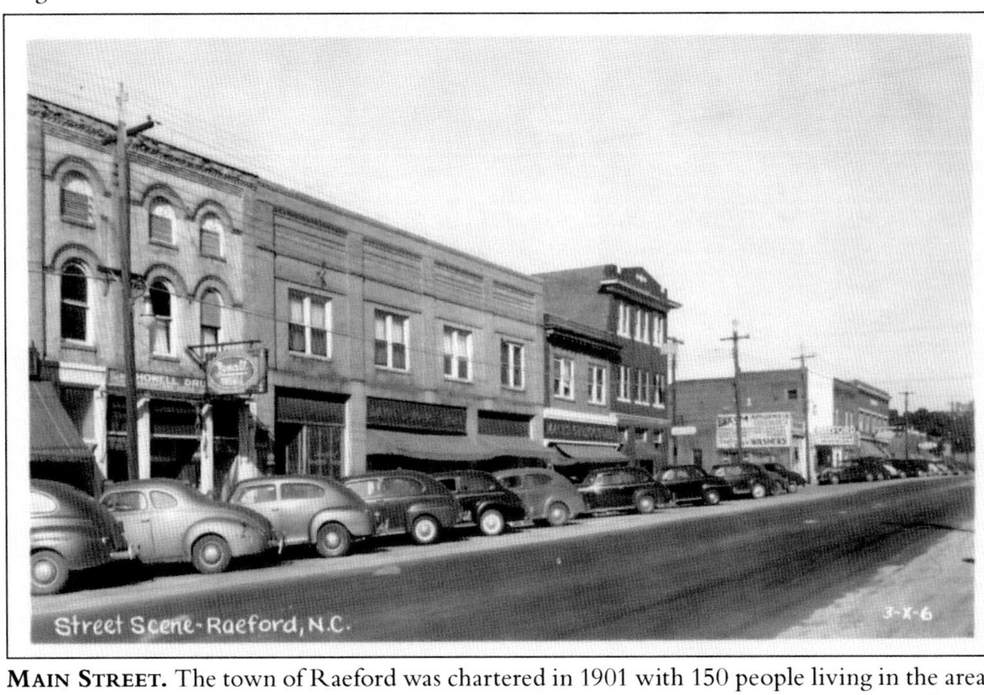

MAIN STREET. The town of Raeford was chartered in 1901 with 150 people living in the area; it took its name from business partners John A. McRae and A. A. Williford. The width of Main Street was determined by turning a two-horse wagon around in the area. There was a well on Main Street in case of fire and three pumps for drinking water.

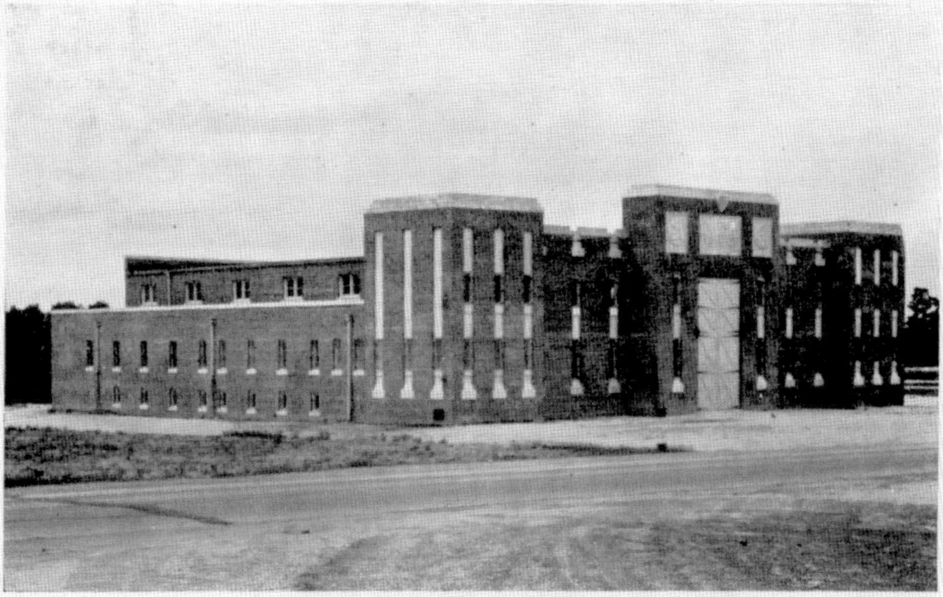

North Carolina National Guard Armory, Raeford, North Carolina

ARMORY. The Armory was dedicated on May 11, 1938, for the use of Battery F and the 1st Battalion of the 252nd Coast Artillery. North Carolina Gov. Clyde R. Hoey spoke at the service. The cost of the structure was $50,000.

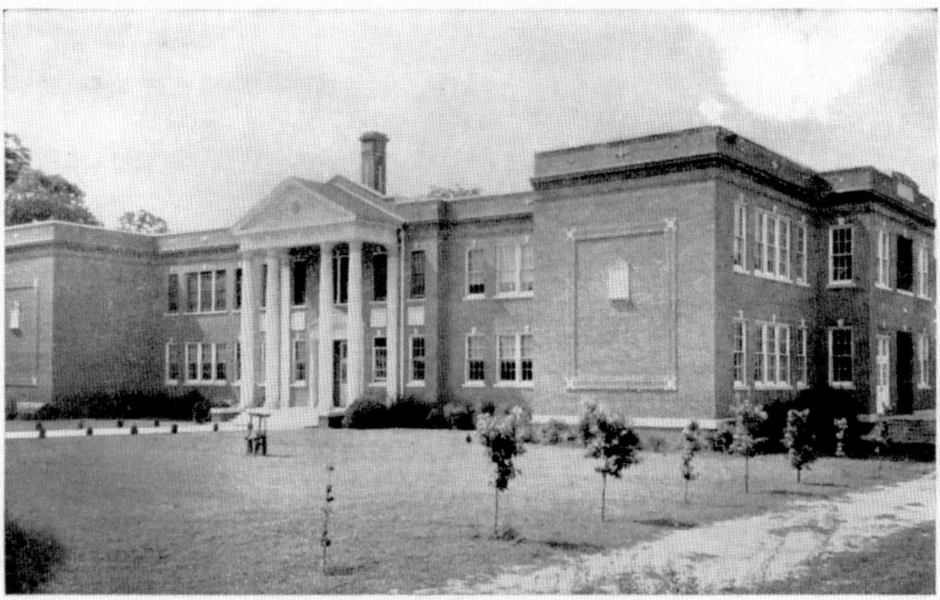

Hoke County High School, Raeford, North Carolina

HIGH SCHOOL. The old Raeford High School was a source of pride for the community for years.

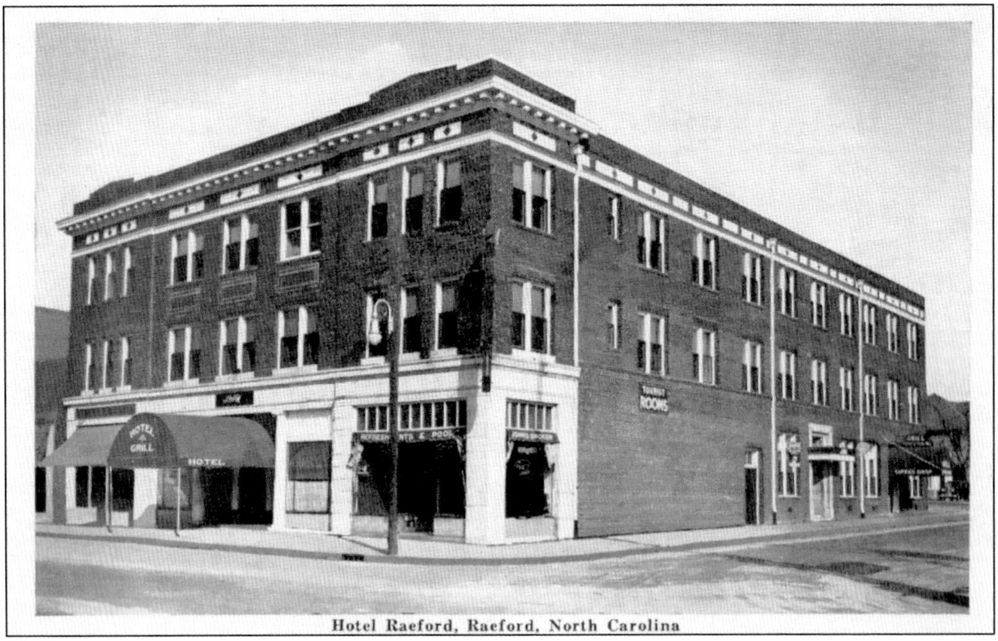

HOTEL RAEFORD. Built as the Bluemont Hotel in 1927, the name was later changed to Raeford Hotel. In the 1960s, the building was converted to apartments with businesses located on the ground floor that included a barber shop, beauty parlor, and doctor's office. The building was located at the intersection of Main Street and Highway 20 and after being abandoned for about fifteen years, was demolished April 29, 2005, as part of the revitalization of downtown Raeford.

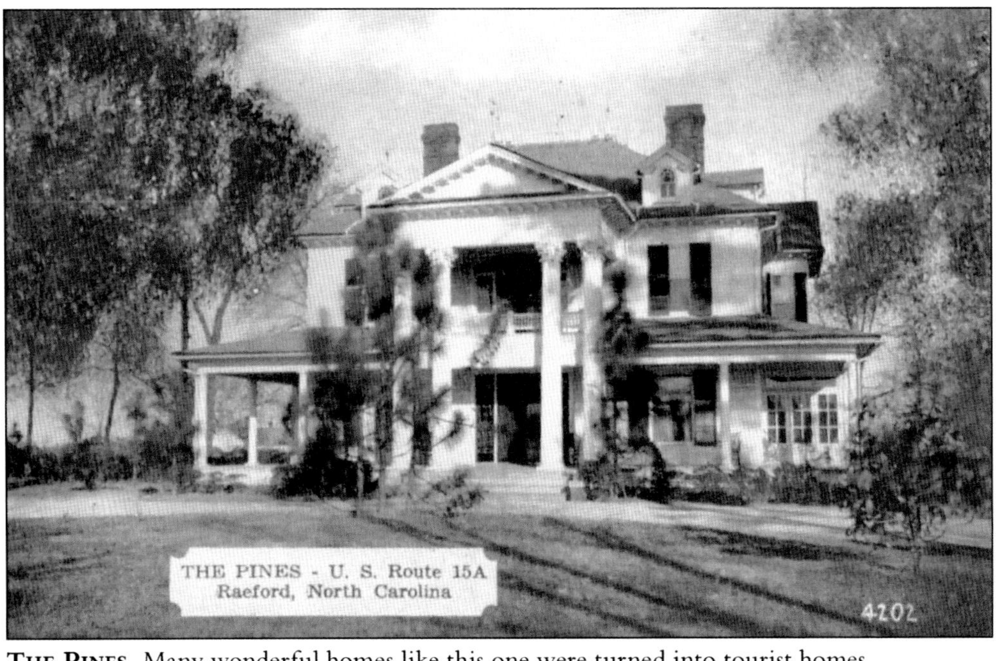

THE PINES. Many wonderful homes like this one were turned into tourist homes.

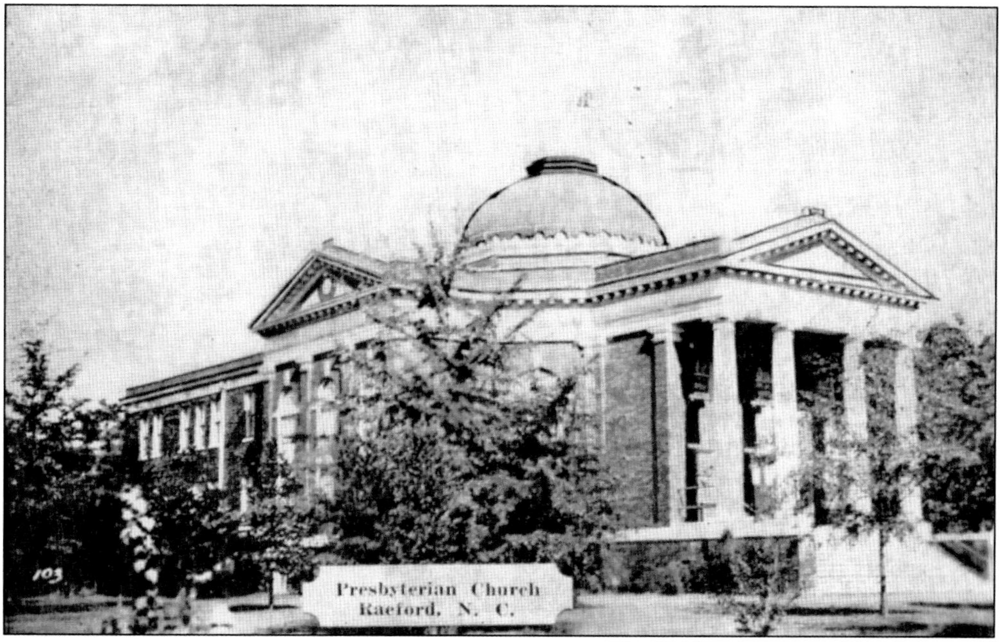

PRESBYTERIAN CHURCH. The Raeford Presbyterian Church was founded in 1899 when 31 men and women requested permission from the Presbytery to form a new church. The sanctuary was destroyed by fire in October 1943, and church services were held in the old Raeford school auditorium until 1945, when the church was rebuilt.

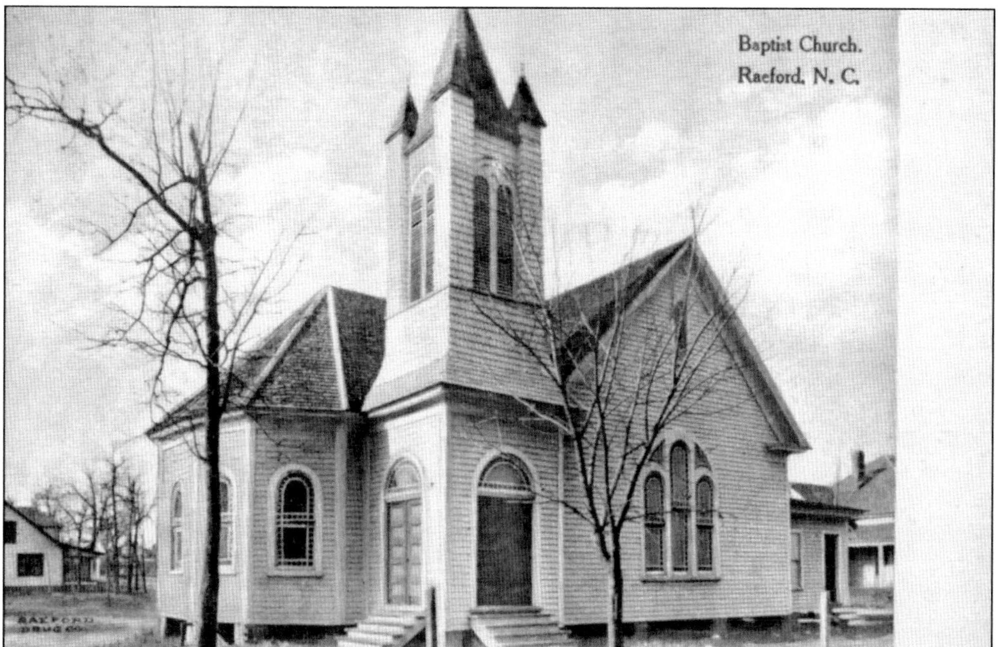

BAPTIST CHURCH. The Raeford Baptist Church was formed in 1899. Fourteen years earlier in 1885 John McRae and A. A. Williford, partners in a turpentine distillery and store, applied to run a post office. The name Raeford was derived from combining parts of their names.

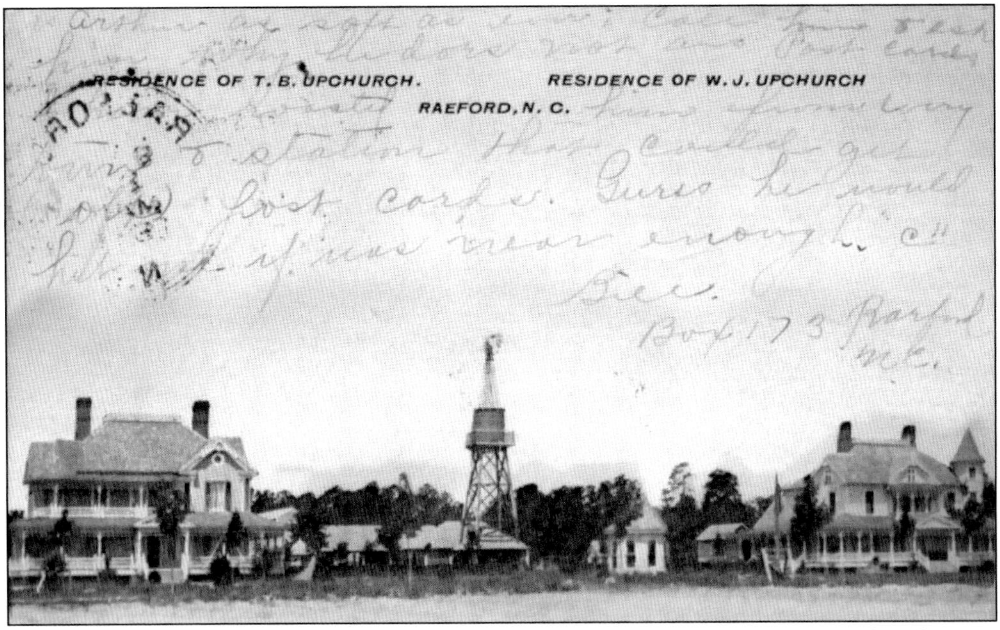

UPCHURCH RESIDENCES. Thomas B. Upchurch and his wife, Mary Johnson Upchurch, were natives of Wake County, North Carolina. Upchurch was a leading citizen of Raeford; he served as president of both Upchurch Milling & Storage Company and the Raeford Power and Manufacturing Company. He was vice president of the Hoke Oil & Fertilizer Company and the Bank of Raeford, in addition to being one of largest farmers in that section. He and his brother, W. J. Upchurch, opened the area's first sawmill in 1896 and cotton mill in 1907.

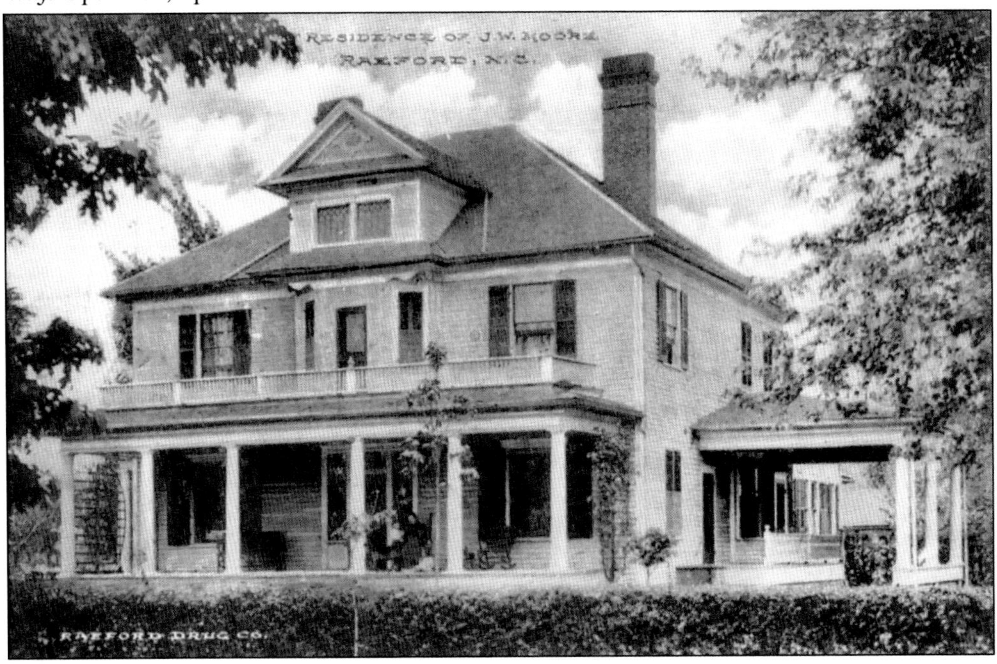

J. W. MOORE RESIDENCE. This large residence is typical of those built by successful farmers and businessmen at the turn the beginning of the 19th century who wished to show their economic success by building larger and more elaborate homes.